MW00388442

AIN'T NOBODY
BE LEARNIN' NOTHIN'

Ain't Nobody Be Learnin' Nothin'

The Fraud and the Fix for High-Poverty Schools

Caleb Stewart Rossiter

Algora Publishing
New York

Library of Congress Cataloging-in-Publication Data —

Rossiter, Caleb S.
    Ain't nobody be learnin' nothin': the fraud and the fix for high-poverty schools /
Caleb Stewart Rossiter.
    Includes bibliographical references and index.
    ISBN 978-1-62894-102-9 (soft cover: alk. paper)—ISBN 978-1-62894-103-6 (hard
cover: alk. paper)—ISBN 978-1-62894-104-3 (ebook) 1. Poor children—Education—
United States. 2. Children with social disabilities—Education—United States. 3.
Poverty—United States. 4. Public schools—United States. 5. Academic achievement—
United States. 6. School improvement programs—United States. I. Title.
    LC4091.R675 2015
    371.90973—dc23
                            2014048301

Printed in the United States

Table of Contents

Author's Note

My purpose in writing this book is bring to the attention of the American public the reality of the fraud of high-poverty schools and my proposals to fix it. As a professor of statistics and research methods in public policy who left a university in 2010 to teach mathematics in high-poverty high schools, I feel that I am in good position to do so. I could only have learned the depth of the fraud by experiencing it day in and day out as a teacher because I could never have imagined many of the things I saw unless I had been there. I can only offer a credible proposal to fix the current, failing "school reform" framework of test-based college prep for all because my academic background allows me to analyze the many studies relating to poverty, ethnicity, and school achievement that are referenced in this book.

My target audience for this book is not the "testing class" of politicians, administrators, and foundation executives who have captured public education over the past 30 years. As you will see at various times in the book, my efforts to engage members of this testing class in debate over the past few years have been fruitless. They appear to be too busy running the system in which their lives are invested and concocting tales of its supposed successes ("things were so bad, but now test scores are up!") to be able to sit back and contemplate its abject and obvious failure. My target audience is the general public because only its awareness of the fraud and the fix for high-poverty schools can create the necessary level of demand for policy changes.

For this reason I decided not to use an academic tone in this book or provide traditional footnotes that provide a formal reference to each study and claim cited. Instead, I use true stories to illustrate my points and include in the text enough of a description of the authors of the studies I cite so that readers can find them on the internet. Many names of people and schools have been changed to representative ones, both to protect people's privacy and to make the point that these stories occur daily in virtually every one of the tens of thousands of high-poverty schools in our beloved but economically and ethnically segregated America. (The first time a representative name is used, it is put in quotation marks.)

My thanks to my family, friends, and fellow educators for their support, both when I was struggling under the stress of trying to teach at open-enrollment schools and when I was celebrating my joy while teaching at selective schools, those that assert the right to bring in students who are ready to take advantage of the opportunity of education and to counsel out those who are not. In my experience, about half of poor black students fall into each category. This book offers plans and hope for both groups.

Most of all, I thank my students and their parents or guardians. It has been an honor to work with you, even when the current system's guarantee of failure frustrated us. The goal of both my teaching and this book is to help end this guarantee of failure and increase the opportunity for all of our students to make a successful transition to the middle class...and beyond!

* * *

Preface: No, I'm Not Kidding

Adults who attended middle and upper class high schools invariably say "you're kidding" when I describe a preposterous incident in a high-poverty high school where I have taught. But I'm simply not imaginative enough to make this stuff up. This is a work of non-fiction. Only the identities — of some schools and streets and of most building administrators, teachers, parents, and students — have been changed.

It was ten minutes after the tardy bell after lunch on a fall afternoon at "Johnson" Senior High in the District of Columbia, but dozens of students were still running down the lavishly-carpeted halls in the new $100 million building. The state-of-the art facility could accommodate 1,500 students, but only 800, all black and nearly all from single-guardian poor families, were on the books, and about 400 showed up on any given day. At the dedication a few days before, the city's elected and education officials had promised that the beautiful new school would give students a greater sense of pride and purpose than the run-down one they had left behind.

Pride and purpose, though, were in short supply as the students came down the hall from lunch, screaming, laughing, and joning. (*Joning* means creatively insulting someone, often starting with the claim that "Yo' momma so ugly that..." It has been a staple of poor black culture since the days of segregation, when it was called "doing the dozens.") The students were staying a few yards ahead of the "Crow," who was striding along while bellowing his standard call, "Teachers, lock your doors!"

The Crow was by title the dean of students, but by role he was the hammer, the boy from the 'hood made good with an education degree from an on-line college. He would wade into fights with glee, in hopes that a student would want to burnish his or her reputation by taking a swing at him before being tackled and pinned to the ground. A star quarterback in high school, he was about 35 years old and in great shape, and had never lost a school fight, even when leaping over the railing to collar an entire crew he saw throwing trash at fans during a school football game.

The ninth-grade students burst into my Algebra class, reliving the details of a fight in the cafeteria that had only been quelled when the entire security team had been summoned on their walkie-talkies: the Crow, the principal, both assistant principals, both of the resident city police officers, the three burly GS ("goon squad") disciplinary assistants, and eight of the 10 security guards. (Two of the guards had to stay at the front door with the screening machines at all times, to make sure that an irate guardian or crew member went to the office rather than wander the halls looking for a targeted student or teacher.)

The security guards were low-wage neighborhood workers who were instructed not to grab disruptive students and drag them from class, but rather simply to stand by them, cajoling until they came along. The GS, in contrast, consisted of salaried graduates of historically black colleges, usually scholarship football players, who had a license to grab and drag at the first demurral. They enforced obedience in the stairwells, where there were no cameras to record beatings. The perpetually disruptive "knuckleheads" gravitated toward them, despite and perhaps because of the beatings, which showed a measure of respect and familiarity with family practice in poor black culture.

The Crow and the GS had finally muscled one of the combatants into the principal's office, where the boy adopted a calm demeanor. Once they had relaxed, he attacked the principal. At 67 years old, the principal had seen his share of combat, from Vietnam to a succession of "urban schools," so he and the Crow knew to go right at it, slamming the boy down so the *po-po* could come and cuff him. "Damn," said the Crow, "he broke my watch and I ripped my slacks. That's the last time I get dressed up!" (The Crow was wearing dress shoes, slacks, and a collared shirt for a rare meeting after school at "downtown," the school district office. He usually dressed like a student, in sneakers, blue jeans, and a white t-shirt.)

The boy had a long history of assault in the school. Just the year before, he had invaded my classroom in the middle of a lesson, ripping things off the wall, cursing, and throwing around spare desks. There seemed to be no reason for that disruption, since neither he nor I knew each other. When I closed the door to keep him in until the GS or security guards could take him away, he grabbed me, muscled me aside, and ran out. I filed the requisite report, but there had been no suspension, just as there had been none for what turned out to be a number of his previous assaults on teachers.

The reasoning provided by the vice principal for this lack of action was that the boy was on probation, as shown by his ankle bracelet that he, like about a third of the boys in the school, proudly used to trigger the screening device each morning. Any disciplinary action would have to be reported to his parole officer, sending him back to the notorious juvenile facility. He was of indeterminate educational status, with very few credits to show for his three or four years in the school, but each student who was put out reduced the rolls by one unit of reimbursement. If cursing at and shoving a teacher were considered grounds for suspension or expulsion, enrollment would have been cut in half in a hurry, putting lots of people out of work.

But cursing at and attacking a guardian of order, like a security guard or administrator? That was always grounds for joining the over 100 students on the Crow's suspension list, which came to all teachers in a daily email with the warning, "Do not admit these students to your class." The warning was necessary because suspended students would often come to school, somehow evading the Crow's presence at the screening devices, and wander the halls until after the free lunch.

As the students settled into their desks, I turned on the Smart Board, an expensive version of a chalkboard that allowed me to type from a computer or write with a "Magic Pen." On the days that it worked, the Smart Board was a minor miracle, calling up textbook pages, music, on-line instructional videos, and geometric shapes, and allowing students to flip to previous screens on which they had shown their work on class problems. On many days, though, the school district's failure to budget for a technical support staffer in each building meant that the expensive tool went unused because of a missing part or a simple software problem.

The schedule for the period was written on the Smart Board, under the heading of the main topic: "Standard A1.N.2: Exponents: *Ex-ponere* — Latin for *put out* (like you *put out* or kick your 'ex' to the curb). So put out the base the power's number of times and multiply." The first item on the schedule was: "Turn to page 156 in your textbook, and prepare to present problems 1 to 3." I asked a student to read the instruction to the class, and began to take attendance on the computer. Immediately, a plea, with a tone as incredulous as that of a basketball player challenging a foul, came from a boy in the middle row: "Naw, Doc, no work. We beat. Ain't nobody be learnin' nothin' today!"

Murmurs and then chants of assent followed. "OK, 'Ramsillah'," I said, "I'll take the bait. Tell us. Why can't you work this afternoon?" Now Ramsillah's tone was humorous, as if the whole class knew the answer, but for some reason he had to say it: "Come on, be real, Doc — you know you fakin'. We was testin' all morning and we is beat, and this class be only 30 minutes. You the only teacher doin' work — all the others is just showin' movies."

The "testing" Ramsillah was referring to in Black English was the first of six Interim Assessments for the DC-CAS, the District of Columbia Comprehensive Academic Standards exam. He and the other students had taken it for three hours that morning in the sort of large-hall, tightly-regulated standardized testing environment associated with the College Boards. Each class was then shortened from 80 minutes to 30, so they could all fit in the afternoon. The testing explained why nearly all of the 26 students on my roll were present, when it was more usual to have about 13. The school district deployed roving squads of temporary workers to bring every student to school for testing days, since federal certification and funding under the "No Child Left Behind" Act depended on 100 percent of enrolled students being tested.

"No Child" was a wishful federal law enacted in 2001 that declared that schools would make "annual yearly progress" on the percentage of students "proficient" on standardized tests, so that after ten years they would all be proficient. The Act's illogic violated the first law of statistics, that of the bell-shaped "normal" curve with half of cases above and half below the midpoint. It required all students — the strong, the weak, the mentally handicapped, and the English language learners, the healthy, tutored rich and the less healthy, untutored poor — to be, as Garrison Keillor, the host of the radio show "A Prairie Home Companion" liked to say of his Minnesota town, above average. In order for their districts to receive federal funds, schools that did not show sufficient annual yearly progress had to be "restructured." The schools would be dramatically "closed" and then "reopened" immediately with new administrations, teachers, and even private or charter management teams. Of course, with the same students returning, the most important factor in test results remained, and the cycle of "school failure" and restructuring would have to continue.

The students took an Interim every six weeks. The stated purpose was to inform teachers of the skills in the curriculum to date that their students had and had not mastered, but teachers already had knew that from their weekly quizzes. The tests had three real purposes, though, within the same overall goal, which was in fact the laser-focused goal of the entire school enterprise: raising by a few points the percentage of students scoring at the "proficient" level on the end-of-the year DC-CAS, so that while not meeting No Child's benchmarks along the way to 100 percent proficiency after ten years, the school would at least be placed in a "Safe Harbor," dodging the dreaded bullet of restructuring for another year. The DC-CAS was actually given in April in order to get the results graded and sorted in time to be used to decide the eligibility of teachers and principals for pay raises — or even their jobs — for the next school year. This effectively cut the instructional year by two months, since students and even teachers breathed a sigh of relief after the well-publicized build-up to the DC-CAS, and little work got done after it.

One purpose of the Interims was to pressure teachers and principals into focusing on test-type questions during instruction. This was achieved by reporting the results throughout the district and using poor results as a reason for giving teachers and principals low grades on their evaluations. Teachers who wanted to get a pay raise, or even just to keep their jobs, would hammer the students with those test questions whenever possible, and principals would hammer on the teachers for the same reason. The second purpose of the Interims was to give students practice in the standardized testing environment and on certain types of questions, so they would perform better on the DC-CAS. Ironically, in the case of these ninth-graders, the pay-off would only come at the end of tenth grade, which was the only high school testing grade for DC-CAS.

The third, most insidious purpose of the Interims was to identify the "bubble kids," meaning those whose scores on the Interims were "on the bubble," within a few points of being "proficient." Only an increase in proficiency percentages on the DC-CAS would place Johnson in "Safe Harbor," so lists of the bubble kids shot around the school, with administrators and teachers making plans to focus on them, inevitably to the exclusion of the majority of students who were hopelessly behind and the very few who were already well ahead. In a violation of the union contract, I had once been assigned a class of 38 seniors for a pre-Calculus class so that the Geometry teachers in the 10th grade testing year could break the "bubble kids" into tiny classes. Only the threat of my resignation and a union grievance got my big class broken in two, divided at the fifth grade math level. The "bubble kid" strategy failed in any event. The school did not increase its percentage of tenth-grade proficiency and the principal had to resign to avoid a No Child Left Behind "restructuring" in which the entire teaching staff would be removed and forced to look for other positions in the district.

From administering a series of grade level tests, I had established that my ninth-grade students averaged 2.5, meaning half way from second to third grade. I learned from the English teachers that the students' reading skills were just as weak. The Interim Assessments were written for the appropriate point in ninth-grade Algebra, and assumed reading, problem-solving, and computational skills at the ninth-grade level. As a result, the students always scored abysmally on the Interims, just as they would on the

DC-CAS, with less than 20 percent scoring at the "proficient" level, which was really about a seventh grade result.

Motivation was low for the Interims and the DC-CAS alike. The test material was so much harder than the students could handle that teachers couldn't use the results in their grades. Most students would look in bewilderment at the first few problems, give up, and then just put their heads down on the desk, discouraged, embarrassed, and wondering why they came to school at all. For them, the tests were really a form of child abuse. When proctors would, as required, ask students to raise their heads and try more of the problems, giving first encouragement and then threats, students would often would shout: "You're not listening to me. I said, I DON'T CARE!" At some point, faced with being taken out to the special testing room for the uncooperative, they would simply fill in all the bubbles randomly, and then be allowed to put their heads down.

The few students who thought they had a chance at proficiency would try familiar problems, in hopes of a reward from the teacher or principal. Administrators suggested that teachers reward the proficient with a pizza party or additional points on a semester grade, and the teachers usually did, because their pay scales and even their jobs depended on these results. Principals paid for their own cash prizes and parties for the proficient.

Bizarrely, for all the work done to establish a standardized testing environment in which results could be compared between classes and schools, and between years for schools and the school district as a whole, the classroom rewards were not the same across classes and the school-level rewards where not the same across schools. This lack of standardization made the comparisons statistically invalid, yet they formed the basis of teacher, principal, school, and district evaluations. Pay, careers, and such "No Child Left Behind" remedies as "restructuring" schools by firing all the administrators and teachers were riding on the DC-CAS, despite it not being standardized in its delivery. However, there was something even more bizarre about the entire edifice of the all-important "No Child" comparison of annual test results, even if the administration of the DC-CAS had been truly standardized. The comparison of one tenth grade to the next is statistically invalid because one is not measuring growth in the same students, but rather comparing one group of students to another. The results depend on whom you are testing, not whether they have improved during the year as a result of instruction.

Right from the start, the math problems were tough, with sequential instructions requiring a sophisticated strategy. For example, the very first question that Ramsillah had seen that day stated that 356 students sat for an exam, and 118 got As, 46 got Bs, 86 got Cs and the rest got Ds. It then asked students to choose the one of five pie charts that correctly showed the percentages in each category. To answer it, students would have to know that a percentage is found by dividing each category's number by the total across all categories, and would have to know how to do long division (as in 356 divided by 86). To do long division, though, they would have to know their times tables. Unfortunately, less than a third of the class knew their times tables to five, let alone 12, and even fewer had a grasp on time-saving long division strategies of estimation. To top it off, "pie charts" would not even be reached in the "Scope and Sequence" document that teachers used as the curriculum until the next six-week period. In fairness, though, the students had been taught about pie charts many times in previous grades, just as they had seen nearly everything in the ninth-grade Algebra text in previous years.

"Percentages" was indeed on the "Scope and Sequence," but as part of a 16-day instructional window along with properties (associative, distributive, commutative, identity), ratios, proportions, rates, union, intersection, and complementary, universal, and disjoint sets, as well as Venn diagrams. It is a tradition of mysterious origin that many students in high-poverty urban schools do not come to school until after Labor Day, despite school starting in mid-August, and that nearly all simply stop coming in early May, despite school running through mid-June. So, many of my students were absent for much of the 16-day window, and when they did come, I first had to test them, like the rest, for grade level over a series of days.

Throw in students changing classes throughout the first month and the slow progress the class made through the curriculum due to disruption and lack of effort in class and on homework, and the students arrived at the Interim Assessment with only a few days of practice on finding percentages. They certainly had never had to find three with long division and then figure out that the difference of the total from 100 would give the fourth. To introduce percentages, I had decided to dodge the frustration of long division, and used primarily single digit problems. Attention to the task was decent, since the students enjoyed hearing that the X in "X over 100 is the same as what-per-cent" could be remembered by reference to Malcolm X and the black separatist Nation of Islam. X is an unknown quantity, and the Nation of Islam adopted it as a way to indicate unknown ancestry due to slavery. (The well-dressed vendors of the Nation's newspaper wear bow ties, like me, which led a student to ask me, a white man, in all seriousness, "Doc Rock, you NOI?")

The students had become somewhat comfortable with percentages by making up their own problems for others to solve, including: "Tiashia and her seven friends go for a hair weave, but only three of them can get an appointment. What percentage of the girls got an appointment?" and "DeJo'hn missed 25 percent of his 8 foul shots. How many shots did he make?" But nothing had prepared the students for this first question on the Interim.

Most students with second-grade skills and perseverance levels shut down soon after they start a ninth-grade test. Those who do try exhaust themselves as they move through the problems. On this test there were 23 problems to be completed in 90 minutes, and most were even more complicated than the pie chart example. We math department teachers complained later that month to the school district's testing staff about the number of problems on the first Interim, their difficulty, and the exhaustion that came from their complexity. The next Interim test had 43 even tougher problems, so we stopped complaining.

I thanked Ramsillah for his opinion, but explained that class time was what I was paid by their parents to use, and I was going to do just that. The eternal battle of high-poverty schools erupted again, in which students effectively are bargaining good behavior for not being made to work. As always, I prevailed on a few to move ahead in the chaos of disruption, but the disrupters fell farther behind.

How did American education come to this? In a gorgeous, state-of-the-art $100 million building, with another $10 million or so being spent a year on the salaries of the people in the building, let alone the millions for the central administration and all their test-makers and curriculum consultants, Ramsillah still can't read — or handle percentages. This fraud, and its fix, is what this book explores.

* * *

Johnson is one of the ten all-black, all poor, nearly all fractured-family "neighborhood" public high schools left in the District of Columbia. What was happening in Johnson on that day, the low proficiency and the misguided curriculum that will result in half the students dropping out and the remaining half being helpless before a community college curriculum, was most certainly happening in the other nine. A neighborhood school is one that has to accept anyone who lives within its boundaries. There is one neighborhood high school in the white part of town, which is bursting at the seams with black and Hispanic transfer students from other parts of town who either behave or get sent back to their home school. There are also a number of "admission" schools for academics, the arts, and Hispanic students that select their students from families that have the wherewithal to apply — and deselect them, too, so that students who can handle the work and the rules can progress.

Johnson's mismatch between capacity, enrollment, and attendance was repeated in the other nine neighborhood high schools, with some actually closing down entire wings so students couldn't roam and hide. Where had all the students gone? Why had public school enrollment in a city with a high birth rate due, in part due to significant teen pregnancy, fallen from 100,000 to 42,000 in the past 20 years? There are two main reasons, and they help explain why Johnson and the other neighborhood schools had 50 percent graduation rates and 20 percent "proficiency" rates.

First, enterprising black families, often with two parents and at least one regular job, began to flee the city for the growing, upscale all-black suburbs in Maryland and multi-ethnic working communities in Virginia. With relief they left behind an ever-more concentrated collection of generational low-income or state-supported no-income families. These households are almost uniformly headed by poorly-educated single women — mothers, grandmothers, aunts, and friends with minimal control over children whose poorly-educated fathers are often hustling, incarcerated for hustling, or hustling again without hope of a straight job because of their prison record.

Second, legislation promoting public funding for charter schools mushroomed at the local, state, and federal levels. Politicians received campaign funding from charter operators who stood to profit handsomely, even those that masqueraded as non-profit corporations. Diane Ravitch was a top George H. W. Bush administration education official. Today she believes that the 30-year results of various "school reforms" like charters and test-based punishment are too weak to justify their continued drain of resources from the public schools. In her 2013 book *Reign of Error* she portrays the charter movement as a privatization drive, a successor to the failed "voucher" movement for taxpayer funding of private schools. Charters too capture the more "together" families, in this case those remaining behind in the exodus to the suburbs who can take the initiative to apply and push for admission. Again, this leaves behind the least "together" families, more concentrated than ever in neighborhood schools.

Anybody can open a charter and get $12,000 per head per year, in addition to bonuses for facilities and special education students. So just about everybody does. Guardians with some sort of wherewithal take the time to find a charter and enroll their child, leaving the public high schools dominated by no-income families. Charter families usually resemble nearby public school families in their demographics, but they generally provide more motivation to their children. Charters counsel out, push out, or just plain throw out students who are disruptive in behavior or lack of effort, sending them back, guess where, to the neighborhood schools who must take them. In Washington, charters enroll almost as many students as the public schools. In New Orleans they have taken over the entire system. In many other cities they are growing, driven by guardians' desire for education without disruption. The irony of the paean to charters, a non-fiction film called "Waiting for Superman," is that the success it attributes to charters is regularly attained by admission public schools. Toss out the disrupters, and education is always feasible.

The heart of the problem explored in this book is the fundamental alienation of a good share of poor, black students, perhaps half, from mainstream society and its aspirations. With no concern for effort or success, these students see school as an entertainment, where fights, food, sex, joning, and smoking form the curriculum. Any pressure to listen, respond, or work is met with a purposeful resistance and eventually a hearty, "Get the (expletive) out my face," based in part on embarrassment about their skill levels. One could call this resistance "massive" in memory of another barrier to black education, the self-styled "massive resistance" of white Virginians to school integration orders in the 1960s. The alienated students taint the remainder who might be willing to work but who enjoy the drama of the revolt and mimic the bargain they demand, of "no work, no disruption — try to make us work and we'll go wild."

The following tale of the "bum rush" provides a good example of this alienation and of the "school reform" fraud of pretending that it does not exist. School reformers have a mantra they repeat, which is that "we know what to do," that students steeped and isolated in black, high-poverty culture can all be as successful as middle class kids in a college prep curriculum, given hard-working teachers with high expectations. So let's ask how the reformers would handle the bum rush.

The District of Columbia school district has a requirement that every high school have an assembly once a month. In the old Johnson facility, this was a recipe for disaster. Students would wander in, ignoring teachers' attempts to keep them in set rows. They also would ignore whatever was happening on stage, which was usually incomprehensible anyway because of a faulty sound system and ancient acoustics. At some point, there would be a rustling in the seats as a few students stood up and looked around, laughed, and sat back down. A few minutes later, a few more students would stand up and look around, yelling a bit louder. Then the buzzing would escalate, the mystified guest speaker, usually a paragon of black achievement, would be even more ignored, and the administrators and security guards would head for the rear doors, because, clearly, the game was on.

Suddenly, with a roar, the entire student body would jump up from their seats and surge toward the rear doors, overwhelming the human barrier there, with even the redoubtable Crow swept aside in the laughing enthusiasm and chants of "bum rush, bum rush." Out the side door and into freedom would romp the few hundred students who had remained after lunch, bringing the school day to an abrupt and early end. Just a few seconds after the bum rush began, the only students left in the auditorium would be the wheelchair-bound and a few serious or cautious souls.

The bum rushers knew that there would be no consequences for the jail break. Too many people involved in too many transgressions means that proper consequences would depopulate the school and put everybody out of work. Hardly anybody did homework anyway, so there would be no penalty for leaving notebooks behind in the mad rush out of school.

To end this tradition in the new school, administrators never brought the whole school together, but rather divided the assemblies into grades and always kept an administrator on stage with a microphone, directing the GS to the rows where students were talking, to have them removed. In the new school the bum rush would actually come in the other direction at times, when assemblies were a reward for good behavior. For example, a fashion show by the Ladies of Distinction was something everybody wanted to see. Boys and girls alike, for different reasons, enjoyed seeing 20 girls strutting sexually around the stage, changing into progressively more revealing outfits, hips snapping and lips pouting as go-go and rap music boomed through the speakers. But sometimes the administration would announce that students could only get in with a pass signed by all their teachers for having gone a week with passing grades and no disciplinary referrals. The security guards and the GS formed a wall at the door, and fought the hundreds of students who had skipped class to bum rush the event.

But the classic bum rush at the new school came during another event that treated the high-poverty school just like any other: the homecoming parade. A motley crew of 300 students milled around the front of the school, by the massive wall letters that spelled out "Natatorium." Unfortunately, the lovely swimming pool behind the Latin sign had never been used. Neither the city recreation department nor the school district had budgeted for staff, guards, and cleaners. The one student on the nascent swimming team trained once a week at a public pool a few miles away, illegally driving over with the unpaid coach, a ninth-grade "Teach for America" history major from the elite University of Chicago.

Four police cars led the homecoming parade through the tough neighborhood known as "Barry Terrace." Nobody from the school but the Crow and an uninformed Korean-American teacher in high heels had ever entered the projects there, where students had witnessed at least three shooting deaths in the previous year, including one of their own. Teachers considered this boy the least likely to be caught up in gang violence, since he was a fine student, a gentle soul, and a poet. But it appeared he had tried to steal a gun to use to avenge his brother's shooting.

When a teacher with over 40 years' experience, "Rosemary Queen," drove a girl home to Barry Terrace after basketball practice one day, the girl's mother and grandmother, both of whom Ms. Queen had taught as pregnant 14-year-olds, rushed out to the car in terror at the thought of her getting "taken off," and shooed away the gathering crew. The Crow, though, was respected and feared, a sort of walking threat that it was better to leave alone, and "Ms. Lee's" appearance at Barry Terrace in her first week at the school to drop off some homework for a girl who had been shot during a drug deal was so startling that none of the crew members thought to "go shopping" and "get paid" with her watch, phone, and wallet.

A couple of teachers on motorcycles followed the police, and then came the marching band. The band consisted only of six students smacking snare drums, since the beautiful new horns purchased by the school district lay in their cases in the music room for lack of reeds and mouthpieces. As a result, the band leader, just recruited from the proud marching band at a historically-black university, had been unable to teach anybody how to play them. He would soon leave in frustration at the bureaucratic logjam blocking the promises of instruments, uniforms, and trips, just like the previous band leader who had been recruited from the proud marching band at an all-black high school. Behind the drummers came a few administrators' cars, bearing the elected homecoming king, queen, and court, waving despite the absence of any onlookers throughout the two-mile march around Barry Terrace.

The students wandered after the vehicles, glad to be out of class for the afternoon, and when they turned onto the main artery that ran past the neighborhood, the game was on. There was a small grocery store across the four-lane highway, just begging for a bum rush by a flash mob. The store, like nearly all the businesses in the largely-poor, all-black, part of town "east of the river," was run by immigrants, in this case from Korea. Even the McDonald's, one of the two restaurants with seats for the 300,000 people living east of the river, was staffed entirely by Asian and Hispanic immigrants. The Johnson students refused to apply there for summer jobs, preferring instead the no-show program the city had offered since it was dreamed up in the 1980s by former Mayor Marion Barry, who still represented one of the wards east of the river despite his conviction and incarceration for possessing crack cocaine. As one Johnson student told me, "I ain't no chump, gonna clean no toilets at no Mickey D's."

The Korean-American owners stood behind bullet-proof glass all day and late into the night, selling chips, candy, cigarettes, and beer, and they taped every entry in hopes of deterring hold-ups. These precautions were useless against the mob of probably 200 students who burst away from the march, ran screaming across the four lanes of traffic, and stormed the grocery.

They grabbed everything they could in the two minutes before the police doubled back, sirens wailing. The parade had become a rolling crime wave, and the police cars stayed much closer to the marchers as they munched on their ill-gotten Twinkies and Coke Zeros for the remainder of the stroll. Consequences? Discipline? Nothing was ever said or done by the police or the administrators. When you are up to your ass in alligators, just getting through the day is enough.

How would those supposed saviors who "know what to do" in high-poverty schools, the charters and private firms, handle a school that suffered from the alienation that creates the bum rush? Well, they had their chance: in the late 2000s when two of the DC neighborhood high schools, Anacostia and Dunbar, were turned over to private parties in the usual desperate attempt to raise proficiency scores and find "safe harbor" from federal penalties. In Dunbar the operator was a New York firm, Friends of Bedford. It was dismissed in its second year, as the school culture deteriorated even further, with gangs roaming the halls. The final straw was an alleged gang rape inside the school. At Anacostia, the Friendship Charter Schools took control and established a collection of small "academies." After two years of press releases claiming wonderful progress, Friendship threw in the towel, as the proficiency scores ran out of opportunities for gaming, and went back to its own charter schools where it could control which students came and which were pushed out.

These examples are not cited to blame the charters for those failures but rather to point out how silly it is to think that rearranging the deck chairs of teachers and college prep curriculum on the Titanic of America's high-poverty schools can "turn around" what decades of class and race discrimination have created. The Fix must be equal to and relevant to the Fraud. This book starts with a summary chapter called "Yes, There Is an Answer," and then has two sections, one on the fraud, consisting of eight chapters, and one on the fix, consisting of six. Read on. And after pondering the true tales from this preface, pleased don't ever say "you're kidding" to either the fraud or the fix I propose.

* * *

Chapter 1. Yes, There Is an Answer

If education is supposed to be the bridge to the middle class for low-income Americans, then the bridge is definitely out for children in high-poverty communities who attend segregated open-enrollment public and charter high schools. Tragically, that is nearly all the children in these communities. Very few escape to private schools or the handful of public and charter schools that function like them by using selective admission to keep out, or academic and discipline rules to push out, weak or disruptive students and troubled families.

In the "admission" schools most low-income students have a parent or guardian who is able to keep them building the perseverance, knowledge, and study skills they need to gain and maintain the free ride that nearly all of them need to complete college. In contrast, in the open-enrollment schools half of the students drop out and the other half are simply passed along until they graduate, years behind grade level, helpless before a college curriculum.

Poor families have been the focus of a 30-year experiment of repairing the bridge to the middle class with a package of "reforms" in public and charter schools, including teaching to grade level tests regardless of students' skill levels, insistence on a packaged college prep curriculum for all students, and most of all test-based "accountability," in which teachers, and administrators are punished for the well-documented fact that being poor, black, or Hispanic correlates strongly on average with weaker performance in class and on standardized tests. These reforms came with the best intentions to produce better teaching and, as a result, better learning, but the experiment has failed spectacularly.

I know this not just because, when you strip away the "gaming" of the numbers that reformers use to make perpetual claims of progress, the exam, SAT, graduation, and college completion statistics continue to show the same abysmal results for the poor and for blacks and Hispanics as 20 years ago. I know it also because for three and a half years recently I left university teaching to lend a hand as a math teacher in open-enrollment, high-poverty high schools, and I failed just as spectacularly. (That "half-year" is the dead give-away. I recently resigned from a charter school because its administration demanded that I record passing grades for the 40 percent of my ninth-grade students who were delivered to Algebra 1 six years below grade level and then made little effort to catch up.)

But really, are we surprised? Was it logical to expect that with the poorest, most stressed families increasingly segregated into separate schools, we could help them overcome the challenges of poverty just by demanding that teachers use a standardized method and work harder? Looking for the bridge to the middle class for children only in schools rather than also in jobs and support for their families meant that we could ignore the toxic legacy of America's unique brew of slavery, segregation, and the passing of the cultures and opportunities of poverty and wealth to the next generation. How convenient!

* * *

Kenneth Clark was the psychologist whose research on black children's self-image, in which most preferred a white to a black doll as a "good" playmate, underpinned the Supreme Court's *Brown vs. Board* finding in 1954 that segregation was inherently unequal for the historically-excluded group. In his work in Harlem in the 1960s Clark discovered that all poor African-Americans teenagers were "encumbered" by the devastation of the black family and of the black, particularly male, psyche by the violence and degradation of slavery and segregation. Clark identified the result as the "tangle of pathology of the ghetto": a sense of inferiority, embedded discrimination and dysfunction, group and self-hatred, "defeatist attitudes," and lower ambition. Remarkably, though, he also found that many children were not derailed by being so encumbered.

Clark was not blaming the victim but rather recognizing what the victim needed to recover. It has been a stunningly tough row to hoe, or chop, or pick, for African-Americans. The brutality and humiliation of 250 years of slavery and then a century of legal segregation and denial of opportunity created a burden of anger, confusion, poverty, and dysfunction that only the strong could survive, and in which only the fortunate could thrive.

Clark's findings ring true today, after another 50 years of segregation and denial of opportunity — this time by practice rather than law. A recent book by psychologist Joy DeGruy Leary reads like Clark could have written it. She talks of the "intergenerational trauma" of black families and the denial of its existence by a white mainstream that fears "retaliation and reparations" if it is acknowledged. Leary says that the black underclass is still in "slave-like" conditions of hopelessness, violence, and lack of acceptance by the mainstream. The underclass then develops "adaptive survival behaviors" reflecting a post-traumatic slave syndrome. These behaviors include "vacant esteem, extreme feelings of suspicion, perceived negative motivations of others," depression, and a self-destructive outlook leading to violence against oneself, one's family, and other blacks. Like Clark interpreting black children's preference for white dolls, Leary identifies a continuing racist socialization in which children internalize white racist views of themselves and develop an aversion to their physical characteristics and group members.

Roughly half of my students exhibited the external symptoms of what Leary and others have called post-traumatic slave syndrome as well as what I have coined currently-traumatized segregation syndrome. The causes are physical isolation and social alienation from the middle class, damage in pregnancy, shortage of intellectual stimulation in infancy, and high levels of violence, threat, and unemployment. The symptoms are stress, braggadocio, "joning" (verbally humiliating others in your cohort), responding violently to being joned, early and sustained language and academic deficits, fear of trying and failing, and looking for affirmation in gangs, crime, and early sexual activity. For the fortunate fifty percent who do not exhibit serious symptoms, there is almost always a strong adult somewhere in the family who guided them through school, demanding solid performance and behavior.

The "tangle of pathology" produced by our history results in behavior that is wildly counter-productive to poor students' chances of crossing school's bridge to the middle class. The Duke of Wellington described his troops' misbehavior during the Peninsular War of the early 19th century by listing a few transgressions and then cautioning that, once "out of sight of their officers...there is not an outrage of any description that has not been committed." Similarly, by listing these realities I am only providing a sample. Whatever outrage you can imagine, these students have witnessed it, committed it, or been victims of it.

A partial litany: virtually no men in the homes, shootings by and of students, nearly half of boys involved in the criminal justice system, nearly half of girls pregnant, drug-running students and drug-chasing parents, violence and murder in the home and on the street, teenage prostitutes pimped out by family members, a third of the students classified special education or emotionally disturbed (four times the rate of middle class schools), 50 percent daily attendance, endless joning and fighting in and out of class, and worst of all a massive, active, nihilistic resistance to caring, planning, or doing homework or classwork that leaves students years behind, even as they are magically passed along with their grade cohort.

This last condition, a resistance that is externally-driven but self-imposed, is the primary constraint on poor black students, far more important than poverty itself, or having a young birth-mother, early health problems and language deficits, or an absent father. All of those can be overcome with a student's modest effort, so the cultural resistance to making that effort is the linchpin of today's tragedy.

During my teaching stint in open admission schools I would regale friends, family, and strangers in coffee shops with these outrages, and they would invariably ask: "But what's the answer?" I would demur, saying that we teachers couldn't think about overall policy when we were focusing all our creative energies on helping one kid and supporting one family at a time. I could say that I had quickly learned what didn't work: "school reform." The reformers claim that they can improve college prep performance to middle class levels by browbeating teachers with daily packaged lessons, firing the reluctant ones, and "teaching to the test." This latter method is so all-consuming and so aligned with the expected test format and questions that I prefer to call it "cheating to the test."

Reformers repeat and repeat that "we know what works" and that, in the words of the Edward Brooke charter schools in Boston, quite typical for this genre, "research tells us that the number one predictor of student achievement isn't race...or socio-economic status," but great teaching. According to The New Yorker, the Atlanta superintendent who was indicted for presiding over a massive answer-changing operation stubbornly continued to argue that "an effective teacher three years in a row will completely close the gap between a child born in poverty and a child born to a middle-income family," even after criminal investigators had documented that any gap-closing in Atlanta was due to fraud, not magical teachers. Such claims constitute a fundamental, willful misreading of the strongest research finding in educational statistics, which is that segregating children into schools by race and socio-economic status dwarfs any teacher-related variables in predicting their performance levels. There is a reason why all the National Merit scholarships go to suburban high schools rather than high-poverty high schools, and it's not because the teachers are so wonderful in the suburbs. It's because of the students who walk in the door and the academic and behavioral background they bring from home.

The reformers' "teacher-based" claims arise from complex "value-added" computer models that compare high-poverty students' test scores to their "expected" scores, factoring out their own and their school's socio-economic status and previous years' scores. These models often show that some teachers move their students far farther than others in a particular year, but they rarely show that these same teachers have such an advantage over, say, a decade. That is because the variation due to, you guessed it, who walked in the door outstrips the variation due to teaching skill, even within the high-poverty population.

The reformers' cheerleaders among politicians and newspaper editors tell us every year that they have "done wonders" in this or that classroom or school or district because "test scores are up." But repetition doesn't make any of it true. In fact, they don't know "what works," because after nearly 20 years of school reform no non-selective school has changed the basic trajectory of its poor children. The claims of progress invariably dissolve under examination of who is being tested in year-to-year comparisons and which comparisons are being picked and which ignored. The top predictors of average student success in America are still, and for a long time will be, class and race.

I also knew what might help but couldn't be used: integration, by race and class. If you have a solid majority of white or wealthier students in a school, their families create the dominant learning culture by getting them to focus and behave in class, complete homework, and succeed. Research in cities such as Berkeley and St. Louis that have used integration plans to spread lower-income black children out into largely middle-class schools has consistently found "significant, if not dramatic" improvement for the black students, particularly in graduation rates, with no reduction in white scores. In addition, middle-class and wealthy families are far more active than poor parents not just in advocating for their children with teachers and administrators but in taking part in school activities and, most importantly, demanding resources for the school from the central administration and school board and in the media. However, creating a norm of largely white, or for that matter black, middle-class schools with a small share of low-income families is demographically and socially impossible in America as a whole.

America's race and class-based residential patterns create initial school segregation in urban and suburban areas. When school districts try to promote integration, middle-class and wealthy families choose private schools, move to wealthier jurisdictions, or bring lawsuits that have recently been validated by the Supreme Court. In small towns throughout the South, most white children still attend "private academies" that were set up to resist integration. Nationally, black isolation is returning to the levels from before *Brown vs. Board*. Over 40 percent of black and Hispanic students attend schools that are over 90 percent non-white. For the indefinite future, the front line for the education crisis for poor minority children will be in schools in which they are the overwhelming majority, and our strategy must be planned accordingly.

Now I am back in the cozy confines of both a university and a selective high-poverty high school, where I tell my students every day, "Thank you for doing your homework and not throwing anything at me," and I tell my administrators, on the rare occasions I see them, "Thank you for letting me teach." I have finally been able to find time to think through the crisis facing my previous students. And I am happy to report that yes, an answer has come clear to me. It's simple, and its principles, though not its practice, have already been proven in private schools and in public schools for wealthier families. The principles are, at heart, just common sense: (1) schools should be built around the needs and likely careers of the students, and (2) families must be strengthened so they can safeguard health and develop intellect in the critical pre-natal and early infancy period.

Wealthy families already know that these are the two keys to success. They demand and receive a college preparatory curriculum because their children typically go to and complete college. Their children benefit from healthy, low-stress pregnancies and intellectually stimulating early childhoods because the families are intact and have resources. Either one parent focuses well-developed mainstream social and verbal skills on the child all day, or the family pays handsomely for an experienced one-on-one care-giver while both parents work at a professional level. Families in poverty need, and deserve, these same two keys.

The easier half of this proposal to implement — restructuring high-poverty schools to fit students' needs, rather than forcing students to fit theirs — can be handled within existing school funding if federal and state school reform requirements are waived or rescinded, putting curriculum back in the hands of local boards. This would allow school districts to offer top-quality vocational and college prep programs for students who keep up and don't act up, as well as a remediation track for those whose skill level or behavior requires temporary separation so that the other students can succeed. The harder half — hammering at the legacy of poverty and slavery by promoting employment and setting up programs that help poor families provide a strong base for their infants — could cost as little as $120 billion per year. We would probably get that investment back in spades in a decade through increased economic growth and taxes and reduced poverty payments and prison expenses.

* * *

There are three things that must happen for high-poverty schools to prepare poor students to have a productive life in the middle class. First, schools must pursue behavioral goals that keep students alive and able to thrive; second, families must be offered a choice between vocational and college prep; and third, weak effort or disruption should never result, as it often does today, in suspension and then a return to the same class, but rather in separation from the students who are working hard, with intense remediation intended to allow a new start in a new class the next quarter.

Pursuing appropriate goals can rescue some students from crime, disease, and pregnancy. Vocational education can rescue more from being drop-outs. Remediation and the end of automatic promotion can give on-task students a chance to gain a credible degree and off-task students a chance to pull themselves together. Many of the most encumbered students will drop out, as they do now, but many more will be able to take the bridge to the middle class. Those failing to cross the bridge could be reduced from nearly 100 percent today to perhaps 25 percent, and the long-held goal of transforming high-poverty neighborhoods into working class settings could take place over a few generations. Selective public and charter schools could continue to "cream" off the students whose families have the wherewithal to apply and therefore are the easiest students to teach, but they wouldn't really be necessary. Each open-enrollment school would have become selective within itself, able to offer families an environment within the school where effort and success, rather than lethargy and chaos, would be the norm.

Appropriate goals: I used to tell my students that it was a waste of time to work on math problems if they wouldn't first pledge to "take no life, make no life" each night — short-hand for staying out of violent situations and using a condom. To have even a chance of getting to the middle class as an adult, you first have to make it out of the teenage years alive, without a criminal record, without a baby, and healthy enough to work. This reality is one that high-poverty schools need to acknowledge by providing lessons and counseling for every child on these topics. Once that is in place, the next goal is to gain the social skills needed to hold a middle class job: be ethical, cooperative, reliable, creative, perseverant, and confident in mainstream settings. Again, that is a huge challenge in a high-poverty neighborhood, and it must be met in a structured manner as in any course, with curriculum and assessment.

Next comes the ability to read, interpret, write, calculate, and strategize as needed for an entry-level job. Currently, most poor students are dazed and discouraged from elementary school on up because they have not solidified these basic skills before they are buried by the required flurry of college preparatory "Common Core" objectives. Only when the basics are solid should we turn to the supposed primary goal of high school, and the only one that gets a structured curriculum today: develop the more advanced skills that are needed for a career or college.

Vocational Choice: In a sort of reverse racism and classism, reformers who are mostly rich or white have claimed that offering vocational high schools to the poor or people of color is, to quote President George W. Bush, evidence of a "bigotry of low expectations." But at best about 80 percent of all Americans graduate from high school, and then only about 60 percent start and 35 percent complete even a two-year college degree. When 65 percent of your clientele end up not needing your service, you'd better rethink your approach. For poor children all the percentages are far lower, on the order of 50 percent graduating high school, with 30 percent starting college and 10 percent completing a degree. Combining in high school classes with a college prep curriculum poor students who could succeed in college and poor students who cannot, or who want to move more quickly into a blue collar career, means that hardly anybody can succeed at either.

Parents deserve an honest appraisal of their child's skills and interests, so they know exactly how their children compare academically with college-bound peers. Then they deserve a choice between college and vocational prep. It should first be offered after elementary school, because today's middle school curriculum already looks like college prep, which turns many students off to any schooling. The choice should be offered again after middle school for families who want to go in a new direction.

A minimum-wage job pays about $18,000 a year. That is all that dropouts or fraudulent graduates of a watered-down college prep curriculum can obtain. Careers that will easily pay twice as much for the indefinite future include plumbing, carpentry, electrician, cosmetology, hotel and restaurant management, fire-fighting, police work, computer technician, audio tech, web and social media design, computer programming, heating and air conditioning, medical records and technology, and bricklaying. In rural America there are many programs in which kids go to a home school to take practical, rather than college prep, academic courses half of the day and then go to a trade school the other half. Practical academics means checkbook math, not number theory; percentages, not calculus; angles for construction, not for Euclidean proofs; the physics of plumbing, not molecular motion; and analysis of newspaper articles, not Shakespeare's plays. Success, not stigma, is associated with these programs. In urban areas, though, they have fallen into disarray.

There are many mildly-challenged special education students in high-poverty schools. Our legal framework places far too many of them into mainstream classes that are simply overwhelming, but parents rightly resist the alternative of isolated classes and a dead-end special education diploma. Vocational training would often be a viable alternative for helping these most vulnerable young people prepare for a middle class career.

The vocational option would have to be exempted from the start from the school reform curriculum and punitive testing because Common Core standards and improvement rubrics are illogical for it. For the college prep option, school reform may, unfortunately, hold sway for a while, but it does far less damage to administrators, teachers, and students when the students can largely handle the work and the tests.

Discipline and Remediation: Whichever program a family chooses, student effort and behavior will determine success far more than the quality of teachers and curriculum. College prep or vocational, schools must build their rules around a recognition that the culture of poverty so well identified by Kenneth Clark in the 1960s is alive and not well today. To neutralize the culture of poverty we need to have two tracks in every course, from French to gym, from refrigeration to cosmetology, in high-poverty open-enrollment schools: the regular class for kids who are trying and succeeding, and a separate remediation section for the rest of the quarter, at most ten weeks, without credit, for those who have disrupted class or earned a failing grade.

All students would start the course together in the fall, but in contrast to today educators would quickly remove students from class for disruption or earning a failing grade, so that all students can get the help they deserve. The high share of students, up to a third, who are now under disciplinary measures, including suspension, on any given day in high-poverty schools, would indicate that these two tracks could be almost equal in size for the first few years.

Being removed from a course for disruption or failure to work enough to keep up would knock students out of their graduation cohort. After completing the quarter in remediation, they would be a quarter behind, and have to start that quarter's material the next time it is offered with a new group of students. Remediation could include basic academic methods and skills in the subject, but would largely consist of students and families working with counselors and administrators to identify and address the students' behavioral barriers to success in school.

The largest subgroup of poor Americans is white. However, the greatest barriers to school success are found in poor black communities. The kids themselves acknowledge the reality of the culture of black poverty, saying, "I can't help myself. Sometimes I just be so ghetto." In the television drama "The Wire," teachers classified high-poverty middle school students as "stoop kids" or "corner kids" based on what they did when they were elementary school students and their parents told them to stay on the stoop of the house. Those who stay on the stoop as ordered typically have parents who, while poor and stressed, have the strength and perseverance to rise above their deluge of problems and maintain control of their children. Those who ignore the command to stay on the stoop and just head on down to the corner, rarely have an adult in their life who can control their behavior at home, on the block, or in school.

Stoop kids can respond, and actually want to respond, to structure and academic challenge. When they are taught as a group, without distractions from the corner kids, they can thrive in college preparatory or vocational classes. With strong funding and follow-up in college or post-secondary vocational training, they can make it to the middle class. They will comprise the bulk of the regular class track. Corner kids actively resist taking direction from parents or teachers, and they melt down in dramatic misbehavior when pushed to work. They do little work and quickly fall behind in early grades, and only get to high school by being falsely promoted for years. They will make up the bulk of the remediation track, but after each quarter will get a chance to be back in the regular class again, with a new cohort.

Today the stoop and corner kids are mixed in every class and setting. The corner kids' personal dramas and low skill levels deprive the stoop kids who are ready to learn, given the chance to do so. We owe it to both groups to separate them so that stoop kids can succeed and the corner kids can address whatever is keeping them from trying. One of Wellington's officers in the Peninsula campaign described the effect of the miscreants on the soldiers who were trying to obey orders: "The man of education could not help but be lowered to the standard of a beast of burden. Blackguardism held sway." Indeed. The Duke's officer might have been talking about corner kids and their impact on stoop kids.

On the surface it seems like a policy of separation would amount to cold-hearted triage of those who can't handle school, be it college prep or vocational. But that is misleading: we are already losing not just the corner kids, but the stoop kids as well. Establishing clear rules for attendance in courses for credit would permit the stoop kids to learn and put the corner kids exactly where they need to be: in a separate setting within the school that is devoted to finding their deficits, be they behavioral, psychological, family, or academic, and providing support so that in the next quarter they can try again. Far from cold-hearted, this recognition of their reality would be a warm-hearted landing for them.

As one of my funniest students, "Jayvon," used to say when he used a new math method, "Boom, there you go." Simply by setting rules for staying in class, we will free half of our kids to succeed and give the other half a clear path back to success. Good teachers will stay in such an environment, and even if we can't end the school reform paradigm right away, it is far easier to teach and learn in the absence of chaos.

* * *

Social worker turned congressman Ron Dellums once told me that the motto of his former profession was, "You have to take people where they are, not where you want them to be." So, where are our poor children? Where their families are. And the families are weak, largely father-absent, alienated, and under crushing medical, psychological, and economic stress. There is no solution to the educational disaster for high-poverty kids without reducing their families' challenges.

In the case of poor black families, there is an additional challenge from our long history of racism and discrimination. The reduction in overt racism since the 1960s cannot magically wash away that history. This is an international phenomenon of violent race rule, in which some share of the oppressed are extremely affected. At about the same time Kenneth Clark was writing about America's "dark ghetto," psychiatrist and revolutionary Franz Fanon concluded that the source, or at least the compounding agent, of the mental illnesses he treated in his Algerian patients in the 1950s was colonialism by race, the daily drip and sometimes deluge of segregation and structural abasement that some transformed into self-doubt and self-hatred.

Assistant Secretary of Labor (later Senator) Daniel Patrick Moynihan completed a study in 1965 called "The Negro Family: the Case for National Action." In a memo to President Johnson on his study, he called for the government to confront the history of "unimaginable mistreatment" of blacks and the "racist virus" that continues to live in white America's bloodstream, and to make a national commitment to move the segregated, dysfunctional, black lower class into a successful and largely integrated middle class.

Moynihan borrowed much of his logic and language from Clark's studies of Harlem youth. He too identified the "crumbling" of the "Negro family structure" under a "tangle of pathology" as "the master problem," and called strengthening this structure "the work of a half-century." After just half of that period Moynihan looked back in despair at the lack of funding and commitment, and the resulting lack of progress for the lower, as opposed to the middle, African-American economic class. Now the full term has passed, and the poor black family is even more distressed. If we falter again we will be having this same conversation in another half- century.

If we want to improve school outcomes, we must be take on Moynihan's national commitment to do whatever it takes to disrupt the transmission of poverty. The strongest research shows that the best two ways to do that are by assuring living wage jobs for parents and by promoting health and intellectual stimulation in the crucial pre-natal and infancy period.

Jobs: There are 16 million children living in poverty in America, in about eight million homes. The federal government should offer a $30,000 public sector or subsidized private-sector job to each pair of parents (or guardians), with the custodial parent given the first crack. Perhaps three million parents might want such a job and be able to retain it by showing up and performing well. Eligibility would depend on parents bringing their children in to school on time each day, before going off to their assignment. For men, there would also be the requirement to stay up to date on child support payments if, as is usually the case, they are not living with the child.

Local governments and non-profit organizations have experimented widely with this sort of employment program, and have stockpiled lots of plans, particularly in infrastructure repair and maintenance using basic skills. Even if some jobs were make-work rather than directly addressing needs in the community, they would be delivering a benefit by strengthening at-risk families. Some families may be able to move to a middle-class black or integrated area, which is the hidden, unspoken goal of poverty programs anyway.

The cost of the program would be 3 million times $30,000, or $90 billion, to which might be added another $10 billion for administration and planning and evaluation. The income should be uncounted for taxes and social services, so as not to reduce existing assistance, such as Medicaid, food stamps, or welfare.

Whether it is direct services or jobs, we must acknowledge that some families are too distressed to benefit. The program need not be distorted to chase them down or give them multiple chances. It should focus on those who can benefit. In the 1970s I worked in a poor county in upstate New York for the Appalachian Regional Commission and its Home Start program. I recall a meeting of all the government-funded social agencies trying to help a legendary, extended rural family, which squatted on abandoned land, living in burned-out school buses. The men hauled junked cars for cash, the women scavenged for surplus food from public and private sources, and the children were malnourished, inured to scabies and lice, hampered by escalating medical problems, and lost in school before they even showed up.

The family members were trapped by violence, illness, poverty, and chaos, before even considering the psychological damage of being the poorest, unhealthiest people in the county. When I went to the meeting room in a shiny new county social service building I could barely get in the door: health clinic staff, social workers, psychologists, special education teachers, food stamp administrators, anti-poverty organizers, probation officers, heating specialists, cooperative extension agents, job training managers... it seemed like virtually everybody on the federal, state, county, and town payrolls except maybe the grave digger was there. All of us, this phalanx of two dozen helpers, had extensive and useless experience with the family. I remember thinking that if one-tenth of our salaries went to the family, just for one month, they all could move to a mansion in Malibu. We should accept the fact that some families cannot be helped, and focus on the large number that can be.

Neo-natal and Infancy Support: America is expanding pre-school programs for poor three and four-year-olds, but we also need to focus on the far more crucial developmental period between a child's conception and first birthday. In graduate school I worked as an analyst with Cornell University's Longitudinal Early Childhood Consortium Study, which studied pre-kindergarten programs that featured high teaching hours, highly paid professional teachers and intense verbal stimulation, and heavy interaction with and support for families through home visits. Such programs (which should not be confused with typical Head Start programs) can have surprisingly solid, but not dramatic, benefits on such long-term behavioral variables as high school graduation, employment, and prison rates, and age at first child. However, their impact on cognitive variables like test scores recedes quickly. This is because brain development and learning style are set much earlier than three years old. In fact, from conception, the longer you wait to intervene in poor children's development and families' interaction styles, the less intellectual benefit you get.

In my Home Start program in Appalachia in the 1970s I visited the same 15 pre-kindergarten children each week in their homes for an hour and a half. I was 21 years old with a child development degree, and my job was to encourage poor parents to talk, play, and read with their children in ways that would stimulate their cognitive growth and prepare them for kindergarten. As condescending as that sounds, it was a great model, and it was guided by rigorous research. A consistent finding, then and now, about social class and cognitive development is that poor children, on average, have millions (by one study, 32 million) less words, questions, and demands for responses directed to them by their parents in the first few years of life than middle class children. This gap, which I sensed literally the second I walked into the eerily quiet Appalachian homes, creates significant developmental and social lags that more than explain the so-called "achievement gap" between poor and middle class children. Because black families are poor at three times the rate of white families, the ethnic achievement gap is also exacerbated by poverty. In addition, for a variety of cultural reasons, there is also a word gap between black and white parents, controlling for income, with black children on the losing end of the gap.

To help block the transmission of poverty, a home visitor should be sent out to every expecting low-income father and mother for up to two hours twice a week, from the middle of pregnancy to the middle of the first year of life. The visitor would collaborate, teach by example how to interact to increase stimulation, make suggestions about healthy living, and simply help navigate the burden of being a parent of limited means. Pilot programs are already underway in a variety of guises, backed by public donations and a half a billion dollars of annual federal funding for local efforts under the much-maligned "Obama-care." For about $20 billion, the programs could reach nearly every high-risk family.

At-home support for infant development would dramatically increase many families' ability to send children to school ready and able to achieve, while living-wage jobs would do the same for their ability to maintain discipline and support throughout their children's school careers. Knowing what we do about the importance of these middle-class supports to school, the question is not whether we can afford to spend public funds on such programs, but whether we can afford not to. The most powerful predictor of a strong student is a strong family. If we want to help educators in high-poverty schools do their job, we'll stop kicking them for the fact that their students are not middle class, and put our efforts into helping those students' families attain that status. To expand on the name chosen by school reformer Michelle Rhee for her advocacy group, you can't put "students first" if you don't put their families there with them.

* * *

PART I. THE FRAUD

Chapter 2. Phony Grades

I don't think they're gonna like that downtown, Doc.

In the spring of my second year at Johnson, I notified the school district that I would not be back in the fall. I wasn't completely sure it was the right move, and by contract I had until August to decide. If I waited that long, though, and finally did decide to leave, I would reduce the school's choice of applicants to replace me. One year the district failed to remove me from a list of teachers seeking jobs after I took a college position, and I had been called two days after school started by a desperate principal, offering to hire me sight unseen. He was so desperate, he actually offered me the job on a voice mail.

One of the vice principals, "Don Marcellus," came by to see me when he saw the district's lists of returning teachers. He was disappointed I was not on it, and asked me why I was leaving just when I had mastered the ability to manage a classroom of the "urban child." I had great respect for Don for his patient energy and connections with the students. He could calmly bring a roaring crowd in an assembly down to a fairly respectful semi-silence with a mix of platitudes and imprecations, albeit with a healthy dose of GS ready to haul out the defiant. Don was a former music teacher and continuing opera lover, and he counseled me that while I might want the students to take more ownership of the classroom, I was the bandleader whose job it was to make it work: "Every class is like being on stage. It's show-time, Doc, three shows a day!" He also properly treated the various requirements to show progress on tests as icing on the cake of our true mission, telling us: "You don't teach math, and she doesn't teach English. We're all teaching the same thing: middle-class social skills. That's what they need if they're ever going to succeed!"

I tried to explain my thinking to Don: "Yes, I can manage a class now, but it's too much like baby-sitting. I came here to be a teacher, not a baby-sitter. I have a usually calmer classroom because you've backed me up on putting out the worst offenders, and making a guardian of the less worse come in before I readmit their child, but hardly anybody is doing homework, or working hard enough in class to master the material. I have to teach college prep to students who can't go to college, and it's not working. Even the students who care about passing know they don't need to do the work to pass. They tell me exactly how they'll get credit for the course when they fail, through summer school and after-school 'credit recovery' classes, where they don't need to work and rarely even show up."

After I left, I wrote a memo for Don and the head of the DC schools, who is grandly styled a Chancellor rather than a Superintendent, and then met with her to discuss it. The memo harshly criticized credit recovery and called for students to be forced to take any course they failed again in a regular school class. I wanted to keep working with the students, so I became the volunteer SAT math coach for the athletes that fall. Three times a week, after school, I met with the athletes in their homework hour before practice. It was just a little bit less useless than regular teaching, with many of the athletes coming irregularly and socializing more than studying, even though college scholarships were on the line. An experience I had going in the door one day led me to write this piece for the Wall Street Journal under the title of "How Washington, D.C., Schools Cheat Their Students Twice."

I recently bumped into a former student of mine outside the high-poverty public high school where I used to teach math. Quaniesha, as I'll call her, was on her way home, and I was on my way in for the SAT tutoring sessions I hold with athletes trying to become "NCAA-eligible" so they can accept sports scholarships.

Quaniesha feigned anger as we walked past the school's metal detectors: "Why you do me like that, Doc? I gotta start Credit Recovery next week." She was smiling and knew full well how our back-and-forth was going to go. She'd say I failed her in math. Then I'd say no, you failed yourself. She'd say I was a bad teacher. Then I'd ask her how often she had come to class, done her homework, or even brought her notebook and done the class work rather than cursed and fought and joked around.

Once I invited her mother to school for a ceremony celebrating Quaniesha's award as "improved student of the week," but her mother said she couldn't come because she—the 30-year-old mother of the 15-year-old student—had been barred from the school for cursing and fighting with security guards.

But if Quaniesha was feigning anger, I was really angry, because the Credit Recovery program she was starting is a fraud to which I alerted the chancellor of Washington, D.C., schools last summer in a memo and at a one-on-one meeting. In Credit Recovery, students who have failed a semester-long course attend a special class after school for a few weeks and magically earn credit for it—without taking a mastery exam. It is a big reason why the 50% of high-poverty, public-school students who actually graduate from high school are generally helpless before a college curriculum.

The dirty little secret of American education is that not only do half of students in high-poverty high schools drop out, but most of those who graduate—as I found in my two years teaching and testing students—operate at about the fifth-grade level in academics, organization, and behavior. These graduates must then take noncredit remedial courses should they try to go to college.

Of my ninth-graders last year, only 10% were present in class more than three days a week, and a full 50% attended two days a week or fewer. When they did attend, the chronically absent did virtually none of the class work or homework. As a result, I thought it remarkable that a mere 68% of my ninth-graders failed—which, by the way, was typical across the ninth grade in the math department. Instead of insisting that students retake failed courses and actually work, the school system allows students to take Credit Recovery or equally bogus summer-school courses. Thus students "age-out" of middle school with second-grade skills and "D-out" of high-school courses they rarely attend. That explains why my so-called pre-calculus class of seniors last year entered with an average fourth-grade math level, just like my freshmen: They had learned little in the previous three years while "passing" algebra I, geometry and algebra II/trigonometry.

What can be done for the Quanieshas of the world, of whom there are literally millions segregated into the high-poverty public schools of America? Clearly, if students enter high school with elementary-school skills, graduation is a long shot and college is a mirage. Schools should drop the fraud of pretending they are doing grade-level work. Instead, schools should rework their reading and math curricula to prepare them for trades that can support a family, such as being a bricklayer, hairdresser, plumber, nurse's assistant or computer technician. From my experience, 80% of high-poverty high-school freshmen are at elementary-school level, which includes the 50% who are going to drop out. The remaining 20% who are within striking distance of high-school standards should have the option to remain in the academic track. These well-behaved and well-prepared students have been cheated of most of their learning time throughout their school careers by the disruption of the disaffected, and they can probably get to grade level—and to college—if the disruption ends.

Triage? You bet. For now, at least. I don't know anything about teaching in elementary school, but I suspect that an end to standardization and a change to relevant curricula would help there, too. In any case, when the majority of high-poverty high-school students are within two years of grade level in their skills, then we can try the "college is for everyone" thing again. For now, let's end the fraud of Credit Recovery so students can be taught where they truly are, not at the level where we pretend they are.

The heavy response to this article surprised me. I began to realize that lots of people knew about the fraud of improper grading, but that it was so imbedded in the system that nobody felt they could do much about it. From all over the country I began to receive emails and calls from teachers with similar tales to tell. In Albuquerque, Chicago, Seattle, and Los Angeles, school districts were finding devious ways to inflate graduation rates by giving phony grades. Even community college professors were under pressure to pass students who were not showing up or doing the work. Two of the most interesting calls came from people in the DC school system itself. One was from Erich Martel, a veteran teacher at a high-performing high school. His school served a largely white and wealthy zone, although it admitted hundreds of "out of boundary" poor black and Hispanic students. A few years before, Erich had been shocked by seeing students walking across the stage at graduation who he knew had just failed his required course in DC History. His persistent and public investigation led to the reluctant discovery by a government inspector that every year hundreds of students with incomplete transcripts were being given high school diplomas on a "principal's judgment."

Erich was eventually hounded out of his school by the administration of Michelle Rhee, the chancellor who was padding her already phony résumé with improved graduation rates, by hook or by crook. Rhee had built her reputation by claiming dramatic results in her two years teaching in a tough Baltimore elementary school, "moving 90 percent of the students to the 90th percentile" in national tests. Unfortunately for her, education researchers were able to unearth the test results for her school when she became chancellor, and showed that anything even vaguely resembling her claim to be, of course, impossible. Her response was that her principal had told her so.

The other DC call I got was from a senior official in the central administration who knew about how Credit Recovery had originated, and how it was administered. The official asked to meet me for lunch, but "off-campus," so as not to be seen with me. Over lunch, I learned that Rhee had started Credit Recovery as a way to boost graduation rates. Once, as Rhee complained to her that graduation rates were still too low, the official had had jokingly said, "Just tell me the number you want, and I can easily deliver. I'll just hand out that many diplomas." That was one of the ways the "Texas Test Miracle" was generated by Rodney Paige, the football coach and school board member who got himself appointed as superintendent of Houston's public schools and then became President George W. Bush's Secretary of Education and promoter of No Child Left Behind. Paige's other tactic was simply to classify students who disappeared from school not as dropouts but as students seeking their education elsewhere. Under his guidance and definitions, Houston's graduation rate in its poorest schools rose magically from 50 to nearly 100 percent, but the reality remained the same.

Like gamed tests results, phony grades and graduation rates are systematic whenever success, salaries, and reputations demand a demonstration of improvement. When I went to teach in the Friendship Charter schools the next year I was told that there "cannot be" failing grades because it would be "bad for the school" to have the school board think that the students are not "on track to graduate." The Washington Post wrote an article on my claims, but I think I will just let my memo to the Friendship board speak for itself:

I recently resigned from a position as a ninth grade Algebra 1 teacher at Technology Preparatory because of unremitting pressure from the administration to alter failing grades and the return to my classroom of two students whose actions threatened the safety of other students. These issues are related to a fundamental question about Tech Prep's mission: can it successfully implement a college preparatory, let alone a STEM, curriculum for the ninth grade when a significant minority of that grade has math skills that are below the third grade level or consistently exhibits disruptive behaviors that keep both this minority and their peers from achieving?

There appear to be strong institutional pressures on administrators to achieve high enrollment figures, pass rates, and scores on grade-level standardized tests. These pressures flow down to the classroom, where they collide with the reality of severe academic and behavioral deficits, creating the sort of situations that led to my resignation.

The administration pressured me to raise failing grades for the first quarter to grades that students had not earned. I was told by a supervisor that my intention to report 30 percent of my students as having earned a failing grade — due to low rates of doing class work and homework, which led to poor performance on assessments — "cannot be." I was told that this would be "bad for the school" because it would have to be reported to the Public Charter School Board as evidence that students "were not on track to graduate" and that it also would be "bad for me." I was asked to raise grades or to change the weighting of the different categories of grades listed in my syllabus that had been sent to parents so that the grades would rise.

The pressure was not successful with me, but I know that it was with teachers of these same students in other courses who had similar provisional failure rates. This casts into doubt for me all the grades reported for the ninth grade. When the second quarter started, the supervisor met with me and continued to press me to raise grades, including suggesting that failing students who completed one homework assignment in a week of five of them be given credit for all of them.

At this point I decided that the emphasis on "crunching the numbers" (as the supervisor called a review of the homework, class work, and assessment grades reported each week) to improve students' grades artificially would predominate in our planning over finding proper placements for students who cannot, or will not, work on a ninth-grade curriculum. I began to reconsider whether I could be successful in this environment.

The condition of an unsafe classroom arose soon after, when the administration ordered me to take back into my classroom two students who had thrown over heavy desks, in one case hitting another student. The administration insisted in writing that this was not dangerous behavior. The two students have Special Education status (because of emotional and behavioral challenges rather than learning disabilities) and have been on "Behavior Improvement Plans" since the previous academic year. The incidents occurred after these two students were informed that they were failing the first quarter. They came into class in a disruptive fashion and were assigned detention for disrupting others' learning. At this point they erupted with yelling and cursing, as they often had previously in this and other classes and school settings, but escalated the behavior by throwing over desks.

I asked that they not be returned to class without a meeting with me, them, parents and administrators, but the administration placed them back in class without such a meeting. It responded to my request at that point for assistance in preventing dangerous behavior in the future by these students by advocating "planned ignoring" of their behavior, so as not to irritate them and lead them into disruption. At this point I decided to resign, because I lacked the authority to provide a safe environment for my students.

The fundamental question: Both of my reasons for resigning arise from a failure to address a fundamental question about Technology Preparatory. What are the criteria for students to be enrolled and to remain enrolled in a college preparatory high school? I realize that both enrollment and dismissal are governed by complex legal standards. However, even if the law requires Friendship to accept and retain all students, no matter how poorly prepared for a college preparatory curriculum and no matter how disruptive their behavior, Friendship must decide if they can be educated in the same classroom as students who are ready to take on ninth-grade work.

Skill level: I tested my incoming 9th graders with a grade-level assessment tool and found that the mean level was third-grade. This conclusion is consistent with their mean performance on the first of six "Achievement-Net" standardized tests for the year, despite the administration's decision to provide teachers with not just practice tests to guide the curriculum, but the actual test. Given the presence of a significant number of seventh-grade levels and a few ninth-grade levels, this necessarily means that many the students were at the second-grade level on skills. This group does not appear to lack the intelligence to handle grade-level work; rather, for a variety of reasons, its members consistently arrive at school without school materials and homework, and are disproportionately late and absent, unwilling to attempt and complete assignments in class, and disruptive of others' learning.

When I reported all this to my administration, it agreed with my assessment of the six-year deficit in math skills, which it blamed on the DC Public Schools, even though many of these students have been in the Friendship system for years. I also reported my belief that these students must have been given passing grades for years without mastering grade-level content in math, including in the previous year, when many failed, but then passed a summer school course with no required exit exam.

Disruptive behavior: I have followed the school's behavior code, which calls for, in order, a warning, a phone call to a parent or guardian, a detention after school, and finally removal from the classroom to a "focus room" where a staff member counsels the student. These steps are called "consequences," as all the students know — even turning the noun into a verb ("He consequenced me!"). However, there really is no credible consequence for some students, because there is no number of detentions or referrals that results in a student being removed from the classroom or the school. If you look at the detention lists for this month, 14 weeks into the school year, you will see over well 100 students, up to a third of the school, listed on many days. This means that hundreds of hours of instruction are being lost each week for the students who are not engaged in disruptive behavior.

Can Technology Preparatory fulfill its mission of preparing the majority of ninth-graders who are ready and able to work on a college preparatory curriculum when it retains in the same classrooms the significant minority who are not? My answer, after 14 weeks of effort, was no. I hope you will rethink the model you are using. I am eager to talk with you about any of these issues.

* * *

Despite my dramatic allegations of fraudulent grades masking system-wide failure, I never heard back from any member of the Friendship board, and the only response from the DC Charter board was a member's angry response on the comments page after a Washington Post reporter wrote an article about the incident. The gist of his argument was that he had met the principal and she seemed like a wonderful, dedicated person. Again, though, the news story resulted in my email box being flooded with notes from teachers around the country who had felt such pressures, and generally had to succumb to them keep their jobs. Typical was this response from a foreign language teacher in a DC school for students who had been expelled from neighborhood schools — and that takes a lot of doing: "How can students miss 120 out of 180 classes and pass a foreign language? It's a mystery to me, since I report them as failing, as per district rules. Yet they somehow get the credit and are on track to graduate. I keep my head down, I do my job. I don't want to end up like Erich Martel."

The pressure for phony grades becomes even more intense as students drift up towards graduation. As mentioned in the Preface, I was once assigned 38 seniors for pre-Calculus, because teachers in the "testing grade" of 10th grade Algebra were given tiny classes of "bubble kids" who might be able to score "proficient" on the DC-CAS test that would determine the school's future. My first move, as always, was to test my class with grade level assessments, where I found that I really had two classes. While the overall average was at the fourth grade level, similar to my entering 9th graders, about half showed some competence and work ethic, and were clustered at about seventh grade, while half were either so devoid of basic math skills or were such weak readers that they could not decipher, format, or compute a second-grade problem such as: "John spent $1.18 on pencils, $1.45 on paper, and 30 cents each for three erasers. How much did he spend in all?"

Putting these two groups of seniors together in a course starting with sines and cosines and moving on to the secrets of calculus derivatives and integrals was, to put it mildly, challenging. The lower group did not have enough background to study anything resembling pre-calculus, attended sporadically, rarely brought a binder and pencil, would purposely disrupt the entire class if pushed to do any book work, and responded to homework being an admission ticket to class by copying it from others. The higher group, in contrast, was game to be slowly guided into any topic, came to class with a binder and pencil, would try to complete class assignments, and would at least start and struggle a bit with homework. After a week I went to see the principal, noted that the union contract limited class size to 25, asked him to split the class into the two logical sections, and said I'd be glad to take either one. He said he'd get back to me shortly, so I continued on for two more weeks, keeping the material basic and fun rather than rigorous for the time being, so that everybody could participate.

For example, instead of practicing trigonometric examples on paper (which one definitely must do repeatedly to cement the concept and the method of calculation), I formed mixed-ability groups of four and gave each group a ruler, some string, and a protractor, and had them compete to see which one could come closest to estimating the true height of the room. You do this by measuring the distance from a point on the floor to the base of one of the walls, and then eyeballing a protractor placed at that point beside a string held up to point to the top of the wall, to estimate the angle formed by the ground and the string.

By the definitions of trigonometry, the tangent for that angle (whose numeric value, found in a table, is valid for right triangles of all sizes, since those triangles would be proportionate to each other) is the ratio of the height of the wall and the distance from your point to the wall. If you measure your distance as 18 feet and estimate your angle as 30 degrees (which has a tangent of .58), then your equation is .58 = height/18. Multiplying both sides by 18, you would estimate the height at 10.4 feet. After all the groups had made their estimates, we had the tallest student stand on a desk and use a yard stick to find the actual height. By listing their estimated angles and associated tangent figures, students could see how an error of a few degrees in the angle would have put them far off their estimate of the height.

While the stronger students warmed to the task, and after a few guided efforts were willing to defend their estimates to their classmates by illustrating them on the board, keeping the weaker students on task without a constant presence was a never-ending battle in which I finally surrendered. They mostly just let their group mates do the work, while they joked and joned. I went to see a guidance counselor with a list of the names in the weaker group, so we could pull up their academic records and confirm that they had indeed passed Algebra II, the prerequisite for the course. Knowing the difficulty of Algebra II even for 11th graders with decent skills and work ethic, I was sure that these students could not have passed that course. However, all of them had been awarded the barely passing grade of D. Given the high turnover among teachers in high-poverty schools, only two of the five teachers who had registered these grades the previous June were still at the school.

The first teacher I went to see was "Mwalunthu Mwunguthi," a Malawian immigrant who for 20 years had taught special education math. He had passed "DeJarius," a voluble, bubbly, massive, and mentally challenged all-district football lineman and shotputter, in a "self-contained" class consisting entirely of special education students of different grades taking different courses. Mwalunthu was known by one and all simply as Mr. M. By tradition, students and staff alike called most teachers who were not African-Americans by their initials, as if their last names were phonetically bizarre. A white American of Hispanic descent became Mr. O., not Mr. Ojeda; a Filipino became Mr. P, not Mr. Pangalinan; and a Nigerian Ibo became Ms. N rather than Ms. Nguzina. (I manfully resisted becoming Dr. R., but had to settle for "Doc" with the staff and "Doc Rock," pronounced Dock-a-Rock, with the half of the students who could comprehend, but not speak, standard English.)

It was difficult for me, and the students, to understand "Mr. M" with his broad Afro-British accent, which may have explained why he had been unable to move to a job at an easier school, like so many of his former colleagues. But I couldn't miss his shock at being told that DeJarius was in the one pre-calculus class being offered to seniors, alongside the few students who were truly college-bound. As best as I could tell, he said: "Huh! That boy can't add two plus two and doesn't care! What is he doing in pre-calculus? Yes, of course I passed him — that's a gentleman's D. Everybody knows that a D for a Special Education student means nothing but that he came in once in a while."

There was no doubt that DeJarius had some gentlemanly qualities. He was always friendly, laughing at his embarrassment over his inability to perform basic math or follow simple directions. Unfortunately, he never stopped being friendly, as he happily chatted with his seatmates and called out to friends across the class and in the halls, and lightly joned with them throughout the lesson. As a senior, DeJarius had clearly learned the mechanics of getting a gentleman's D, because he and his position coach would come around at the end of each week to ask what he could do as "extra credit" to keep his grade up enough to stay on the football team. He also tried to round up a few credits toward passing by copying others' homework, which was more of an after-class effort than most of the students made. But his tested level was at the first grade, and his presence deterred and disrupted others' efforts.

Mr. M. dragged me over to his computer and proudly showed me the latest of his lengthy letters to the Chancellor, in which he challenged his low classroom evaluations from an assistant principal whose written assessments read the same way he always talked, in Black English, and so were replete with grammatical errors. Mr. M. put a lot of time into his letters, and the one he showed me included a detailed analysis of the many grammatical errors made by the assistant principal in the latest evaluation. Each letter officially started a lengthy appeals process in which he was usually able to raise his scores and preserve his job. Mr. M. compensated for his poor classroom scores by following to the letter the requirements for every portion of the score based on writing and filing lesson plans. He also documented every request he had made for materials and information on students that had been ignored, and kept files for years to submit in appeal, should he not receive a perfect score for those portions.

The second teacher was, like me, the rare white man on the faculty. While the ratio of black to white teachers for women was about three to one, for men it was more like six to one. All the staff responsible for keeping the school ticking and maintaining contact with the guardians and the community — administrators, guidance counselors, social workers, security guards, office staff, and Goon Squad members — were black. "James Arbent" had moved to Washington midway through the previous school year, leaving behind his job at a tony all-white private school in a southern city so his wife could take her dream job. He had replaced a young white woman who had broken down from the strain of her classes. Tired of her tears and her students' disruption and lack of effort, she had suddenly fled one night to her family and Midwestern hometown, not even coming in to pick up her belongings. There are always openings at the high-poverty neighborhood schools, and the rare ones that are rumored to be about to pop up at the admission schools and schools in the white neighborhoods are filled by teachers there reaching out to friends and getting them on the inside track before the announcement can even be made.

James did not challenge the administration's low classroom evaluations, laughingly admitting that he was certainly "minimally effective" in this environment. He also didn't bother to document the administration's ignoring his requests for disciplinary meetings with guardians, teaching materials, keys, and necessary parts for his Smart Board. His response to all this was simply to intensifying his search for a job in a private or charter school. James was in an obvious and open state of perpetual disgust and despair at the lack of support, but his first child had been born over the summer and he needed the money, so he was forced to stay on into a second year.

James' excuse for "D-ing out" "Malita," a frequently-absent and aggressively disruptive gang girl, from Algebra II, was refreshingly honest: he didn't want to have her in class ever again. She had already flunked the year-long course once, and then she had failed to show up for the easy summer school course because she had been hospitalized after being shot in the leg. With her original math teacher, Malita had failed the first half of the year, recording virtually no work the few times she attended. Under a little-noticed regulatory trick, though, she had needed only to pass the second half of the year with James to get the all-important check mark for one of the four years of required math.

Those four years were a classic college prep sequence of full years of Algebra I, Geometry, Algebra II, and then one semester of either pre-Calculus or Statistics. While each of the first three math courses were for an entire year, students only had to pass the second semester to complete that year's requirement. Of course, they would only have one unit of credit from that year instead of two, but the graduation requirements only averaged about five credits a year, whereas passing a full load of four courses each semester would have provided eight, leaving lots of wiggle room for failed semesters.

Nobody at the school was prepared for Calculus, let alone the Advanced Placement Calculus courses offered, often to juniors, at the white neighborhood and admission high schools. The principal once asked me to prepare an AP statistics syllabus and have it approved by the College Board so that Johnson could have the course listed on its books. The approved syllabus packed into half a year what would take a full year in a typical college introductory course. Fortunately, scholarly disaster was averted because only two students showed up for the course. The AP course had to be cancelled, Assistant Principal Marcellus explained to the angry pair of seniors, tongue-in-cheek (perhaps), because I would have been attacked in the parking lot by other teachers who had more than 20 students and often 30 enrolled in their classes. The listing stayed on the school's website and was counted as one of its AP courses.

After another week went by, I returned to the principal to check on my request for dividing the 38 students into two classes. He told me how as an Army sergeant he had taught 100 high school dropouts to repair helicopters, and dismissed me with, "Just teach 'em, Doc, just teach 'em." Quite certain that I would not be given the power of Army sergeants to encourage attention with pushups, latrine cleaning duty, dismissal, and ultimately execution for failure to comply with orders, I went to see Don Marcellus. I knew that his usual preoccupation, come each spring, was helping seniors massage their porous transcripts into diplomas. He and the guidance counselors would certify the lamest descriptions of hours and duties toward the required 100 hours of community service and find redefinitions to make waivers for courses and experiences that plausibly could meet the various overall and subgroup requirements for a diploma. So I put it to him bluntly: "If I keep all 38 students, I can tell you that the weaker half will fail and be unable to graduate. They will have to take pre-Calculus again in summer school or at the community college next fall in order to get their diplomas."

"I don't think they're gonna like that downtown, Doc," he replied, and he promised to check back with the principal for me. But the next day, now almost a month into the semester, he told me it was not going to work. "I simply don't have the teachers. Tell me what I'm supposed to do. Give me a solution." I told him that's why he was paid the big bucks, and went off to find the real power in the school, Rosemary Queen. Rosemary was, like many of the black teachers, a proud Aggie, meaning a graduate of North Carolina Agricultural and Technical, one of the two or three strongest historically-black universities.

Rosemary's power did not derive from being the head of the math department. In fact, in violation of all the written, contractual powers of that position, I had been hired by the previous principal, white man to white man, without her knowing. And her power did not derive from being the union representative in the building, because she had given up that position years before. Her power derived from her knowledge of personalities and procedures, acquired not because she sought it but because staff with problems sought her out as I had, and her reputation as someone who said absolutely nothing of substance to any administrator unless absolutely necessary.

Rosemary always came and sat next to me at the frequent "professional development" sessions before and after school and the one day each month when students would stay home so "PD" could go all day. She knew I was irritated by the theft of class and preparation time by these largely nonsensical meetings, in which district staff and various consultants would guide us through discussions of the latest fad being foisted on us. One of the first sessions I had to attend had ended in acrimony when I told the leader of the session that I wanted to discuss ways to improve teaching, not ways to improve my score on the classroom evaluation for one of the eight categories in the untested evaluation system. The principal had erupted and demanded an end to all comments that were not germane to the topic. Since then Rosemary made a point of sitting next me so she could pinch my leg each time I stirred to ask a question, and would whisper to me her mantra for surviving 40 years under a dizzying succession of fads, professional developers, principals, and superintendents: "Quiet. Smile. This bullshit too shall pass."

I told Rosemary on a Thursday that if the class wasn't divided by Monday, I would resign and send a letter to all the guardians of the kids in the class explaining that I could not in good conscience agree to an arrangement that was bad for all their children. Later that day I saw her in the hallway, calling out pleasantly to the principal, "Come here, boy. We need to talk." Then she saw Don nearby and said, "You come here, boo, because you need to hear this too." I don't know what she said in the brief meeting. I doubt she threatened that the union would file a grievance over the number of students in the class. She wouldn't have needed to, since it would have been obvious that it would happen if I resigned. The union's legal teams always go all out to defend teachers. I have seen them do that for the truly incompetent and the truly evil, so I suppose they would have gone to bat for me. But the powerful don't need to threaten, in any event. Simply by saying her first words of substance of the entire year to the principal and Don, the same words I had been saying about the current arrangement not being good for the students, she was laying down a marker that could not be ignored.

The very next day, Friday, I got the word from Don: the class would be split, with the lower half going to a special education math teacher and the upper half staying with me. "Robert Shick" didn't think he was prepared to teach pre-Calculus, but Don had decided that he could teach his group basic math material and call it a course in statistics, the only other possibility for the advanced math credit needed for the students' graduation. Robert was a wonderful presence in the school, quiet and pleasant with his special education students who seemed to draw calm from his magnificent presence. He was, as the old-school saying went, tall, tan, young, and fly. He was also my sartorial role model as the best-dressed man, always in crisp shirt and tie, with outsized cufflinks and elegant, sparklingly-shined shoes. After school, though, he would change into his gym clothes every day and become the devoted athletic director, available to pick up the slack when nobody would coach a sport at the minimal pay offered.

The dumping of this new duty on Robert created some tension between us, especially when four or five new students were added to the course. Students coming into school so many weeks late were liable to be the less committed ones. By their results on their grade-level tests, they didn't belong in the pre-Calculus group, but placing them all with Robert violated whatever promises Don had made him. Freed for the first time in their careers from classroom disruption, my students were pleasantly surprised to find themselves moving faster and with more effort, and more enjoyment, than they had ever imagined they could. The few weaker students I had to add were almost immediately scared off by the amount of work being done, and simply disappeared. Of my original 19, only the weakest two failed, and that only because they skipped too many classes and assignments to master the material.

That is not to say that my group was always a bed of roses. We had the predictable classroom dramas of anger and reluctance and family traumas of violence and dysfunction. One of the two best students, who had transferred from a Catholic school because he wanted to get a football scholarship and could start on the Johnson team, suddenly turned into a cursing, physical terror halfway into the semester, requiring the same sort of security removal and parent meeting as a troubled 9th grader. The football coach explained the tantrums as "a big head" because he had been offered a Division I scholarship, and his mother managed to turn him around after I explained at our meeting that he would be barred from my classroom, and fail the course, the next time he erupted.

The popular and confident star of the vaunted girls' basketball team had a violent encounter with her mother's boyfriend, and dropped off the team. For at least a month she was also more liable to erupt than to enlighten when asked to come to the board to explain a homework problem, something she had previously enjoyed doing in dramatic and humorous fashion. While the work done in class was solid, the exams were often as disastrous as in my other classes, with students performing well below their abilities because they wouldn't prepare for them. They had always passed their courses without studying for exams, and they weren't about to start in 12th grade. A typical exam would result in two A's (over 90) and 17 F's (under 65). But in the end, it was the best result I ever had, and the students constantly remarked on what fun it was not to have to wait for the knuckleheads to stop jiving and the slower students to "get it" so we could move on.

And what of the lower group, in Robert's "statistics" class? All passed, all graduated, so there was nothing for "downtown" not to like. But the two boys who failed in my class didn't like it one bit. They came begging for "make-up" work, arguing that they had done far more work than many of the students who had passed Robert's class. Their friendly demeanor showed that they had every expectation, given their experiences, of an "arrangement" that would D them out. But my standard response to "What can I do to raise my grade?" remained: "You can take the course again and do what you should have done this time." The friendly demeanor changed to tears and threats, but they still came away unsatisfied. Somehow in the next semester they met their requirements, even though they did not take the only pre-Calculus course in that semester, which I taught. Who knows, maybe they got a statistics credit. I'm no brave soul like Erich Martel. I didn't question the students who walked across the stage. But I know that nearly every diploma was fundamentally phony, that the students had been cheated at some, at many points in their school careers by being passed without proper attendance and effort. Graduation rates are up, the district claimed in a recent press release. Indeed.

* * *

Chapter 3. The Culture of Black Poverty

As a charter secondary school principal with a decade of experience teaching poor black children, "Vanita Mills" rarely strikes a wrong note in her interactions with them. But she made two uncharacteristic mistakes, one personal and one institutional, when she confronted "Malanii," a ninth-grade girl who had been in Vanita's charter system since kindergarten, over her disruptive behavior in the halls and her loud, disrespectful remarks to the security guards who admonished her. Vanita told Malanii: "Young lady, we're not on the street in Barry Terrace, now. We're in school. Don't be bringing the street into the school!" Malanii blew right past the usual restraint the students showed with the ultimate authority figure in the school and went ballistic, cursing and threatening Vanita: "(Expletive) bitch, that's my block. Don't you be runnin' down my block. We know what to do with niggers that run down my block."

Vanita suspended Malanii for three days, and probably had to if the school were to maintain any semblance of order. This was the first time Malanii's mouth had been turned against the principal the way it was almost daily against her teachers if they asked her to stop talking and start working. Those incidents of cursing and threatening had only resulted in her going to the "focus room" for 20 minutes for a chat with an administrator before being returned to class, and then taking part in a "restorative circle" in which she would promise never to do it again and be threatened with suspension if she did. Of course, over and over, she would do it again, and she wouldn't be suspended. The implicit message to Malanii and the other students in her suspension was that you can curse and threaten teachers, but not the principal.

Vanita had momentarily forgotten that it is a losing game to challenge any teenager's roots by criticizing their block or their set of friends, and by implication their family and their culture. Teachers learned never even to imply that there was anything wrong with students' situations, because that would only build resentment with a child with whom one needed to build trust. When a 12-year-old from the neighborhood died riding in a stolen car, the mere discussion of the incident in my class dredged up angry dissents from students who knew the boy. They warned me, "don't be talking 'bout a person's personal business," even if that person was now dead from poor choices.

Letting slip her awareness of the threat that street culture poses to school culture also contradicted Vanita's usual institutional adherence to her charter company's claim that schools can succeed regardless of their students' streets. The ideology of school reform holds that it is bad teaching, not the culture and reality of black poverty, that holds students back. But Vanita had in fact put her finger on the main challenge for high-poverty schools: the street is of necessity brought into the schools, because the kids are of the street. Reformers say the schools are failing. But it is the culture that is failing. After so many years of oppression, the culture of black poverty has become black children's own worst enemy, raising them in a self-destructive alienation from mainstream society and its requirements of effort and decorum. When the kids say they don't care, they really mean it.

* * *

Vanita's charter school is in the poorest neighborhood in the poorest section of town. She is the prototypical "school reform" acolyte. She is a true believer. She probably has to be to come to work each morning, dodge the urinating drunks as she drives down the alley behind the run-down block of black-run hair weave and nail salons and Korean-run convenience and liquor stores, and adopt a mindset that denies the objective reality that the vast majority of her students are not going to make it out of this low-income, virtually no-income neighborhood symbolically placed at the intersection of Malcolm X and Martin Luther King avenues.

Like most teachers and administrators in charter schools, Vanita did not take the traditional path to a career in education, that of education majors who spend much of their four years in teacher training and classroom internships. Instead, she studied English at her elite historically black college and then answered the siren call of a program that promised with that a summer's training she could help deliver the black underclass to college. These programs have an ideology of elitism, following as they do in the footsteps of the Teach for America program, a creation of Yale undergraduates who thought they could do a much better job than the state teachers college graduates who populate the public schools.

After 20 years the research on this claim is inconclusive, as might be expected when teaching ability is hard to define and its impact is harder to measure, and in any event is outweighed by income, health, race, parental education level, and the many other variables that account for low performance in high-poverty schools. Vanita differs from the vast majority of these non-traditional teachers in that she stayed in the profession. Most leave after a couple of years, their résumés padded with public service and their student debt lowered by the incentives the federal government offers for teaching in high-poverty schools.

What Vanita believes is that her charter company "has the answer" that can prepare all poor, black students to attend and succeed in college. That company is a 15-school, two-city empire, with annual revenues of over $100 million, most coming from the $12,000 in public funds it receives for each of its 8,000 students. A good share, though, comes from foundations and individuals who have faithfully backed the "school reform" movement of charters, vouchers, less job protection, rights, and flexibility in the classroom for teachers, and the misuse of tests to reward and penalize staff and schools.

Vanita frequently says that every child in her school is going to college, because, by definition, her charter company sends all its students to college. She says this despite having taught many students who did not start college and many more who did not finish. What Vanita most deeply believes, though, is something she tells her teachers daily, which is that "we know what to do, so just do what we tell you." If a student is not progressing toward college, she just knows it is because of a teacher's failure to implement her system faithfully and energetically enough.

Vanita's belief is at the core of the school reform movement, and of the fraudulent claim that the culture of black poverty presents no barrier to success. Peggy Cooper Cafritz, a Washington philanthropist who was elected to run the public schools in Washington, DC, in 2000, told one and all that "there is no reason" why DC should not reach her goal of averaging as high a score on the College Boards as the suburban districts of Virginia, just a few miles away. Anyone pointing out the impossibility of that goal, given the strong correlation of test scores with poverty and ethnicity, and then given the segregation of the school districts, was seen as a racist whose low expectations for the black poor of DC were the very reason they were not achieving like the wealthy white and Asian children of Fairfax County.

When Peggy finished her six years as president, the district's black and poor children were, of course, very much at the same spot on SAT scores as she found them. Her dreams had been based on the wonderful DC public arts high school she had help found in the 1970s. Why, she asked, couldn't all the students in the district have schools like this, and get just as many college acceptances? But Duke Ellington was an admission school, where students had rigorous auditions to be accepted, and could and would be sent back to their neighborhood schools if their attendance, behavior, and artistic or academic studies lagged. The successes Peggy saw at the Duke were, as always, as much a function of the survivors' strong families and individual attributes as of the strength of the curriculum and the teachers.

The system developed by Vanita's company to prove Peggy right is a hodgepodge of behavioral tricks, incentives, and penalties that teachers are instructed to use the same way in each class. The 80 minute classes are to be programmed to the minute, with catchy rubrics such as "I do, we do, you do," which means demonstration of a concept by the teacher, group practice with teacher guidance, and individual work. For each component of the period students receive worksheets that guide their work. Teachers are told to take notes constantly on a computer system, recording positive acts like following the posters that use an acronym to remind students to sit up straight, hold a pencil for immediate note-taking, follow the teacher's eyes, and ask questions with a raised hand, and negative acts like being late, talking, or not following the acronym of attention.

These computer notes automatically translate into "merits and demerits," with points that are summed for weekly prizes like candy bars and monthly prizes like electronic devices. Too many demerits earns "consequences," which escalate by rule from a warning, to a phone call to a guardian, to a 30-minute quiet detention period after school, and finally to "referral" out of the classroom to a "focus room" with an administrator who then calls a guardian in for a meeting or plans a "restorative circle" in which all the participants in an incident relive it and come up with a solution.

On paper it's a great system, apparently accounting for every eventuality. But in real life it's not working for Vanita. The classrooms, hallways, and lunchroom are rife with disruptions, especially from the many special education and emotionally disturbed students who are being more integrated into the regular classrooms each year. Charters are under pressure to show that they take in as many challenging children as public schools, and actually have financial incentives to do so, since federal aid for special education students follows them to their school. More importantly, the first set of interim test results this year at Vanita's school accurately reflected the many years her average student is behind national levels. Pressure came down from the revered founder of the cult-like charter company to improve the scores. Vanita is not one to challenge the founder, a social entrepreneur of national standing whom she refers to in a tone of awe: "If he knew you were using precious class time to discuss teen pregnancy, I am scared to think how disappointed he would be."

As a believer in the system and its promise of success, Vanita had to find someone to blame for the poor scores. First she blamed the DC public schools, telling the staff that the public schools' failure had created this lag of many years that they would have to overcome. The fact that most of the students had attended the company's elementary school, and not the public schools, was conveniently ignored. Then she blamed the teachers, taking all the pressure that was being placed on her and turning it onto them. She invoked the founder's public warning to the entire staff at convocation each fall that, "If you can't move these children forward, I'll find someone else who can."

The young, white, Teach for America types responded to their blistering sessions with Vanita by increasing their work hours, every night correcting each day's many papers and trying to reach by phone every guardian whose child had disrupted class. But "Stacey Christian," a 30-year-old veteran teacher from an historically-black teachers' college who had spent some of her childhood in that very neighborhood before her family moved to a suburban school, was having none of the blame or the extra hours. The tension between the two proud black women escalated into a months-long battle, with angry meetings each day that Stacey would refuse to leave without an apology, even when classes had started.

Vanita would say: "I am heartsick, literally sick to my stomach, when I look in your class and I see the students not working. Those black children are our future, and you are destroying them. You are not putting in the time to teach them properly." Stacey would respond: "I am not leaving here until you tell me you will not talk to me in this fashion again. You are making this a hostile workplace. It's outrageous, blaming me for the academic level at which students enter, or for their disruptions, which are throughout the day, in all their classes and in the halls, not just in my class. That's not on me and I won't accept it. I am a professional with ten years' teaching students, and I will not be talked to like a child. I have a life and I will not be told to work until midnight each day." Other teachers and administrators had to be asked to "cover" Stacey's classes until another of these frequent dust-ups was over.

Many teachers resigned during that first semester, just disappearing overnight, tired of the impossible demands, reminiscent of Peggy Cooper Cafritz, that the students somehow just act like white, middle class kids, and of the vitriol that Vanita would heap on teachers if they did not. Not Stacey. Unlike the youngsters, she had been a teacher so she knew she could teach; she knew the culture so she knew the odds of success were low; and she was a grown-up so she knew she deserved a paycheck and a life. She stuck out the year before leaving the classroom for an administrative position.

The middle and high school Vanita runs is open-admission, but it is grandly named Science and Technology. This name is a nod to the fashionable

Science, Technology, Engineering, and Math (STEM) concept that in recent years has drawn federal and private funding to city schools. STEM is more a vision than a curriculum, and the vision is that by being exposed to robotics and science labs, poor black students will want to, and be prepared to, study science and engineering in college. The only problem with Vanita's school appropriating this vision is that her students, like those at most open-admission STEM schools, are just like all high-poverty cohorts: on average reading, calculating, and behaving about six years below their grade level.

In fact, "Science Tech" came about largely as a target of opportunity. It is really just a classic neighborhood, open admission school with about 75 students in each grade, created to absorb the graduates of its charter company's elementary school next door. Like most STEM schools, the only thing "STEM" about it is the bold sign on the door. Students from high-poverty neighborhoods are deeply loyal to them, and most of them are secretly scared of unfamiliar surroundings. The graduates of the charter elementary school were not showing up at the charter company's middle and high schools, which were in other neighborhoods. So, the company decided to create Science Tech for these graduates right next door, in trailers and an ancient public school that had been abandoned as the surge of charter schools cut public school enrollment in half over a decade. As Science Tech added a grade each year, the charter company began building a stunning new building on the same block, with a capacity far beyond current enrollment. Vanita has to fill that school, giving her another reason, along with her belief in the system, to be loath to push out students, no matter how ill-prepared or disruptive.

* * *

But why are so many poor black children so ill-prepared and disruptive when packed into a school with their neighborhood set? Why do most children in high-poverty schools do little class work and no homework and then say, "I don't care" when they see their grade go down? What is at the heart of the matter?

DeWayne Wickham, the dean of historically-black Morgan State's school of journalism, titled one of his regular USA Today columns in 2014, "Why are preschools expelling black boys?" Wickham was "dumbfounded" to discover in a federal panel's report to President Obama that children were being suspended or expelled from pre-schools, and "outraged" by the fact that black children received this discipline at more than twice the rate of whites. Implicit in his bald recitation of percentages is his opinion that racism, or at least insensitivity to racial issues, is at play. But as the column continues, hints trickle out that Wickham gets it, that he understands that black pre-schoolers children are being disciplined more often than white ones primarily because they are exhibiting a higher rate of behaviors that disrupt other children's learning or might harm them. The experts he interviews point out that black children tend to have "education deficits" even at this early age, and that "kids who have psychological problems or come from dysfunctional homes" need special resources.

The remedies the experts suggest themselves acknowledge the problem: "Schools have options: Social workers, parent liaisons, counselors, advisers." But what pre-school can afford to have this special staff, especially if they need a lot of them because, by segregated residences, it has a concentration of parents who have not "done their part to ensure that their children are well-behaved and emotionally ready for school?" And how do we know that all these staff can change the fundamental dysfunction of a highly-stressed family in poverty, or ease the alienation the child feels from mainstream society? By the end of the article Wickham is still worried that a pattern of expulsion for "young blacks who come from single-parents homes" can be "an early step in the pipeline that funnels black youngsters from school to prison." But by acknowledging that losing both his parents led him to misbehavior in high school that got him expelled, he makes the outrageous actions of the pre-school administrators now look a little more logical.

The school reformers are caught in a bind on this crucial question of poor black children's culture and their alienation from mainstream expectations. Under their ideology, the weak results in Vanita's school must be a function of there being bad teachers with low expectations, yet the school reformers themselves are middle and upper class and make sure that their children have a background entirely different from that of the poor kids.

The reformers have carefully-planned pregnancies and put their kids in socially calm and intellectually stimulating day care and schools. They hire tutors from first grade to 12th, covering everything from reading to SAT prep. They arrange music and computer lessons, gymnastics, soccer, family vacations to the country and to Europe, summer camps, healthy food, trips to museums, and constant activities and conversations. They seek high school internships for their kids through businesses and government contacts. The reformers must think these things are important, or they wouldn't do them, but then they argue that the poor black kids who don't have them are none the worse for it, because with great teachers in their segregated reform schools they can be just as good students as the privileged kids.

Some of the leading school reform philanthropists also make donations to programs that give poor children more of what rich, white children have. They advocate employment programs for parents, improved health care for children, and home visiting and early childhood programs that focus on verbal interaction and intellectual stimulation to address the multi-million word deficits of poor infants. But any implication that not having these programs results in children being more difficult to educate for college prep and families being more difficult to engage in supporting them intellectually and academically at home is seen a way for teachers to get off the hook for their laziness and low expectations.

Where the school reformers really miss out, though, is in dismissing not just the importance of middle class methods of preparation for life, but of middle class culture itself. Let's let "Diamonita," a burly, funny, blustery Science Tech 9th grader, show that importance. Wherever you find Diamonita you can be sure to find noise. She invariably puts on an act of angry disputation if somebody "jones" her, and she can overhear somebody doing so from 50 feet away in a noisy cafeteria. So of course she is always being joned, and always reacting dramatically. When she finally calms down and returns to the classroom from one of her many removals by security guards, she will explain herself this way: "I'm sorry. I can't help it! Sometimes I just be so ghetto."

The word "ghetto" is so important in their life that poor black students use it as multiple parts of speech: We in the ghetto now; That boy be pure ghetto; Don't you go ghetto all up in my face; She be ghetto dancin'. The kids know they are different from the mainstream they see on TV. They know that not just whites, Asians, and Hispanics, but even middle class blacks are wary of them. They know they have a ghetto orientation. And as Malanii's reaction to her principal's comments on her street ways shows, they are proud of it. The kids indeed "be so ghetto," and many cannot overcome that orientation enough to embrace anything resembling a middle class approach to school.

Yes, there is a poor black culture, and yes, it can disrupt education. In fact, it is all-powerful. It is their thing, their *Cosa Nostra*. You can work with it, you can work around it, but you can never ignore it. When we pretend that our high-poverty and our middle class schools are essentially the same, and can be successful with the same curriculum and expectations, we are setting our poor kids up for failure.

Unless you've been in the culture, you can't imagine it and its importance in school. After a career as a college professor, I decided to teach high school. The vast majority of the open jobs were in high-poverty schools because of the constant turnover of burned-out teachers. At a recruitment event I talked with the Johnson principal and was invited on the spot to give a practice class and have an interview. The practice class consisted of eight of the registered 20 juniors in Algebra II, which I found out the next year was a typical attendance rate, scattered around a giant classroom. One boy had his head down and was pretending to sleep, and after a couple of tries even the principal felt it prudent not to disturb him. With some friendly cajoling the other students played along politely enough in an easy proof of the Pythagorean theorem at the board, in which they used markers to break up each side of a square into a long and short piece (lengths A and B) and made a smaller square and four triangles inside the original square using lines between the pieces (length C, the hypotenuse). They were able to show that the area of the square could be calculated either by simply multiplying length times width (A squared plus B squared plus two times A times B), or by adding up the different triangles making up the square (C squared plus two times A times B). Subtracting the last term from both sides of this equality, they had proved Pythagoras right.

I was surprised that by 11th grade the students did not recognize the Pythagorean rule, and more surprised that when we began to do some examples most of the students could not square small numbers or subtract larger ones accurately. I expected to talk about this in the interview with the principal and other administrators after the class, but the first question, from "Ms. Billy," a young assistant principal, stopped me in my tracks. She bluntly asked me what I would do when the first student said to me, as she predicted he or she would, "Dr. Rossiter, get the (expletive) out my face. I be too tired to do no (expletive) work today!"

The question was completely alien to my recollections of high school, where I had been the bad boy, the suspended and expelled one, for actions that would never have approached this level of disrespect, and to my experiences as a professor, where I had endured anger over grades from entitled students without a hint of cursing or threat. So I stumbled for appropriate words to address a clearly ridiculous hypothetical situation: "Well, um, I suppose you have a school policy about cursing that will tell me exactly where to send the child. Ah, I will follow whatever rules you have for this." Ms. Billy laughed and said, "Come on, think on your feet! The only rule around here is to solve your own problems!"

Well, there I was the next fall, standing in my very first class, ten minutes after the bell with only about ten of my registered 25 students in their seats, when "Heston Littleton," a handsome, rangy 10th grader, bounced into my door. "Hey y'all niggers," he yelled out happily, "Bitches be glad, 'cause the (expletive) himself is back!" Well, I solved my own problem by telling him to try again tomorrow, but that nobody who cursed would be coming into my classroom until he came back to see me and talk it out at the end of the day. In the coming weeks I discovered that Heston's mother was sick with AIDS, that he was essentially homeless, bouncing around from house to house at night, and that he had done so little work and had so few credits to his name that it was hard to say what grade he was in. We developed a decent relationship, so he did not repeat this particular antic, but he was never really a student. He came to school because it was warm, safe, and had food. He spent all his time trying to get into the girls' pants, right during class, and none of it studying; but he was a good kid, who for his own protection certainly needed to be in school and not on the street. That first day, though, I wasn't having any of it.

Except that I was. Minutes after I tossed him out, Heston came back to the door, towed there by the notorious dean of students. This was my first encounter with the Crow. One of his jobs was to get students out of the halls and into classrooms, and he was doing it that day. "You can't put someone out for a Class 1 offense," he said, for all the class to hear. I was nonplussed, unaware of any classes of offenses. "District rules: cursing is a Class 1 offense. Handle it in the classroom," he said. So in came Heston and out went my excellent plan for dealing with cursing. When I finally read the rules for classes of offenses that night, I could see why cursing was put into the lowest one. There needed to be classes and penalties available for higher crimes and misdemeanors than I had ever imagined in a school setting, like lighting fires, carrying weapons, punching teachers, and starting gang chants in the cafeteria.

I had parked my motorcycle by the sports field, and when I went out to it after school that day, there was Heston, up along the railing on the bank above the field, watching the junior varsity football team practice. He was in his street clothes, tossing beautiful spiral passes to his friends. "Whoa," I said, "You'd make a great quarterback. Why aren't you out there?" Heston looked at me like I was crazy: "Oh, I could never make the grades for any sports."

Just then a boy came riding on a bicycle up to the field. He was wearing his uniform and clearly expected to jump right into practice. The Crow, who was the coach of the junior varsity team, stopped him in his tracks, his voice ringing out, all ghetto and commanding, so that Heston and I could hear it 50 yards away: "Oh no, nigger. Don't even think about it. You get right on that (expletive) bike and pedal your black ass away. On time is on time and we don't have no late niggers on this team!" Heston turned to look at me, clearly enjoying my surprise at hearing an administrator use the same language that I thought merited getting him tossed from class. I was clearly in another world.

It was the Crow's world, not mine. What he was doing with his fine instincts for reaching these students and keeping a modicum of order was absolutely right. He was my go-to guy for rescuing students from descending so deeply into the logic of resistance to the mainstream that they could not return to it. "Jalonte' Smith" was a ninth-grade man-child with two special attributes: his size, which made him a starting and feared linebacker on the varsity team, and his intelligence, which made him so quick at grasping math concepts that he was bored to tears by the slowness of classes in which most of the time was spent quelling disruption. In my class, as in his others, "Jal" would chat and curse and, if he felt like paying attention briefly, would yell out the correct answer almost at the instant that I asked a question. I tried all sorts of ways to move him forward, like having him show groups of students how to do their class work, and take on assignments from the next year's text. But Jal's sense of pride as the only freshman starting on the varsity had puffed him up to where he couldn't back down from showing that the rules just didn't apply to him. "Man, I know this (expletive). I already took this course in 8th grade. Let me out of here or get out my face," would be one of his less objectionable responses to being assigned work.

I finally got Jal's attention in November, when he started playing on the junior varsity basketball team. The coaches loved his crazy energy but only dared put him out on the floor for brief periods, because his response to somebody driving by him for a layup would be to tackle him into the stands. It would certainly set the tone for the game, and it helped the junior varsity wend their way toward the city championship game, but after such an assault the referees would confer with the coaches and suggest that maybe Jal should sit down for a while and regroup.

The coaches were two of the school's "goon squad" roving disciplinarians, wonderful young men who connected with the students. I walked over to them during the warm-up for an afterschool game. The players, who could not or would not follow a simple direction in the classroom, were performing a sequence of complicated joint warm-up drills without a single reminder from the coaches. I told the coaches that Jal had been so disruptive in class that day that he had to be removed by security officers, and that I was not happy with him being able to play sports on the same day. "No problem, Doc," one of the coaches said. "Jal, shower up and change," he yelled, and went back to his discussion of game plans with the other coach, turning aside Jal's protest with "Student athlete: student comes first. Work it out with Doc."

I went back to my classroom, and Jal came running in, in his uniform, apologizing, crying, begging, and promising bliss in class. I accepted his apology, and told him I looked forward to his success, in class and on the court, but that I wouldn't let anybody play on a day they had been tossed out for disrupting a class. I admit it, after weeks of his disruptions, my motivation for hanging tough was no longer to mold Jal into a better young man but simply to force him to shut up so the other students could learn. If sports could help me with that, I'd take it. The next day, I asked the Crow to track down Jal's mother, as part of my rule of not letting a student back into class after a disruption without a conference with a guardian. Often

I would settle for a phone call from an unlisted number, but in this case I wanted to get it done right. As was often the case with poor families, I had been unable to track her down by the various phone numbers, most of them disconnected or fake to begin with, that she had provided the school or Jal had provided me. The Crow somehow found her and brought us all together in a conference room for one of his patented talks, the type in which he did the talking.

"Jal, you see your mom here," he said, referring to a woman in her 50s who was exhausted from just climbing the stairs to the meeting room. "You know she works all day cleaning, you know you disrespect her, don't listen to her when she says to mind your teachers. You know she deserves better than she has, trying to provide for you. Don't you want her to have a good house someday? Don't you want to take that check from the NFL draft and buy her the house she deserves?" By this point Jal was crying again, nodding yes, yes, to this vision of him turning his football millions over to his mom. Whereas I always insisted that boys not write down sports star or rapper for their career choices when thinking about the future, and would give a little lecture about how it was important to have the schooling needed for a permanent job because of the high odds of getting hurt in sports or ignored in rapping, the Crow was playing right to Jal's improbable dream.

The Crow ended the meeting, still the only one to have spoken, in violation of all the educational theories about getting everybody to talk through a problem, to explore their actions, and participate in decisions affecting them: "We never going to have this meeting again. This is it. You screw up, you're on your own. You're gone. No sports, no school, no life. We done here." Jal finished out the semester in fine form, requiring only a few reminders of the Crow's threat. He continued on brilliantly in sports and functionally in academics, a tribute to the Crow's touch with his culture. Ironically, when I finally got around to checking out Jal's complaint about having already taken the course, he was right. The guidance counselor had previously dismissed this as unlikely, since she had never heard of someone taking Algebra I in 8th grade at his particular junior high school, but when we dug through the files, there it was, unique like Jal. For the second semester, he joined the 10th grade class in progress. With the minimum effort someone with his brain needed, he caught up and coasted with the low-performing class.

* * *

One of the most important attributes of the culture of black poverty is that it has its own language that cannot be penetrated by the middle class white world. Black English is a rich dialect that developed with two overriding social purposes during slavery and segregation: to bind the tribe together through adversity, and to communicate without being understood by the master and his people.

Like the universal "soul brother" hand shake, Black English reaffirms the unity of the black nation that is superimposed on white America. A white foreign service officer once heard some men hooting with each other in low-down, impenetrable ghetto Black English around the corner of a hallway at the State Department, and assumed it was the always-rowdy custodians. To his surprise, as he rounded the corner, he saw some custodians all right. They were the custodians of U.S. foreign policy, three of the highest ranking American diplomats, sharing a brief and welcome respite from their formal roles. Every African-American, no matter how integrated into upper-class America, can speak Black English.

Nearly all communication between the students at high-poverty schools, and between them and school staff like security guards and secretaries, is in Black English. A secretary upbraided me once for leaving a note for her that read, "Please ask the principal to drop by my class." She was upset that I was teaching students but didn't even know how to spell "ax," which is how "ask" is pronounced in Black English. Black teachers generally don't use dialect during lesson time, but when they have to make a point with disruptive students, or to maintain order in the halls, they slip into it as deeply as necessary.

Black English is a way poor children maintain pride and identity. Since lessons are conducted in the mainstream language of standard English, there is a sense of disconnection between school tasks and real life. While all of my students could comprehend standard English, only about half could speak it, and so naturally expressed all their class comments in dialect. This group often could not even grasp the distinction, like a foreigner being told the four different pronunciations for "cz" in Polish but not being able to hear the difference. If I corrected "I ain't" to "I'm not," a student might look at me blankly and say, "That's what I said, I ain't!" Most students understood the concept of being bilingual, though. "Tanika," a bright, disturbed, and very pregnant 14-year-old, responded to my corrections once by rolling her eyes and saying, with a laugh and perfect British accent, "Jawly gude, Dawctor Rawssiter, shall we transpawt ourselves to the doining area promptlay?"

Black English is a slack-jaw language: things are pronounced less clearly the more the speakers want to avoid comprehension by white people. *All right* becomes *ah-ite* becomes *ite*, until even other dialect speakers have to ask what was said. One day, as my seniors finished up a card game, playing "war" with a deck by multiplying two cards together and comparing the result with other students, I overheard a group of girls in animated conversation. Since I couldn't understand a word, I asked "Rahnika" to slow down so I could at least hear the syllables of the sentence she had just said. I wrote it down as it appears here, with what she then told me were implied words in parentheses, and then asked her to translate.

> We be at Chipotle, and the triflin' thot be kirkin' on me, not (up in) my face or nothin', so I be fakin' on her, all up (in) her damn business, and she ain't nothin' (for) all that.

Rahnika did some translating for me: "trifling" means bothersome, "thot" is an acronym for "that whore over there," "kirking" means talking rudely or threateningly about someone, "faking" means to pretend to slap someone, to see if they flinch or respond with real punches, and "being nothing" means to talk tough but not dare to fight. For Rahnika, dialect is a shield against the middle class, because it immediately distinguishes her and places her in her protective community. While a conversation like this is similar in some ways to that of any users of a first language in multi-ethnic America, like Indian immigrants speaking Hindi with friends, Black English has one big difference. It is the only dialect among all primary languages that is a pointed barrier to integration, because it is a constant reminder of the brutal history of white rule and black resistance in America. By using it, one is declaring *Cosa Nostra* and reaffirming W. E. B. Du Bois's daily duality of being American, yes, but always being black. Facility with the language is a celebration of difference from the white culture and oneness with the black culture.

Cheerleading has become a ritual in black culture with a role very different than it has in white culture. That role is rooted in the unifying use of Black English. Crowds at black high school and college football games don't leave their seats at half-time, because that is show time! The large, well-rehearsed bands are looking to make a name prior to their end of year competitions, the largest of which for the colleges is in the Superdome in New Orleans before the Grambling–Southern football game. The bands are fun to watch, but the real show is the tightly-clad young women. Cheerleaders, flag girls, fashion girls, marching girls, and all manner of other groups of girls strut their stuff. The stone-faced, blatantly suggestive bumps and grinds and the complex and creative movements receive a lot of attention, but one of the attractions is the language, the rhyming, the chants dreamed up to affirm one's team and demean the other.

"DayeSean" was a student in my last class of the day. She was very smart, so smart that despite being absent more than half the time because of conflict and turmoil at home she could easily pass her courses. When she was in class she would constantly be slapping her head with her hand because of the sting of the chemicals she used to maintain her shellacked helmet of hair. DayeSean's disrupted home life kept her from being on the formal cheerleading squad, but she was always breaking into moves and rhyming chants just for fun. We developed a ritual, as the witching hour drew near and the students would gravitate toward the door, in which she would lead the other students in an improvised round of claps and rhymes. She would pick a student, dance next to him or her, and make up a chant about them. A classic she just pulled out of thin air on the spot was: "There go 'Nita, bobos (cheap sneakers) on her feet-a, she can't sleep-a, dreamin' 'bout a Peter." Since there was nobody named Peter in the class, I have to assume that the screams of laughter had to do with an alleged affection for the male member, but I never bothered to ask. It was good enough to send them home happy.

* * *

Alienation from middle class culture is fundamentally engrained in black poor culture, but it is also purposely controlled. Students who want to show their alienation as a point of pride to each other and an act of resistance to authority can turn it off and on. For them, it is an amusing sport of disruption, one they can call up when things get boring. Courtland Milloy, a Washington Post columnist, has written of being at an awards ceremony for black high school students. The boys at his table were acting as atrociously as possible, but rather than reprimanding them for what they knew full well was wrong, he simply took out his notebook and began writing down what they were saying and doing. The boys became curious, and when he told them that he was going to put in a column exactly how they were acting, they switched off their knuckle-heads and became the thoughtful students they preferred to appear as in the newspaper.

When a trio of proud and true ghetto girls were screaming with laughter as they competed to see who could disrupt my class the more, one of them said, as an aside, "Doc, you ain't gonna make it here. We got more energy to play this game than you." They were in complete control of themselves, and they were simply trying to achieve a purpose: have fun rather than have to try to do some work. For them, disruption is purposeful. It is always there, just below the surface, ready to emerge if a teacher demands effort and attention, thereby violating the unspoken bargain of calm high-poverty classes: don't push me to work and I won't disrupt the class much.

I often brought visitors to my class to give students a sense of what lives were possible if they applied themselves. There were few professionals or even employed people in their lives, and the example of the black professionals in the school for some reason rarely captured their imagination as role models. My visitors were entrepreneurs, policy wonks, friends from Africa, and virtually every black professional I knew. The students, like Courtland Milloy's tablemates, invariable showed with the visitors that they knew full well how to act with respect. Of course, they also knew that the longer the questions went, the less time they had to work.

Jadwong Olweny, a friend of mine from Uganda, remarked to the students that he was simply stunned by their constant, albeit friendly, chatter while he was trying to talk to them. He said, "In my school in Kampala, if you had spoken when the teacher was talking, the headmaster would have called the school together to watch him whip you with the dreaded hippopotamus tail." Jayvon called out, "no way," making Jadwong's point by interrupting without raising his hand. "My mom finds out, she come to that school and kick his behind. Nobody layin' a hand on her boy." Jadwong laughed, and said, "Oh, she'd find out. The whole village would know. And she would indeed come to school the next day, but only to thank the headmaster. And then she would whip you again with the hippo tail too, right there, for embarrassing the family." The students, steeped in their culture's tough talk about never letting anybody in authority get away with pushing you around, simply could not believe Jadwong.

Our school had received a feeler from an organization run by civil rights legend Bob Moses. His Algebra Project sees mathematics for black students as the civil rights challenge of today. Without it, he argues, they will be as powerless as unregistered voters in Mississippi in 1964. In anticipation of a visit to the school by some of his staff, I passed out photographs of Moses from the 1960s, showing him speaking to voting rights volunteers and being attacked by a white mob. Just as we finished our discussion, unplanned, in he walked, not his staff but Moses himself, a slight, bespectacled, taciturn older gentleman, but very recognizable from the picture.

Led by a respectful Heston, the students teased information about the civil rights days out of Moses. They listened carefully but simply could not relate to the tactic of non-violence, shown by the pictures of him and his workers accepting violent attacks from the police and the mob without fighting back. Then he said, "So what are you working on?" And lo and behold, my students took him to their "bricks," the rectangular concrete pieces of the wall each had appropriated for a Pythagorean project, and tried to explain how they had predicted the length of the diagonal they had drawn by squaring the lengths of the sides and taking the square root of their sum. Most explanations were rough, because the students had spent far more time decorating their squares with chalk pictures and neighborhood "crew" slogans than actually pondering the workings of the theorem, but with a visitor like this, they were trying to show respect.

Thinking of our visitors, I can't help throwing in this tale. Whether or not it has a clear link to poor black culture, it's too good to pass up. Two professional friends, both men, a lawyer and an accountant, came to our class to talk about their jobs. After a lengthy, respectful hearing, "Shalonda," a 14-year-old mother who rarely attended and was usually halfway between comatose and belligerent when she did, asked them how they knew me. "Our son goes to school with his son," one of the men said. "What you mean 'our son'," said another girl. "You brothers or something?" In the moment I had been waiting for since inviting them, the men held up their left hands, showing their wedding rings. "No, we're married," they said. Shalonda smiled, and laughed for the first time in my class: "I knew it, I knew it. You is gay!" Unfortunately, "Malcolm," the boy whose constant homophobic comments were the true target of the visit, leapt up yelling, "Gross! Faggots in my classroom! I'm not sittin' here. I'm gonna tell the principal!" And be bolted out the door. The other students, though, ignored this outburst, and then had a discussion of gay rights and gay people that indicated they all knew some. Shalonda summed up the mood: "Well, I guess you happy, so I guess it's your own damn business."

* * *

It was a Monday, halfway through a period, and from the turned heads of the students who were supposed to be looking at me and the Smart Board, I knew that somebody must be looking in the class window. In the new school this was a constant problem. Students who were skipping class and even non-students from the neighborhood often roamed the halls, staying a corridor ahead of the security guards and GS, and disrupting classes by peering in the windows, acting up for friends' amusement. At the old Johnson, there were just tiny rectangular windows in the doors. Most teachers disregarded the principal's instruction to leave them clear, and covered them. The 40-year Spanish teacher covered hers with a picture of a monkey that read: enjoy the mirror. Some architectural genius had decreed that the new Johnson have long glass windows covering the entire length of the classroom, with panels under them that students could jump up on for even more dramatic disruption from the halls.

To my surprise, there was not just a couple of knuckle-heads mugging at the picture window, but an excited crowd of maybe 20 students, giggling and gesturing at something in my class. They began to pound on the window and yell something that sounded like, "Give him to us. We want him!" Within minutes there were over 100 students there, covering the entire length of the window, and the braver ones opened the door to call into the class. Quickly I pushed the door shut and locked it, but they began to bang on it, chanting louder what was now more clear: "Give them to us! We want them!" The window was shaking dangerously from the fist-pounding. I tried to contact security, but the intercom system wasn't working, and my cell phone couldn't get reception in the building's mass of concrete. However, because students must have been streaming out of classes to join the fun, I was hopeful that somebody would notify security.

"It's his shoes, Doc Rock. They want his shoes," a student told me. She was pointing at "DaShiki," a boy who rejected his even more Afro-proud name of DaShikiAshante, sitting glumly at his desk. It turned out that DaShiki's father, who did not live with him, rarely saw him, and was years behind on support payments, had blown into town the weekend before with a special present. He had been in New York when Nike released a new sneaker and had managed to grab a pair roughly in DaShiki's size. The shoes cost $350 retail, and had all manner of straps, colors, and pumps on them, so they must have cost at least $10 to make in an Asian factory. A rumor had gone around the school like a flash that, because the shoes had only been released in New York, they were being sold on-line in DC for $3,000. That's what had emptied the classrooms and brought the students to our window, the promise of getting paid by stealing DaShiki's shoes.

The pounding on the door took on a deeper tone, and I could hear the Crow calling me from behind it. I opened it up and he and the three-man GS burst in and locked the door behind them. "Boy, what you thinkin'? Get your bag, get over here," commanded the Crow. He and the GS surrounded DaShiki, opened the door, and muscled him through the screaming, grabbing crowd. They drove him home and made him change into his usual sneakers, and then took the new ones with them, pointedly showing people in the neighborhood that they had them, so nobody would try to rob his house. They held the sneakers in a locked room in the school office for the father to pick up after he promised not to give them back to DaShiki until they were available at stores in DC.

What was DaShiki's father trying to express with his gift? Was he trying to show him how a man looks out for his children? DaShiki certainly needed to know that, because he was a 14-year-old freshman who was already in the social worker's discussion and support group for young fathers, in preparation for the upcoming birth of his baby-mama's child. Young people in poor black culture are immersed in sexuality from an early age and see nothing untoward about high school pregnancy. Our rate was at least 25 percent by the end of 10th grade and the explosion of drop-outs. Despite all the lecturing by teachers and health workers they had received in school, neither DaShiki nor his "baby-mama" believed their lives would be worse for the pregnancy. Their mothers, who had their babies early too, would help, and they knew from neighborhood lore exactly how much money they would receive and what benefits the baby would receive from various government agencies. The school was even opening a special on-site daycare for its many student-mothers.

The culture of black poverty that produced DaShiki's father was now producing DaShiki's first child. In our egalitarian ideology, we want to believe that father, son, and grandchild have as good a shot at grabbing the American ring as anyone. That is why school reformers insist that everyone can succeed with a college prep curriculum, and then go to and succeed in college, "regardless of zip code." But it just ain't true, and pretending that the culture and reality of black poverty is irrelevant to success is a guarantee for failure. DaShiki's shoe adventure could never happen at a wealthy school. Oh, the parents there do spoil their children with ostentatious gifts, but the response of the children's peers is not to bust out of class and "go shopping" in the Black English sense, but to call their parents so they can really go shopping.

The three brightest stars in Johnson's firmament were "Mia," "SoLayla," and "Kileshe'a," who also rejected her Africanized name and preferred to go by Kiley. They were among the few students from my classes who graduated and went to a four-year college. Of the 50 percent who graduated rather than dropped out, about half went to college, but nearly all of those attended the open admission DC community college or one of the weaker, essentially open admission historically black colleges. Even two of these girls, who had been academic successes and made a game of getting straight A's throughout their schooling, were so deeply separated from mainstream knowledge and concerns that they struggled with college and dropped out to regroup. That separation was evident when I took the three girls on a field trip as a reward for having the best grades, indeed the only A's, in my classes one year.

Mia and SoLayla had been in the same neighborhood schools since kindergarten, usually in the same classroom because of low enrollments, always competing with each other to have the highest scores. They told me they had figured out early that if you did just a little bit of work right away, you could spend the rest of the period relaxing and chatting as the teacher focused on getting the knuckle-heads to quiet down and try something. It was the same with grades: making a little effort went a long way. They hadn't put in the time to build enough knowledge to be able to compete for A's at a middle class school, but they could have survived with C's. At Johnson, though, they were the top of the pops. Kiley had been expelled from a rigorous charter school because, as its head said, "she just didn't believe the rules would apply to her," since she had always been able to use her intelligence to get by, and indeed have the top grades, at her neighborhood schools.

Mia had been raised primarily by her grandmother, who was only in her 40s. Her mother was still having trouble with drugs and alcohol, as the grandmother had earlier in her life as well. Mia's grandmother was a severe woman who guarded her emotions and her space relentlessly and never smiled with me. Mia exhibited precisely the same behavior. I spoke many times with

Mia's grandmother, both on the phone and when she was one of the very few guardians to come to the supposedly required parent conferences. Whether I was congratulating her on Mia's performance or asking for her help in stopping Mia's at times stunningly surly misbehavior, she would always tell me, with Mia listening, the same thing: "She is here for herself. She does not help anybody else. She looks out for herself. Nobody else will look out for her." This was her mantra, and it certainly made it hard to appeal to Mia's concern for others when she was disruptive, or unwilling to help weaker students, even when I explained that teaching something makes you understand it better yourself.

We left school to drive to the Capitol, where I had arranged for some Members of Congress and staff to meet with them. The three girls decided to sit together, squashed into the back seat of my car, rather than have one of them be separated from the others and sit up front. When I interrupted their dialect discussion to ask what landmarks they recognized, they said that they rarely went over the bridge to the "other" part of town. I could tell that they were even unfamiliar with the Eastern Market shopping area as we passed through it, even though it was no more than two miles from their neighborhood. As the dome loomed over us on our approach, SoLayla said, "So what is that Capitol thing, anyway? What do they do there?" I tried to draw on their memories of U.S. government classes, and on analogies to the local work of their infamous councilman, Marion Barry, but it wasn't working.

The high point of the trip turned out to be the congressional staff cafeteria, because the portions were essentially unlimited and the girls fell to boxing up everything they could to have meals and snacks for their family that night. With the members and staff, they sat nonplussed and unconnected. Because they couldn't grasp the function of the Congress, they would ask me and each other after a meeting, "What was that about? Who was that?" The formidable Houston congresswoman Sheila Jackson-Lee kindly took them with her to a committee hearing, where she delivered a searing interrogation of a government witness. I hoped that the image of the colorfully-dressed, crisply-spoken black woman out-thinking the white bureaucrat might stick in their heads as a vocational inspiration, but after the hearing and the photo session, SoLayla just said, "Why was she so nasty to that guy?" None of the girls could recall the topic. As I dropped her off at her house, Mia said again to the other girls, "What was that all about?" These were three very sharp kids, so that question doesn't mean she couldn't have figured it out. She just didn't want to, or need to, to be successful in her isolated world, and in fact had a historical, cultural bias against doing so. That is the crux of the challenge the culture of black poverty poses to educators.

* * *

Chapter 4. The Trauma of Black Poverty

Soon after I published an opinion piece in the Wall Street Journal in 2012 denouncing the fraud of "credit recovery" courses at my Washington, DC, neighborhood high school, I was asked to speak to a class at a high school at the absolute other end of the spectrum. St. Albans is an anachronistically elite, all-boys private school that symbolically sits at the geographic peak of the District as part of the magnificent Washington Cathedral, where presidents and chief justices have their funerals. My school was on the flats at the farthest eastern reach of the District's diamond, next door to a tattered Baptist prayer hall where home health aides and teenage victims of drive-by shootings have their funerals. Such stark contrasts were typical of those I saw the day I went to St. Albans.

My host was Edward "Ted" Eagles, a graduate of the school who looks, dresses, and acts like everyone's image of Mr. Chips. Ted had taught at St. Albans for over 40 years. He achieved a small measure of urban fame as the foreman of the jury that in 1992 agreed with Mayor Marion Barry that "the bitch set me up" by refusing to have sex until he smoked some crack cocaine. Ted's jury showed backbone by nullifying the judge's specific instruction that the videotaped incident did not constitute entrapment, and then showed some practicality by convicting the mayor for a different incident, based on testimony rather than video.

The students in Ted's senior economics seminar were a lot like the Ph.D. students in international affairs I had taught at American University: surprisingly diverse thanks to scholarship funds, although tending to wealthy and white, well-prepared, sharp as whips, knowledgeable about national and world politics, confident, and eager to learn. I was to lecture on cost-effective solutions to the conditions I had observed in my school. Since the students had read and taken notes not just on my opinion piece but on a longer article on school curriculum I had sent Ted, I started by covering some new ground about the how poverty hampers child development prior to high school. As I was describing research on the language and health deficits of poor black families, a student raised his hand and, when I called on him, said: "It seems to me that these students are behind us from the moment they're born, and it gets harder every day to catch up, given the advantages our parents can keep buying us."

As he went on to present an idea for sharing these advantages, I couldn't help interrupting him: "I'm sorry, but what you've said gave me an epiphany. Your point is so important I just have to respond before I lose my thought. No, no, no! They are not behind from the moment they are born. That, we could do something about, as you were about to explain. They are behind from the moment of *conception*. That is an even bigger problem."

His comment had made me realize that before there is limited exposure of infants to verbal interaction, before there are no books in the house, before there is the absent father and the drop-out mother who can't control a child's behavior or whereabouts, before there is the violence in the home and community, before there is the constant example of joblessness and hustle rather than regular employment, before there are chaotic, segregated school days, before there are the drug crews using young teens as runners to avoid prison terms, before there are the addicts and prostitutes, the Standells' "muggers, thugs, and thieves," before there is poor health care and stress for children, before there is Du Bois's unremitting alienation of being both American and black, before there is Kenneth Clark's sense of inferiority from being on the losing end of segregation, before it all, right at conception, poor black children are fundamentally behind.

Why? The answer is early pregnancy and, even if not early, unhealthy pregnancy and, even if not unhealthy, stressful pregnancy. Premature birth and its resulting low birth weight are proxies for weak development and health in a baby. They are strongly associated with death and physical and learning disabilities. Teenage mothers, due to immature development, and poor mothers, due to poor health and stress, are at far greater risk for prematurity and low birth weight. High-poverty communities are replete with mothers who are both. Throw in the additional stress of simply being black in America—which is suggested by the remarkable finding that black women who are healthy, wealthy, college graduates have 50 percent higher infant mortality than their white peers—and you have a truly deadly combination. Poverty is a killer. There is nothing romantic about it. And it starts in the womb.

In high-poverty schools the cycle constantly starts again. So many girls are pregnant, as early as 8th grade, that at times classes resemble maternity wards. By tenth grade a quarter of my girls already had babies, and as girls dropped out of school, many more became pregnant. By keeping track of students after they leave my class, I can estimate that a little less than half of all our entering freshman girls had a child as a teenager. I couldn't estimate a rate for my boys' involvement in pregnancy, because so many would happily brag (or lie, I hoped) about their baby-mamas. Certainly, some of the young mothers had been exploited by older men, but it was clear that many of the fathers were students as well. One day I was using a health survey sent around by the central office for a lesson on percentages with 10th graders. I asked them to estimate the number of students of the 16 in the room who were sexually active, based on the 44 percent district-wide figure in the survey. When Mia quickly calculated that the answer was seven students, the class clown, whom everybody called by his nickname of "Jimmy Bones," objected strenuously: "Doc, Doc, that's gotta be wrong. Everybody knows that we is all sexually active — except for Ronald there! So it's gotta be 15 students." The class dissolved in laughter, and I think that Jimmy was probably closer to the truth than Mia.

The high rate of pregnancy is surprising, given the knowledge the girls have gained from the health professionals in the schools, as well as the ease of obtaining an abortion. Sex education has come a long way since the 1960s, when it consisted of gender-specific lectures designed to scare students away from fornication. The school nurse and a health teacher came into my 10th grade class to give a power-point lesson on sexually-transmitted diseases that they told me was the same one they give in early elementary grades. Once they started, I could hardly believe it was my students. Girls who couldn't remember their times tables, or be bothered to try to, were raptly attentive, raising their hands to win prizes for identifying diseases as viral- or bacterial-based, spelling their scientific names, and naming appropriate drugs for treatment.

I asked them how they knew the material before it was even presented, and they told me that they had already been treated by the nurse for some of the diseases and had worked with her in their visits to learn about the rest. This really piqued my interest, so I went to the nurse's office to learn more, and found girls lined up for their regular pregnancy shots. No permission from a guardian was required for these substitutes for birth control pills. So, why so much pregnancy, and why not more adoptions or abortions?

The answer to the first question is that the boys and men who are having sex with the young girls pressure them, and often prevail upon them, not to use condoms. They are seeking to have what they define as the maximum pleasure of unprotected sex, not babies, but they are not concerned about that possibility either. Under the code of the culture it will generally be the girls' mothers, not theirs, who will watch the babies. The answer to the second question is that, once pregnant, many of the girls simply want to have the baby, or at least don't object to the idea enough to take some other action. Abortion is not looked down on socially or subject to religious objections, and adoption agencies are eager to have infants, but among these young girls there seems to be little sense of life's possibilities being undermined by raising a child, as there might be in a middle class home. They know from other girls exactly what the welfare benefits will be for their child, and they see some other girls leaving their babies with their mothers as they return to school, and they just think that's how it will be for them. Despite all the college banners and pictures of black scientists hanging from the walls, they don't really believe in the alternative future of college and the middle class, so pregnancy is not seen as a great loss of opportunity.

Some people posit that girls who get pregnant and keep their babies are often from dysfunctional families, and crave the affection and attention they believe a baby will give them. Some teachers humorously claim that the girls mostly just want their turn at creating a special name in the tradition in the poor black culture that took off in a burst of creativity and ethnic pride in the 1970s. The names amalgamate capital letters, verbs, brand names, images, slightly-Africanized constructions, apostrophes, and modifications of previous names: Flirtisha, Sh'Tara, sisters Tamiesha and Shamiesha, Calvinia, even Kwajalein (probably not to honor the American atoll destroyed by the first hydrogen bomb), and the many variants starting with La, Ja and De: LaQuela, Lawanii, JaVonte', DeSean, DeJohn, Desiria, De'lonte. Maybe three-fourths of my girls and about half of my boys were named in this mode.

But all this speculation about causes misses an obvious point: it is normal in the black poor culture for teenage girls to have unprotected sex and keep their babies, so there is no need to explain it. It holds neither shame nor special status. In most cases, these teenage mothers were themselves born when their mothers were teenagers, often as young as 14, and were raised by their grandmothers. They are simply continuing a tradition.

As I came around to one of my groups of four in a 10th grade class one day, I asked to see how far they had gotten working together on an assignment on basic fractions. I really did intend to get to the day's required standard, which was operations with exponents, but since some of them would be fractional, I could justify taking lesson time to go all the way back to where the students really were, unable to find the common denominator to add a third and a half. All their papers were still blank. "What's up? This is due for group credit in five minutes," I remonstrated. "Lyesiah," a cute, chubby girl who was one of my best students, looked at me like I was a bug on her arm, and dismissed me with an incredulous: "Come on, Doc, can't you see we talkin' 'bout our babies?" That one brought me up short. Indeed, by chance two girls with children (Lyesiah now had two, at 15) and two who were pregnant were at the same table, and they were educating each other. That seemed pretty important to me, so I said, "Well, just do half the problems then." Hearing about how often to visit the doctor, and how much fun it was to play with your baby, might do more to break the cycle of poverty than taking the cube root of 64 (for those of you following along at home, it's four).

* * *

In addition to being born, on average, in weaker physical and mental condition due to prematurity, children in high-poverty communities experience traumatic conditions and experiences far more than middle class children. The worst of these is the prevalence of violence, in the community and in the home. Like all the conditions cited in this chapter, violence is not found only in poor homes. In all walks of life parents beat their children. Indeed, as I have written in a previous book, I was beaten unconscious by my father, an esteemed academic who killed himself when I was 18. But violence is far more common in poverty. Slavery embedded violence in poor black culture to such a degree that today a post-traumatic slave syndrome makes it a norm that constantly drives a new cycle.

Violence begets violence, but the brutality of slavery kept it from flowing back to whites from the blacks they worked, beat, whipped, castrated, and, of equal psychological importance, humiliated by sale and fear. Three centuries of slavery were interrupted by 20 years of protection of black rights and lives under Reconstruction and federal military rule in the South, but the party of Lincoln gave all that away in return for the fraudulent presidency in 1876, leading to another 100 years of demeaning, violently-enforced humiliation and segregation under the Klan, the White Citizens Councils, and the police. Even in the North, blacks moving outside of their segregated ghettos had to tread carefully and faced threats and violence if they protested inequality of opportunity. All this violence done to the black community built up within it, but could not be expressed outside of it, against whites. The result was a disease, a post-traumatic slave syndrome that has transitioned into a currently-traumatized segregation syndrome, that puts violence at the center of poor black culture.

Murder and other violent crimes are tightly clustered around high-poverty areas, and when one of our students was killed it was a normal occurrence, in that most of the other neighborhood high schools experienced the same thing that year. Normal, though, does not mean there is no impact. Any teenager who knows someone who is murdered is going to be scared, scarred, and then hardened. "DaJonte" was old for a 10th grader, having failed many courses because he had such a short attention span the few times a week he attended class. He lived with his dysfunctional mother in a tough corner of the Barry Terrace projects, and was designated special education, but with no particular diagnosis. He was often unable to control his talking, his movement, and his emotions, but was wise enough to come to me some days as he entered the class and say, "I'm wild today. I just feel wild. Please let me walk around in the back of the class for a while."

One day DaJonte was manic, like he was drugged. His speech was slurred and his eyes were darting back and forth as he walked in and told me, "I saw it, Doc, I saw the blood, I saw the brains." I couldn't get anything else out of him as he sat down. A few minutes later, during the calling of the roll in a work time, he suddenly burst up from his chair, threw it against the back wall, and started running back and forth. This was definitely not in the teachers' manual! I tried to calm him, but he lunged at me violently, then stopped himself, and ran out the door and down the hall. The class was stunned into silence. We often had disruptions from DaJonte and many others in this class, but they usually followed a pattern of escalation. A student would talk during a lecture, or yell across the room during a silent work period or forcefully respond to some joning. The class would stall as I remonstrated, warned, and cajoled. If I was unsuccessful, I would eventually decide on a punishment, the student would respond more and more loudly, and finally I would have to go find a security guard to take the student out. It was all very predictable and regular. DaJonte's outburst was not.

Later that day I saw DaJonte walking behind the Crow as he made his tour of the lunch room. I went up to them, and the Crow took me aside. "Let him hang with me for a few days. Police gunned down his friend, right in front of him, at the Terrace last night." DaJonte was simply traumatized, stunned into brain lock and heartache by witnessing violence and death. Whatever promise his semester had held, it was over. He couldn't focus on class work for months. He did return to class after a week of walking the halls with the Crow, smiling as if nothing had happened, yet he could only sit in the back of the room, dreamily leafing through magazines and comic books.

What is crucial to take away from DaJonte's tragedy is not just that it was devastating for him, but that it is a normal condition for many students, perhaps more muted than his, but still powerful. So much violence is present in homes, on the street, and in the school that students' intellects and emotions are distracted by it, making it a barrier to their education. Teachers and administrators secretly cheer when a parent brings the violence to school, ending a disciplinary conference with a warning to the child: "I ain't comin' off work back up in here again. They call me again, I'm gonna whip your ass so hard you never sit down again. Clear?" Desperate to reduce disruption in our class, we stay in the classroom after the conference and don't interfere when we hear the parent add some head-smacking and face-slapping to the berating as they go down the hall.

Fiction simply can't be made more brutal than the truth in works about the black culture of poverty. "Precious," a 2009 movie about a high school girl raped by her father, won acclaim for actress Mo'Nique. It was criticized for demonizing the black culture of poverty, but for those of us working in it, it was a credible rendition of family dysfunction under the strain of generational poverty. The film perfectly portrayed the quotidian urban classroom, where a teacher asks over the din, "and we're barking like a dog, why, Mr. Jones?" The student has no idea why he is barking, but the randomness fits perfectly with the uselessness of being in school. In my schools, teachers have asked the same question about students in class setting their hair on fire or masturbating.

Tanika was a bird-like sophomore, constructed so finely you thought she might blow over in a breeze. She was a talented cheer-leader and a strong student. Designated emotionally-disturbed, Tanika would vacillate from being pleasant, proper, and focused one minute to becoming a screaming, belligerent maniac the next, knocking over desks, scattering papers, and calling out to me, "What you gonna do now, knock me out? Come on, (expletive), knock me out!" In December she had a noticeable bump in her belly, which quickly grew to as big a pregnancy as I've ever seen, while the rest of her tiny body stayed static. Tanika became so uncontrollable around male teachers that I had to exchange her with a female teacher for another student. The social worker helping her confirmed to me what she had seen a number of times: Tanika had been raped by her step-father, who had indeed knocked her out to end her resistance.

Tanika cut an angry, tragic figure, escorted through the halls by her protective friends on the rare days she came to school. By April, after 30 of the normal 40 weeks, she gave birth to an undersized girl. The baby was really being raised by her mother, but Tanika liked to bring her into school on the way to her doctor's visits and show her off to her classes. The office secretaries and security guards would gather around her when she entered school, cooing and praising, instinctively trying to give her and the baby as positive a reception as possible. The protectiveness extended to the administrators, who refused to provide teachers with any information about the case, leaving us to guess as to the current arrangements in the family when Tanika would lapse back into her wild states.

Again, the point of Tanika's situation is not just to show an individual tragedy, but to reinforce the reality that her tensions, in muted form but real, are felt by many girls. They know that older men in the neighborhood are vying for their bodies, and the violence and sexual exploitation in the air makes the danger real. "Latricia," a 9th grader at Science Tech, was often disciplined for fighting after being the target of "thot" comments from other girls, and the rumor spread among social workers and teachers that it was true: her mother was a prostitute and addict who had offered Latricia, "that 'ho over there," up to customers. We had no way of knowing whether it was true or not, but the fact that we believed it could be, based on our experiences, is telling. A policeman who lived in the neighborhood was arrested for running a teenage prostitution ring at about the same time, so the tale of Latricia and her pimping mother didn't seem so far-fetched.

* * *

Drug addiction is the bane of high-poverty neighborhoods. On the other hand, the widespread use of illegal drugs provides a lot of the employment. There is always money floating around that is available for, or derived from, the drug trade. Teachers are constantly telling students who show up in class without their supplies, "Where's your pencil and notebook? You can't afford to buy them? You've got $200 sneakers on your feet and a $500 i-Phone hidden in your designer jeans, and a fancy TV and Xbox at home, and you can't afford to buy a pencil and a notebook? Please. No, I'm not going to give them to you. Borrow from a friend or take an F for the day." The fancy items are often gifts from the absent father, or a crew member who is looking out for the father's reputation and perceived responsibilities while he is incarcerated. Custody payments and regular visits aren't expected, but a real man showers his kids with cool gear whenever he is flush.

Boys from 12 to 15 are often taken into the drug trade as runners, the people who carry the drugs from a holding spot to the customers. They cannot be tried as adults until they are 16, so they are more willing than older boys to accept the high risk of arrest. Even if an older boy is arrested for running, the jails and prisons are so full that only a direct connection to the violence needed to maintain a drug crew will put him inside. The usual penalty is probation and an ankle bracelet to track your whereabouts. The bracelet is actually a status symbol in a high-poverty high school. It triggers the screening bells at the front door, confirming your reputation as a bad mash when the security officer lifts up the cuffs of your pants to confirm it.

At Johnson the runners knew they shouldn't talk about their drug business or their crew and its slogans. The administrators had been in DC schools where gang culture had been tolerated, resulting in gunfights inside the school. Almost any other misbehavior earned at worst a brief suspension, but with the first whiff of gang activity in the Crow's nose — a muted gang chant in the cafeteria, a fight between students he knew were in different crews, a quick sale observed, a flash of a roll of twenties to impress your friends — you would be expelled for the semester and sent to a special school that was really just a holding tank. Despite that school having weak attendance and laughable classes, the students would invariably return with C's and D's in all of their classes, and move on with their cohort.

So many fathers (along with a few mothers) were in jail or in prison that students saw nothing embarrassing or extraordinary about it. After conviction, inmates are sent into the federal prison system, since DC does not have a prison. They can be placed, and moved, all over the country, although the authorities make an effort to keep them near their families. The DC department of corrections arranges buses for children to travel to nearby states to visit their fathers in prison — which is an excused absence from school. Former inmates have formed the Family and Friends of Incarcerated People, which holds picnics to buck up the spirits of the prisoners' children and tries to help what the city politely calls "returning citizens" find legal employment.

In the DC jail, where people who cannot make or are denied bail are placed awaiting trial, there is a public high school called the Incarcerated Youth Program. This is not a juvenile rehabilitation residence, of which we have a number, for young people who have committed crimes and need supervision. This is a jail, with five or six double-lock spaces between the inmate and the outside. The inmates are residents who are 16 to 18 years old and have been charged as adults for violent crimes. Up to 100 young people are resident there at any one time, and the typical stay is over six months before trial or a plea bargain. These young inmates are segregated from the general population, and apart from wearing orange jumpsuits and being locked in their cells at night, it's a lot like being in their school. There are the same classes (and as the teachers laughingly say, attendance is not an issue), the same institutional food, and lots of time to play basketball in the gym, at least until the frequent fights get everybody locked down. Teachers run their classes with guards posted in the room, and just like in the public schools, pretty much everybody magically passes. The biggest difference will be when the students get out. A criminal record makes you far less employable, and few enough people from the neighborhood schools will ever be employed in middle class jobs as it is.

I went to the youth wing of the jail on Sundays to tutor a former student of mine who had been arrested for "going shopping" with two other young men, which in this case meant lurking around white or gay parts of town and assaulting people coming out of bars as they walked home, to take their phones and wallets. By a nasty coincidence I also knew one of their victims from their two assaults on that night of crime, the husband of some friends' god-daughter. By an even more nasty coincidence she was also a DC school teacher. One of the gang smashed the husband from behind with a baseball bat, causing a massive brain injury that despite years of rehabilitation will leave him handicapped the rest of his life, never able to bring his full intellect to his conversations with his young son, let alone his research and advocacy on environmental issues. The three criminals turned on each other in their testimony, so it is hard to know exactly what happened that night, but one of them claimed that my student's only concern in "going shopping" was that he had new sneakers and didn't want to get blood on them.

Despite his wild and aggressive posturing that had led to fights and suspension in school and now to fights and isolation in jail, my student had always been mathematically sharp. I could tell from our jail sessions that he was dominating the limited pre-calculus material his teacher gave him, and would easily pass. He was the only inmate in his math class taking that 12th grade material and was sure to graduate while awaiting trial. The others were moving through lower-level courses, leaving him pretty much to his own devices in class, so I made sure he could convert degrees to radians before I ended our sessions. The sessions had become oppressive to me, since I really wanted to counsel him, not teach him, but I knew that, for legal reasons, we could never talk about what he most needed to.

I had found in meetings with the Family and Friends of Incarcerated People that inmates are largely focused on pulling their own lives together, and on the injustice they perceive in their separation from their families and their permanent stigma upon release. They rarely seem to consider their victims and the responsibility to make things as right as possible for them. Even a supposedly victimless crime like running drugs to willing customers has victims. The victims are all the people in the community who live in fear, and see their neighborhood fall apart, because of the drug enforcers who do, whether a runner sees it or not, kill and maim to protect turf. I couldn't tell my student that I knew his victim, that his family's life was a living hell, and that we had to talk about how he could try to help make things better for them. I couldn't tell him that a criminal can never be whole who has not gone back to address the damage from the crime. To talk about that would force him to acknowledge his crime, which is something good lawyers never want clients to do until all trials and appeals are over. My student had a good lawyer. He was only convicted of armed robbery and assault in one of the two muggings. While the alleged wielder of the baseball bat received a 24-year sentence, his will be between nine and 12. Maybe then I can track him down and ask him to do his duty to his victims and their families.

* * *

A sad manifestation of poverty is the disproportionately large number of special education and emotionally-disturbed children in high-poverty schools. At least a third of the students have one of these designations, roughly four times the rate in middle class schools. Some of this differential is due to the damage done in pregnancy because of the youth of many of the mothers and the stress and poor health and nutrition of many more of them. Some is due to the child's isolation, neglect, poor health and nutrition, and actual trauma during the early years of life. In these cases, the young people are the truly damaged by poverty, children who through no fault of their own are developmentally excluded from ever pursuing a middle class life. A lot of the special education differential with middle class kids, though, is due to the bureaucracy's routine recourse to that designation when a child falls behind.

Like college tuition responding to the availability of federal loans, special education designations have been driven up by the availability of federal funds. Parents are sought out by administrators as their children start testing farther and farther behind and are encouraged to apply for the designation, which will bring more staff into the school. The administrators' actions are motivated by ideology and fad as well as financial practicality. The cause of children falling years behind could not possibly be a curriculum that is inappropriate for their background. The college prep curriculum and the middle class structure must be right for high-poverty kids, because everybody is going to go to college. So, the reasoning goes, the cause of a lag in achievement must be a learning disability.

Once a student is designated, teams of teachers and staff have to draw up an Individual Education Plan. These are silly, lengthy standardized documents that promise many hours per week of special help that rarely comes and predict future achievements that will rarely materialize: "A special education teacher will come into the classroom 8 hours per week to guide the student, and the classroom teacher will prepare another ten hours of special attention in the classroom. By the end of the semester the student will be able to identify plot in a short story 60 percent of the time, and perform percentage calculations from real-world examples with 80 percent accuracy." The plans rarely include a description of a child's learning disability or suggested techniques for addressing it, because nothing specific, other than lagging behind grade level, has been found in the special testing.

Lawyers seek out the parents of designated poor children because the school district has to pay their fees, even if the child is in a charter school. When the special teaching hours and the predicted progress do not occur there are more meetings and more promises. Lost in this mass of students who probably are suffering more from motivational deficits rather than learning disabilities are the many who need, and rarely get, intense support through psychological counseling, both in "self-contained" classrooms of special education kids and in the mainstream classes.

"LacQuan," who was border-line mentally-challenged and prone to class-ending emotional melt-downs of screaming and fighting, stopped brushing her eyelashes and painting her nails long enough to look up at the board as I rearranged $x + 3 = 2x$ into $3 = 2x - x = x$. "Doctor Rossiter," she said politely but pointedly, as if we both knew she had caught me doing something illegal, "what the (expletive) you do with that x?" The class stopped its buzzing, as surprised as me that LacQuan had actually been looking at the board and had actually said anything about schoolwork. We all cracked up, and I said, "That, my dear, is Al-gebra, 'the reunion' of the variables on the balance beam that we've been studying these past six months, and that is one of the best questions I have ever heard."

LacQuan was supposed to be supported in class, and in sessions after it, by a lovely and devoted special education teacher who would talk about her interest in fashion and try to keep her collecting credits in her wholly inappropriate college prep curriculum. However, this special teacher came irregularly, due to a bevy of meetings for "professional development" or writing and presenting the Individual Education Plans. There is no clear path for LacQuan and the many other border-line kids when they leave high school. She is not damaged enough to qualify for the schooling until 21 that is available for retarded students, or the public and private programs that might then help her with a menial job and living arrangements. She'll probably end up in the community, with her own kids, maybe braiding hair or getting public payments. I could see some of her future in my long-delayed meeting with Malita's guardian.

Malita fully deserved her dual designations, special education and emotionally disturbed. School was a wild ride, an extension of the chaos of her large family of half and step siblings, spread out all over Barry Terrace. Her disruptions were so frequent and creative, her manner so distracted and wild, that I despaired of ever teaching anybody anything with her present. Fortunately, she would be absent or suspended for weeks at a time for various transgressions with security staff and administrators. When I finally invoked my rule against a disruptive student not being returned to class until a guardian came in for a conference, it took even the Crow, with his grasp of the neighborhood, two weeks before he could find a family representative who would come in.

The frail, slightly staggering older gentleman slurred out that he lived with Malita, but the exact relationship was never established because it was so hard to communicate with him. He appeared to be retarded or drug-damaged, and expressed himself mainly by slowing shaking his head and saying, "Malita, Malita, why you do all this?" I exchanged a glance with the Crow. There was clearly nothing to be gained by this, and we just thanked him for coming in. My students suffered through Malita for the rest of the year, although she did continue to serve weeks-long suspensions. A guidance counselor had kindly agreed to sit on a panel of teachers and administrators at the end of the year to judge my students' presentations of a geometric proof. (Well, actually she and another teacher were the entire panel that day, since none of the other four invited and confirmed administrators showed up, over a week of presentations.) Usually calm and collected, and inured to all manner of foolishness after 20 years in the system, the guidance counselor simply stood up and walked out in anger after watching Malita babble crudely, with no reference to her supposed proof, when it was her turn at the board. As in most of her courses, Malita failed going away, but she loved to come to school, even when she was suspended, for the food and the friendship and the fun she couldn't find in her bleak home. As a prime candidate for credit recovery classes, I suppose she was eventually handed a phony diploma. She had a baby at 18.

In addition to the wild boys, who had to be transferred between teachers every few weeks because they had spiraled out of control, I knew a number of boys who were either damaged or stoned, unable to muster much of anything besides curse words if asked to work. Teachers were so busy handling the disruptions of the actively inane that these spaced out-souls were mostly just left alone. On my way to the jail one Sunday for tutoring I drove down a side street and saw one of these boys, who had not been in my classes, and I pulled over to talk to him. I was hoping that being outside of school might loosen his tongue with me, but the opposite was true. He stood there like stone, barely registering my presence, or anything else. I decided to save my homily about where I was going that day and how he should avoid trouble. He didn't appear to have the consciousness, let alone the wherewithal, to commit a crime.

Poor parents are caught in a bind when deciding where to place their special education students. They can see that their children fall farther behind when they remain in mainstream classes, but they are rightly scared of agreeing to a placement in the self-contained classrooms. In that setting, they may obtain a special education "attendance" diploma that is still based on a college prep curriculum but leaves the student even less prepared for college than the regular one. The mother of "Martin," a burly football player, resisted the self-contained classes womanfully, assisted by her school-paid lawyer. Martin was illiterate and innumerate in 10th grade. He covered up his academic weakness by being a disruptive class clown. His promised special teaching help never arrived in the mainstream class, and his mother disrupted his learning even more by pulling him without warning for a week here and there to visit relatives in South Carolina, where many DC black families still have roots. Martin's special education team felt that his mother was in denial about his abilities, but she still refused to agree to his placement in a self-contained math class of just four students.

"DeAntonio's" mother had two reactions when she saw his hopelessly weak workbook in a similar review of his Individual Education Plan. DeAntonio was no weaker intellectually than Martin, but his skills at coping with and hiding his disability were not as sophisticated. At first, his mother responded angrily to seeing his pathetic work, cuffing him on the head and called him a lazy fool who could handle the mainstream class if he would stop clowning around. But as he broke into tears of embarrassment and said, "I just don't understand any of it, mom," her heart melted and she acknowledged that he was so far over his head that he should be moved into the special class. Technically, such a decision would be reviewed each semester, to see if he could go back to the mainstream, but she knew that his path was now set.

The parents of emotionally disturbed students know their rights, too, and especially the peculiar one that said that a student could not be excluded from a classroom, let alone suspended from school, for their disability. For these students, the disability was often listed as "lack of self-control." One of my emotionally disturbed students, "Fishel," explained this Catch-22 perfectly to "Bill," a security guard on his first day on the job at Science Tech. Fishel had escalated from talking in lesson to cursing and screaming, and then knocking over desks when told he would be in detention that afternoon, so I had to walk down to find a security guard to remove him. It may have been Bill's first day, but he was no rookie. He knew the protocol and he followed it. He started pleasantly, with "Come with me, young'un. Get your bag." Fishel ran around a few desks to evade him and started screaming curses at him. That led Bill to step two, lightly placing one's hand on the student's shoulder, which led to more screaming, and finally a full-on battle. When Fishel was finally under physical control, Bill told him something that, based on his work in other schools, seemed obvious, "Better get all your gear, junior. You won't be back in this school for a while. You can't be treatin' no guard like that."

Fishel screamed, "(Expletive) you, (expletive), you watch. I'll be right back here tomorrow." And he was, because his indigent mother had a district-paid lawyer who had long since convinced the administrators that he could win a damage suit for disciplining, let alone expelling, a student for a disruption that came from his "lack of control" disability. The previous spring, the lawyer for a girl with a similar diagnosis had driven up to the school and blocked the bus that was taking students with good discipline records on a field trip to an amusement park. Out he sprang with a court order requiring that his client be permitted to attend, because discipline based on her lack of control violated the disability laws. Onto the bus she came.

What is most remarkable about all this trauma, this currently-traumatized segregation syndrome, is not the damage it does to so many young people, but that it does not drag down more of them. About half of the students who share the same demographics as the teen mothers, the ones who were running with a gang, the witnesses to murder, the rape victims, the damaged, and the inmates are able to float through this turbulent sea, feeling the pressure but not succumbing to it. Usually you can identify the survivors by their mothers, perseverant working women who are insistent on respect at home and good grades at school. Perhaps these students also come from the high birth-weight group, which has less to struggle with, physically and intellectually, from conception. Perhaps it is their extended families that are still functional, despite the challenges of the immediate family's poverty. Perhaps it is just the luck of the draw, the magic of individual genetics. Whatever the reason, about half can make it. If they can just get away from the academic chaos created by those who can't make it, they can respond to the many opportunities and programs available to escape the culture of black poverty.

There is hope in the unseen, as Ron Suskind's 1998 book about a DC neighborhood boy who attends and graduates from Brown University is titled. Cedric Jennings' father was in prison for drug-running and gave him nothing but crisis, but his mother was a god-fearing, hard-working woman, straddling the fence of poverty, who respected but could not really grasp the remarkable intelligence and drive that brought Jennings lofty grades in high school. A perfect storm of donors led him to and through Brown: the MIT program that gave him a summer's exposure to the elite scholars of the national black middle and upper class but decided that it couldn't get him ready for the math and science work he dreamed of at MIT; the Brown full scholarship; and the MIT graduate who made equally important private donations that kept him afloat with his peers from the rich and famous at Brown. With all his intelligence, Jennings was still too far behind to stick with a math major at Brown, but he graduated with a degree in education and became a social worker and then the head of youth programs for the DC City Council.

There are as many lessons in Jennings' limitations as in his success. Here was the best and the brightest from a high-poverty school, unable to crack the code of academic success in a technical field and necessarily alienated from the elite culture of Brown. He would come home for a break to find his mother, despite all her work ethic, overwhelmed by poverty's demands, evicted, with her belongings in the street. Yet he had to fit in with dorm-mates who had taken advanced college science courses in their junior years of high school or were jetting off to the Caribbean for spring break.

Perhaps Jennings would have been able to slide up into a scientific field at a top black college, like Morehouse or North Carolina A and T, or a strong white college like Penn State or Arizona. But more likely, he achieved the absolute best he could with the hand he was dealt. Jennings escaped the despair of his school, and unlike nearly all of his competitors for top academic honors actually completed college. How can there be more of him and fewer of them? Certainly not by pretending that they don't face nearly insurmountable challenges from conception.

* * *

Chapter 5. The Parents

The second time I saw a male guardian in our school was at the end of the year, at graduation. Before that day in June there had been 40 weeks of classes, four "required" parent-teacher nights for my 80 students (however, that only generated a total of eight female guardians), hundreds of phone calls home, and dozens of meetings with guardians who wanted their child readmitted to my classroom after a disruption. And the only man in that whole mix had been Malita's retarded father. When it comes to poor black families, to riff off James Brown, it's a woman's, woman's, woman's, woman's world. My contacts were about half mothers and about half others, since grandmothers, aunts, cousins, and older sisters were just as likely to appear for the defense.

And the first thing I heard from the 30-ish man in the baggy shorts and floppy t-shirt? "Nigger, you did it!," he yelled out at top volume, holding up his phone for a camera and dancing in place as his son came down the aisle with 100 other seniors in their caps and gowns to the recorded strains of Pomp and Circumstance, the final tally of diplomas, such as they were, for the 250 who had started as freshmen. The principal had just delivered a stern warning before the graduates came in: "This is a special, family event. No cursing or screaming will be tolerated. The security guards are in the aisles to remove all offenders." I had thought that was a bit over the top, but it turned out the principal sure knew his crowd. The father ducked behind a wall of friends as a security guard came over, probably just like he did when he was a student, 18 years before.

So where are the men? A far greater share is incarcerated than in middle class communities, but still, most are somewhere in the vicinity. You can see them at the Friday night football games, hundreds of 30-ish guys in expensive leather jackets of professional sports teams, filling the stands, cackling knowledgeably about the failings of the coaches and the players. So they're around. And they pop in and out of view, especially with the boys, bearing dramatic gifts like shoes and sports gear and tickets. They just aren't in their children's daily lives by the time the kids are in high school, even if some might have been in the lower grades. It's a tradition, the worst one possible for the children.

That leaves the child-rearing to the women. From many hours spent in students' homes, as pre-school teacher, school teacher, and tutor, I can offer an anecdotal account that is generally supported by current research. The initial approach to child-rearing by poor black mothers is fairly similar. It is the one they have seen, and now replicate, and it can be characterized as survival training. This is not the supportive hovering of middle class and upper class parents. This is the tough and distant style of being a parent. Kids are admonished and if necessary threatened with being smacked into silence at the earliest ages, taught by example that nobody looks out for you in this tough world, so you'd better look out for yourself. In contrast to middle and upper class life, preschoolers are taught how to play and respond by siblings and cousins in groups much more than by parents in one-on-one interaction. Daytime and bedtime reading, guided play with legos and blocks, excursions to museums, the zoo, puppet shows, and quasi-cultural events, all are far more common among middle and upper class parents of young children.

Despite all the huffing and puffing of poor black mothers, obedience and respect appear to be no greater among their children, where it is so valued and sought, than in middle and upper class families. Kids will be kids, and they push until they find their limits. In all economic classes they find that parents generally don't have the time and energy to enforce their many instructions and threats. Ironically, as a result of the energetic pushing back to find limits that is stimulated in poor families by aggressive demands for obedience, about half of poor children develop by the early elementary years a pointed disdain for the mother's commands that would shock the more permissive middle class parents. Children generally divide into two groups, based on personality, which the television series about the Baltimore ghetto mentioned earlier, "The Wire," calls stoop and corner kids. Stoop kids actually stay on their stoop like they are told to when mom goes out; corner kids ignore her and head out to check out the action.

The corner kids break the chain of control at a remarkably early age. "Brian" (pronounced not in the mainstream way, but as Bree-Ann) was a world of trouble to teach in 9th grade. He was extremely smart but dangerously creative, constantly lifting pins and tacks from the poster boards in the room and leaving them on people's seats. His attendance at school was fairly regular, but because he liked to roam the halls and hide in corners and empty rooms, his attendance in class was less frequent. I stopped letting him in if he was more than five minutes late, and he took to lounging on the wall on the hall side of our huge picture window, banging on it and joning with students inside. The Crow said he had no place to take him, since there was a tardy room only for the poorly attended first period. For once even he couldn't generate a single working number for the family, and so could not get a guardian to come in for a conference. It was left up to me how to resolve the disruptive situation, so one day I brought an extra helmet and asked Brian if he'd like a ride home on my motorcycle.

He loved that, so off we went. We parked by a small house tucked up at the end of a long alley, and I said I'd like to come in and say hello to his mother. "Oh, my moms ain't around these days, but my grandmoms is for sure," he said. We went in through a screen door lying to one side on a single hinge, and it became clear from the start who ran the household. "Hey, grandma, say hi to my math teacher," yelled Brian at a small, wizened, maybe sixty-year-old lady sitting in a lounger, watching television, and he went off to his room without further explanation. I sat with her and explained the disruption Brian was causing in school, and asked her if she could help me keep him in the class: "How about I call you at the end of each week, and if he has been disruptive at all, you take away his i-Phone for the weekend?" She looked at me like I was crazy. "Oh no," she said, "he'd beat us up, for sure, and just take it." She indicated another woman, 40-ish, who was sitting in the next room working on her résumé on an old computer, who was another of her daughters. "Since he was eight, I can't tell him what to do, and he just takes what he wants and hits us if we try to stop him."

Some mothers of corner kids seem to revel in their defiance and come to see it as a virtue that will help protect them on the streets. I often called mothers into school for a meeting as a condition for their son or daughter returning to class after fighting in response to joning. I would describe the incident, with the student present, and ask the mother what we could do to encourage a non-violent response, like just ignoring the insult, or telling a teacher. Most mothers would join me in pointing out to their children that the violent strategy would never make them successful, in school or on the job, but three of the mothers used exactly the same phrase, effectively congratulating their sons for upholding their honor, as they would have to do on the street: "I ain't raise no punk." At this point I could only thank a mother for coming in and end the meeting, because disagreeing with a parent in front of a child only makes things worse for your relationships. In one case I made the mistake of pointing out that it was a girl that her son had slugged. "Teach the bitch to shut her mouth about you, that's right," she told her son.

One of the three cases involved the boy I later tutored in jail after his arrest for assault and armed robbery.

At times I would see the same behavior in a parent that I was trying to defuse in a child, which of course explained the child's actions, but offered little hope of correcting them. In these cases I would mumble to myself the Latin question, *Quis custodiet ipsos custodes* (Who guards the guardians)? "Charles" was a rangy senior who rarely came to pre-calculus class, and when he did, often reeked of marijuana and answered questions like he'd smoked a lot. It was the spring semester, and I had 24 students in my class, survivors who had somehow held on as an equal number of their peers had dropped out since 9th grade. The first few weeks showed me that ten students were strong enough in background, homework, and attendance to have hopes of earning a passing D, ten were so hopelessly behind that even if they had tried to do the homework (which they didn't, since copying doesn't count) they would fail, and four were up for grabs. Those four had huge gaps in math background, but when they worked they showed signs of life that could lead to grasping the key concepts. Charles was one of them.

I warned the assistant principal of the impending disaster, but he could not justify organizing a different class for the weaker students as he had the previous semester when I had the contract-breaking 38 students. "You can start planning for a summer school class now," I told him. "The only issue is whether it will be ten or 14!" Charles knew from the start that he would have to work hard to get his diploma, but he acted like the most callow of freshman, and I was soon reduced to my freshman tricks for people who talk in lessons and curse when told to stop, denying him admission to class until his mother came in for a meeting. When she did, she embarrassed Charles into a burst of a few weeks of actual class work by crying, saying she was helpless, that he had refused to listen to her since eighth grade. I felt we were working as a team, and made sure to call her when Charles received his first good grades, on a project about his potential earnings as a record producer, and a quiz on using logarithms to calculate the years of investment needed to achieve a certain amount of profit in that business, given various interest rates.

As we moved closer to the final exam, though, Charles disappeared again. He failed the course, not just because of his dismal grade on the final but because he had so much missing work, as well as weak results on previous exams that he had then chosen not to redo after we had corrected them in class. Of my 12 who failed, three or four came in to see me and ask for extra work so they could graduate. I gave my standard, long-practiced response, which I had noted early and often in every course I taught: "Extra credit and make-up are not words you will find on my syllabus, or in the union contract.

All you can do if you fail is make sure that when you retake the course, you do your work as assigned." They went away in various combinations of tears and rage, feelings I understood well from my own academic misadventures.

At lunch time, the two police officers who were stationed in the school came into my classroom. "We want to escort you to your car so you can leave," one said. "Charles has been making threats in the cafeteria about shooting you, and that child is just crazy enough to do it. The principal says he'll find someone to cover your afternoon classes. Do you want to swear out a complaint for his threatening?" My first reaction was to laugh, because Charles was probably too stoned to organize an armed encounter. My second was to worry that Charles would get a record for running his silly mouth. I thanked the officers, but told them to forget the whole matter and just tell Charles to watch his mouth.

About five minutes later, as I was about to welcome my next class, Charles' mother burst into my room. Thinking she had been called by the police, I smiled and said, "Don't worry, nothing is going to happen. He was just running his mouth, and I am not pressing charges." However, she wasn't there because the police had called. She was there because Charles had called. She let loose on me with every curse word I knew and some I didn't. "You racist (expletive) bastard, you just want to turn another black boy into a street bum by flunking him. (Expletive) liar, you told me he had gotten some good grades. I have worked too hard to get him to his diploma to let you get away with this (expletive). You tell me right now what he can do to pass this course, or I am going to (expletive) you up." Taken aback, I explained that he would have to take a summer school class, and actually do the work throughout the course, and then explained that I thought she was there because she was concerned that he had threatened to shoot me."

That brought out even more venom, and a threat that she'd like to do the same. She slammed the door on the way out, as my 9th graders were starting to trickle in, and then a few seconds later stormed back in for more cursing and screaming before a final exit. Shaken, I emailed the assistant principal to report the incident, saying that a very irate mother had somehow gotten past security without waiting in the office. He emailed me back almost immediately, and humorously, that the same irate mother had just come into in his office, but that he had sent her away happy by finding a credit from Charles' sophomore year that could be applied to his missing math credit, and he could graduate. I never asked how many of the other 11 failing students also benefitted from such creative accounting. I had already told the school I was not coming back, and it was no longer my fight if the district wanted to hand out phony diplomas.

In an earlier chapter I told the tale of Quaniesha's mother, who had been barred from the school herself for using the same belligerence and curses on the security guards that Quaniesha used in class. Many times I have listened to other female guardians interrupting and bullying me as they read me a riot act of excuses during disciplinary meetings that, had I closed my eyes, could have come directly from their children's mouths. Children will, of course, model their behavior on what they see at home from guardians for hundreds or hours a week rather than at school from teachers for a few dozen. Most guardians, though, supportively take the teacher's side in such meetings and express frustration at seeing the same behavior in school that they see at home. Their problem was mostly one of passivity. They had given up on controlling the behavior, and just hoped we could do better. A few guardians, though, both held the line against disrespectful behavior at home and had no trouble helping us hold the same line at school.

Malcolm's sister was a good example of this. Malcolm, my leading homophobe, was a nasty piece of work, as a veteran black female teacher said. He was simply crazy, as a middle-aged white teacher, a former lawyer who had decided to serve society more directly, put it. Yet he was also one of the sharpest knives in our drawer, able in his brief periods between joning, joking, and defying orders to stop and focus intensely and reason his way to the right answer alarmingly quickly. On a field trip with the former lawyer to a museum on the national mall, Malcolm had suddenly jumped down onto the Metro train tracks and danced for a while until the light of the approaching train came into view. On a field trip with me to my university he had smacked the emergency stop button on the longest escalator in the Metro system, so we and the other patrons had to walk up the escalator. Other than barring him from the Metro, I didn't know what to do about his constant disruption of class, which escalated into cursing and threatening when I remonstrated.

Malcolm and a friend made a point to use "nigger" as an appellation in class as often as possible, and I finally sent them both to the principal with a note: "I have tried to explain that the N-word is cursing and unacceptable in school, and that even as a sign of friendship outside school it is damaging. Could you try to explain the same?" His note back to me was a classic that I still have: "Dr. Rossiter — I don't think you'll have any more trouble on this score." Neither the boys nor the principal would tell me about their conversation, so I don't know if the discussion was physical, emotional, or intellectual, but he was right. I had no more trouble on that score.

My efforts to reach Malcolm's mother failed, but the Crow was able to bring in his older, professionally-dressed sister, who was probably in her late '20s. Sitting with me, Malcolm, and assistant principal Don Marcellus, she listened quietly and carefully to my litany of complaint and to Malcolm's response that he was bored, and had to respond when people around him joned him. She skipped the details and went right to the heart of the matter: "I hear anything like this again, I'm going to find your daddy and bring him over to the house and watch him beat you silly. Then I'm going to put you out of the house and dump your clothes out into the street, and then I'm going to tell the school to just put you out too, because I am never, never, going to leave work again and come up here to listen to such nonsense." She got up and walked out without a good-bye to any of us. Don suggested a system in which Malcolm would sit away from others, way in the back of the class, so they wouldn't be close enough to whisper jones, and I would promise not to call on him unless he raised his hand. He also could raise his hand and point to the door when he felt that a breather would keep him from getting angry at somebody.

With this system, we survived the rest of the semester. I had talked to Malcolm's other teachers and realized that while he confronted and challenged every male teacher, he was docile enough with women. I traded him with a young white woman for her most difficult child, and all went well until she suddenly quit over a weekend. But by that time he was off my radar, and we only exchanged nods in the hall. I saw Malcolm over the next two years, off and on, as he made his way to graduation. He was still a bit touchy, a bit rowdy in the halls, but he kept it regulated in a way he had not before the meeting with his sister.

A parent at my charter school, a father who came in when his cranky but usually successful daughter had caught the fever from my rowdiest class and threw something at me when my back was turned, used a softer approach than Malcolm's sister, but was similarly supportive. "Joliana" was taking 9th grade Algebra rather than 10th grade geometry only because she had missed too many classes of a special before-school offering for the most talented students the previous year. By chance, her older brother had been sent out of his class the same day, so when I came over to the meeting room they were both there with their dad. After hearing me describe Joliana as one of my best students, and hearing her say that I was picking on her, "consequencing" her for things that other kids got away with all the time, he said:

> You know, sometime people be expectin' more from the best. You
> know, I been working for Mr. Smalls 20 years, hauling his auto parts
> to the other dealers. Why you think he call me with a big job when I'm
> 'bout ready to head home, and not one of the other guys? It's 'cause he
> think I'm the best, and he want me to do it. You the same way with
> this teacher here, 'Liana. I hear him saying you so good, it jump out at
> him when you do bad. You should be happy he see you that way.

That was one of the most effective talks I ever heard from a parent, or teacher, or anyone. Joliana settled in, scored far higher, and kept texting and calling me after I resigned over phony grades, bitterly disappointed that I was leaving her.

This sample of guardians from disciplinary conferences is obviously biased toward the weak and uninvolved. The disciplinary poster I put on my wall read: "First, self-control. Then Rossiter control. Then parent control. Then Crow-control." It meant that the first disruption would lead to spending time with me after school, the second would require a parental visit, and the third would be suspension into the loving hands of the dean of students. Guardians generally wouldn't be in a meeting about a lack of self-control if they had achieved control over their children at home. Roughly half of my students habitually avoided trouble, even if they avoided doing too much work, so most of their guardians I only knew over the phone. I would call to congratulate their child for good work in class, or to make a rare complaint about them mimicking the behavior of the knuckle-heads, and get only support and enactment of the rewards or penalties I suggested.

Even these parents, though, were overwhelmed by the notion of looking over homework each night, let alone advising on it, like middle class parents often do. Realizing that parents were simply not confident enough about their ability to understand the assignment, let alone the answers, I suggested that they tell their kids to do their homework or quiz preparation in the afterschool tutoring classes put on by friendly students from local universities. These volunteers were embarrassingly under-utilized, particularly given the dozens of athletes who had a mandatory hour break before practice could begin in which they sat chatting in a supposed study hall. The parents and I just couldn't get students to stay for the tutoring. The share of students who never did a bit of homework remained constant at about 80 percent, and the volunteers remained lonely after their long, altruistic trip across town.

What can we learn from these tales of parents that will help us rethink the "urban school?" Most importantly, we need to realize that while all of us as parents feel helpless at times before the mystery of our teenagers, that doesn't mean we all face the same challenges or bring the same resources to the table. It is fundamentally incorrect and unhelpful to paraphrase F. Scott Fitzgerald and say that black, poor parents and guardians are just the same as other parents, only blacker and poorer. The black poor live in a separate culture with its own rituals and standard ways, one that stands quite apart from the middle class mainstream. This culture especially has its own challenges, and they are legion for families.

Mimicking a middle class experience in schools helps prepare students for what they can expect if they break out and leave the ghetto behind, but it does not allow the integration of the family into the support structure of the school. A back-to-school night that looks superficially like a middle-class one only discourages teachers when five percent of children are represented by their guardians, as opposed to nearly 100 percent at middle-class schools, black or white. Assigning homework on the assumption that parents will ensure it is being done just discredits homework when the parents can't follow through. When the children of poverty are packed together as they are in America's urban schools, it guarantees that a system of social workers and special education staff operating at ratios and with tools appropriate for the middle class will be overwhelmed by a flood of dysfunctional families.

What we can learn from the guardians portrayed in this chapter is that they need support as much as their children do. Indeed, many times teachers would say after a meeting with a guardian and child, "the child is the parent in that family." Poverty is a brutally stressful condition, and the only way to relieve the stress is to have a job. Stability and predictability are in some ways even more important than income in addressing the family dysfunction that at a minimum leaves kids to fend for themselves in school and more usually knocks them off the academic track. No force of nature can bring the men back into the families, but some intelligent investment in public and private employment can put some regularity into guardians' lives and put some cash into their pockets. Not all guardians could take advantage of a leg up, because showing up on time without drama is a bridge too far for them. For those who could, though, the payoff would come in the form of a better connection with the promised benefits of education, both for families and for their children.

* * *

CHAPTER 6. THE TEACHERS

Legendary Georgetown University basketball coach John Thompson was once asked by an interviewer, "When did you become such a great coach?" His answer was: "When I recruited Patrick Ewing." This tongue-in-cheek, disarmingly true response tells us a lot about teaching, and about the very notion of "failing" schools, administrators, and especially teachers. What are these teachers failing at? Technique? Effort? No. They are failing at luck. They just happen to have masses of students who come in the door dramatically weaker than middle class kids in academic achievement, mainstream behavior, family stability and support, and cultural connection to a college prep world. Teachers in high-poverty schools persevere through the chaos, providing a source of stability and a bit of improvement for the students that nobody in the school reform movement wants their own children to go to school with. These teachers vary in quality, of course, but in my experience most are heroes, finding small satisfactions in tiny victories, and soldiering on through the daily heartache of their students' lost potential and even lives.

John Thompson has never lacked for an ego. It is doubtful that he really thought he was a bad coach, with poor techniques and lazy efforts, as he taught skills and motivated young people during the nine years he coached at Georgetown before luring Ewing's mother with a promise of constant tutoring and guaranteed graduation for her learning-disabled son. In none of those years did his team win a national championship, as he did with Ewing. Nor did Thompson think he was doing a lousy job when he couldn't win a championship, or even get to the final four, in the 14 years he coached after Ewing graduated and went on to stardom with the New York Knicks.

The point? Only what any teacher could tell you: we play the hand we're dealt. When sharp, well-prepared, highly-motivated, well-behaved students walk in your door it's easy to look like a genius as you engage their attention and help them score at and above grade level; when damaged, weak, alienated, unmotivated, and poorly-behaved students come in, Jesus Christ and the 12 Apostles couldn't move them to grade level with a bulldozer. When National Merit scholarships, stunning average SAT scores, and consistent admissions to top colleges are announced at wealthy schools, and when 50 percent drop-out rates and illiteracy are reported at high-poverty schools, it's the realities of the families, not the quality of the teaching, that is primarily responsible.

Case in point: two famed teachers from Washington's elite National Cathedral prep school for girls, each with over 30 years experience, walked, or in one case rolled, out the door in the 2010s to start new phases in their lives. English teacher and dean of students Roger Barbee retired to the Shenandoah Valley of Virginia and French teacher "Camille LeBlanc" went to join a former NCS principal who was now running a DC charter school. At NCS parents had ferociously sought assignment of their students to these teachers' classes. Roger and Camille were widely recognized and fêted as magical with teenagers, and in their classes it had been pin-drop quiet as rapt students read out their college-level homework or pondered the Socratic lead of the teacher before raising their hands to respond.

Roger began to volunteer and then substitute teach part-time at a public high school in the Valley. He became the coach of the wrestling team, using his experience as a country boy growing up in rural North Carolina and his record as a national class wheelchair racer to reach his boys. In the classroom he was still working the old magic, but now it was to help the son of Hispanic migrant workers prepare for the Virginia Standards of Learning standardized exam he needed to graduate, an exam that was at least six years over his head, or to help a classroom of kids at the third-grade level struggle with the standardized sixth-grade college prep curriculum. However, when he applied for a full-time position he was suddenly not the NCS star, but rather a troublesome critic of the administration's need to pretend that students were years beyond where they actually were. Worse, he was a failed teacher, because not enough of his students had passed the all-important tests. The magic teacher at NCS became just another substitute tossed to the side. The job he wanted went to a young recruit who the administration hoped would do as told, and try to raise those scores by hook or by crook.

Camille was in shock from the first minute of the first class. Her French queries evoked no response from a French II class other than chatter and cursing. The word she used to describe the students' behavior was "horrible," and a short quiz revealed that they could not conjugate the simplest of verbs.

She went to see the principal, and told her, just as she would have when they were back at NCS, that nearly all these students had no business being in French II, and would have to be placed back in French I. Impossible — they had their credit and having them take the course again would cause all sorts of problems with parents and the boards of the charter school and the charter school system. Camille warned that few would be able to handle anything resembling the French II level, and so would fail. Impossible — if they came to a class and worked, they would have to pass. Very quickly Camille got the message: teach them what you want, but give them a phony French II credit. She and Roger had gone from being great teachers with one group of kids to being largely ineffective ones with another. It was just a matter of geography.

* * *

Rosemary Queen had been a math teacher at Johnson from its grand opening in the 1970s through its demolition and reconstruction in the 2010s. I introduced her in Chapter 2 as the North Carolina Aggie who engineered the separation of my large senior pre-calculus class into two manageable sections. Whenever I saw her coming down the hall, lurching her substantial form back and forth due to a hip problem, even the wildest students respectfully parting in her path with a "Hi, Ms. Queen," I thought of the power and grace of elephants on the march in South Africa. These characteristics are what lead the traditionalists among the Zulu, the largest national people in South Africa, to praise the arrival of their king with *Wena we ndlovu* — "here comes the elephant." I told her the chant was even more appropriate for her, given that our school was probably the only one in America to have its teams named the Warriors and not be criticized for insensitivity to American Indians. The image of our warrior was an African man in Zulu war garb, holding the classic short stabbing spear and cowhide shield introduced by Shaka Zulu himself. More broadly, all teachers are elephants, the dominant beast in any crowd, the one whose conduct is the most important in determining if the school is a fraud or a benefit to anybody.

Other teachers, from novices like me to the school district's "teacher of the year," often called on Rosemary to take students who were disrupting their classes. "Shalondra" was a special education student 10th grader who delighted in disruption from the moment she was brought to my room during class by a guidance counselor after taking off the first few weeks of school. She sashayed her considerable bulk through the aisles, smashing into desks on both sides, greeting her friends, and trying out the classic "Get the (expletive) out my face" when I told her to sit down. No notebook, no pencil, no effort. This was gonna be tough. A week of notes, reminders, incentives, penalties, and fruitless attempts to reach her mother later, I asked Rosemary

Queen what to do. "I know that girl," she said, "and she's worthless. I taught her mother, and she was worthless too. I'll take her. You get back to teaching."

When Shalondra wandered in the next day, loud and late as usual, I walked her over to Rosemary's room. Shalondra walked in, showing off to the students with the same sashaying, braying routine she had used in my room, but didn't get into the second stroke of it before Rosemary herself sashayed menacingly up to Shalondra, and they stood belly to belly, two massive and immoveable objects, glaring into each other's eyes. Instead of her usually impeccable King's English, this is what came out of Rosemary's mouth: "Little Missy, there ain't but one bitch of a 'head nigger in charge' in this classroom, and it ain't you. Now sit your ass down and shut up, because you won't like the way it feels if I have to sit you down myself. Just ask your mama if you don't believe me." Shalondra cracked up: "Sorry, Ms. Queen. Just messin' with you." She sat down meekly.

Shalondra behaved for Rosemary, keeping her conversations to a respectful murmur, and peeking at her supposedly banned cell phone fairly discreetly, but she didn't experience any academic miracle. Rosemary didn't try to make her come more often or push her to do the assignments that would be written on the board. She had learned long ago not to splash her water on stone. No fancy handouts, none of the sequenced, power-pointed, standard-based lessons the administrators kept demanding, because Rosemary knew her population. The students who were going to work would, and the students who weren't going to work wouldn't, almost regardless of what materials and encouragement you gave them. Just tell the kids to pick up the book and read, and do the examples and then the problems.

If they did it, they did it. If they asked for help, they got it. If they blew it off, they got a zero. If they failed, they failed. It was all documented, day by day, so Rosemary could show a dissatisfied child, guardian, or administrator. Rosemary got the same percentage returns we all did, or as anybody would who is working with kids with no fundamental connection to the curriculum or school culture: about 10 percent doing real grade level work, another 40 percent or so making a feeble, passable effort, and 50 percent wasting everybody's time. She just got them with a lot less drama.

Where teachers shine, and really show their worth in a high-poverty school, is not in promoting academic excellence but in engaging kids in social lessons that will help them first make it to adulthood, and then maybe earn a living with sound moral standards. "Caroline," a feisty young black teacher, loved to be told by her students that they just couldn't tell her which other kid was the perpetrator of a misdeed, because that would be "snitching." Snitches, as the popular saying went, ended up in ditches, at least in this neighborhood. That was true enough: there were many cases in the previous few years of witnesses gunned down by the allies of a jailed drug warrior. This was music to Caroline's ears.

Well, tell me this, do you feel it's safe for your mother to walk down your block after dark, to go to the corner store? No? Gee, why is that? Maybe because there are criminals lurking about to take her off? Well, over in Georgetown, mothers can walk anywhere they want at night. Do you think criminals are lurking about in Georgetown? No? Gee, why not? Oh, because Georgetown is full of snitches who call the police the second they see something fishy outside their window?

Would you let someone just walk up and beat up your mother? No? Because that is what you are doing when you don't snitch when you see something bad: you're just guaranteeing that someone will someday take your mother off. Maybe kill her, too. Why don't you just kill her right now and get it over with? No? Why not? You're already a mother-killer, because you don't snitch.

"Mark Tully," a gym teacher and football coach, taught his lessons with caustic humor, too, confronting a boy in the halls between classes with: "Vagina! I said Vagina! I love Vagina! I'm a Vagina-man. Want to see a Vagina. Why you showin' me your ass, your drawers out your pants all hangin' down like that? You think I'm a homo-sexual, a gay boy, you think I want to see your ass? You saying I'm gay? No, no, no, I love Vagina, so pull up them silly drawers before I start thinkin' there's a Vagina in there! Vagina!" The laughing boy would pull his pants up out of the gangster look, developed to mimic heroes in jail who had their belts taken away. Maybe it would only last a few minutes, but Mark had done his job. He could have ignored the boy's look like most teachers, but he took the time to deliver a lesson about middle-class living, using ghetto humor.

As a veteran teacher, Mark's method was the same as Rosemary's: he showed the kids how to use the archery kit, the volleyball court, the flag football gear, and the softball diamond. But it you came to class without your regulation gym clothes, or if you screwed around and took away from others' instruction time, he just sat you on the bench and recorded a zero, as if you had not attended at all. The majority of his class would usually be on the bench. Kids only had to take two semesters of gym over the four years of school, and most failed the first time, as freshmen, just like they failed Algebra I. The difference was, there was no credit recovery for gym: you had to take it again sooner or later. Since a lot of the knuckleheads would drop out anyway, Mark had small classes of seniors who knew they needed to come, change clothes, and behave if they wanted to graduate.

Was Mark teaching middle class social skills, as assistant principal Marcellus always said we were, or was he just being lazy? Does it matter? If he'd let the students play who couldn't be bothered to bring their gym kit, they would have brought their insouciance into the class, disrupting it for the others. Mark's realistic approach to gym even extended to the academic study halls the district forced him to hold for his football players for an hour after school, before practice. If they wanted to take advantage of SAT prep classes, fine. If they didn't, that was fine too. They could just sit around and chat. I volunteered to run those classes for all the varsity athletes, but it was soon only the girls' basketball team that came, because their coach made it a requirement for practicing. A couple of motivated football players came on their own volition or their guardians' instructions. By Mark's logic, they were probably the only ones who would have tried in any event, had all the players been forced to come.

New teachers were constantly told to work on their "classroom management techniques" as if using tricks rather than judgment based on a few years of experience was the key to closing down the drama. Roger Barbee says that when he looks back on his teaching for the first seven years he wonders why he wasn't just taken out and shot. It takes that long to get good. Not that the tricks didn't help. Using the actual students' names in examples and on quiz problems usually helps focus the mind, at least of the named student. And if you start a new activity every few minutes, and record prize points toward some treat from each activity, you can always capture more kids' attention than if you had a couple of longer assignment they have to work on throughout the class. But the flip side to spoon-fed lessons is that the 50 percent who are ready to work are being actively un-trained, away from the middle class norms they need, and the 50 percent who had been vaguely captured don't put in enough sweat to remember the material later, and might never learn to work without immediate incentives.

It was the same with behavior. My teaching partner in a mandated "film club" for credit each afternoon at the charter school was "Arthur Jensen," a young African-American teacher of history whose middle-class family had lived in a white area, and who had gone to a mainstream high school and college. Arthur and I would crack up when one of the wildest boys in our supposedly low-stress, last period club, who had to be dragged out every few days by security guards because he couldn't just sit and watch a movie and take a few notes, would say: "You're bad teachers. You can't control us." Arthur told him: "But we don't want to control you. You're not an animal. You have to learn to control yourself." We could have spent hours devising minute by minute tasks and rewards, but we felt high school was time to fish or cut bait. Kids know what should be done. It infantilizes them to pretend otherwise.

When they witness pathetic misbehavior and inattention to work, particularly on one of the many days when it feels like the entire class is in a childish funk, some teachers feel pushed over the line of professionalism, and feel the need to hammer their charges about the importance of appropriate behavior in the school and workplace. I am dubious about the usefulness of these lectures. The tone is really all that the kids take in. Was it fury, sadness, or disgust? The kids already know what's right and wrong. Those who are driving the misbehavior don't care, and those who are just along for the ride are ready to get back to work. It's better just to laugh, take a breath, and move on. Still, I have seen some angry beat-downs that helped clear the air and allowed a resumption of teaching. The rule of thumb, though, is that you should only lose it and scream once each semester.

The ghetto challenge is one form of beat-down; the ghetto appeal to pride is another. A white teacher in a charter school got her miscreants' attention with a rousing imitation of an angry black teacher: "You think you're bad, you little babies? I was in the Baltimore schools for five years, and you wouldn't have made it to lunch time with your little games. Think you're a little gangster? They'd kick your ass on the corner making noise like you do in here. You're chicken-(expletive). You don't dare to look me in the eye and refuse to work. You just fritter away your assignment time. Show me some courage. I dare you to come up here and say you won't work, so I can put you on the street and you can explain it to your mothers."

A black, ten-year teacher at the same school went with: "Shameful. That means full of shame. You are bringing shame to your family, to your street, to the black people of America. People say, 'Oh, those ghetto kids, those gang-bangers [Black English for running with a gang], they don't know how to act, they're too lazy to work.' Well, you are proving them right. I came from this neighborhood. You are shaming me, because people will say I come from a neighborhood of chumps, hustlers, and fools." She got a few minutes renewed attention out of that one, but in the context of an alienated student body it seemed like a lot of energy to make a point the kids already knew full well.

* * *

An important subclass of teachers in high-poverty public schools is the first-generation immigrants. Recently-arrived Filipinos, Indians, Central Americans, Chinese, Jamaicans, and especially Africans gravitate to unionized schools because of the job security and benefits. A mortgage is a beautiful thing to have, and a terrifying thing to hold. With the disappearance of union manufacturing, teachers' unions are a last bastion of tenure for people drawn to America by the dream of building a stable future for their family. Immigrant teachers were usually high achievers in their native countries' school and university systems, and they bring comprehensive knowledge to their classes that is more than equal to that of the American-born teachers. Unfortunately the immigrants also frequently bring accents that, for Americans, are almost incomprehensible at routine speed. Students and even teachers are often mystified by these teachers' pronouncements. It is, of course, good practice and an intellectual challenge to follow someone who is speaking good English with an accent different from yours, be it Scottish or Nigerian, but this task necessarily interferes with the academic task at hand.

The immigrant teachers are among the most attuned to the rules for teacher evaluation, because they are the most grateful to have a job in this uncertain country, and the most worried about the consequences of not protecting their position. Nearly all of them, as well as a minority of the other teachers, will study assiduously, down to the last category, whatever rubric based on the latest fads is being used for scoring teachers, and whatever rules, down to the last appeal, apply to the process for challenging and changing the scores awarded by the district's evaluator and by the principal. A Jamaican-born teacher, who sees her evaluation instrument as simply silly and the process as hopelessly subjective, yet still studies and tries to meet every demand and challenge every score with almost maniacal vigor, told me that, "It's just like a game in the neighborhood, growing up. If they keep score, then score matters, and I'm going to win."

The "gamers" spend hours decoding the bulky instructions, consulting with each other about ways to meet the rubrics for materials on the walls and actions to take during the evaluators' visits. They routinely challenge not just a low score on their overall evaluation, but any score on any part of it that is not the very top one. Most teachers can't be bothered to develop such expertise, but they do pick off some of the lower-hanging fruit. For example, the DC evaluation instrument allowed teachers to set a goal at the start of the year, with their principal, and then get credit or debit based on achieving the goal or not. Johnson's principal must have had some language about "80 percent" in his contract, because we were all told to have our goal be "80 percent of students passing the final exam." With at most half the students attending class more than twice a week, this goal would be nearly impossible to achieve. Teachers quickly learned how to slip in qualifiers like, "80 percent of students who have attended more than 75 percent of classes will pass the exam," which limited the students who counted to the most serious fifth.

If an evaluation instrument has a minor component requiring teachers to demonstrate to the classroom evaluator that they can teach a concept, often called a "standard," to students who learn primarily by seeing, by listening, or by doing (fancily labeled as visual, aural, and kinesthetic learners), then the gamers will have a three-method plan ready to go for each of the standards that are scheduled for the week. They will write the three activities on the board each day, for that day's standard, and if the evaluator walks in for one of the unannounced evaluations, boom, they will go right to them. Of course, no systematic psychological testing has been done to categorize different students in the class into these learning styles, and both teacher and evaluator know that the teacher will never use the listed activities unless the evaluator is in the room. But that is what it takes to play the game, and get to reach the top categories, which will extend your contract and bounce you into a higher pay level.

The gamers have reason to game. If you don't watch the process like a hawk and cover all the myriad check points ("teacher checks for understanding by asking higher-order question as defined by Bloom's Taxonomy of knowledge") within each of the myriad categories of teaching skill ("teacher engages students appropriately") during the evaluation visit, you will certainly find yourself staring down the barrel of a "minimally effective" or "not effective" annual rating. I once was scored poorly on this checkpoint because I was observed asking a tenth-grade student to add two single-digit numbers without then guiding him into a "higher-order" discussion of the day's standard on the "triangle theorem," under which none of the three sides can be longer than the sum of the other two (a straight line being the shortest distance between two points on a flat surface). The evaluator, a "master teacher" who roamed the district's schools, had no way of knowing that the student was a special education kid years behind, and that I had silently cheered myself for the rare victory of getting Martin actually to do any intellectual work in class, even if it was counting up 8 plus 5 on his fingers. I should have asked her to teach him the theory.

Under complicated "school reform" contracts negotiated in recent years between school officials and unions, one or two low ratings can lead to automatic termination, consistently high ratings can lead to dramatic bonuses, and lower scores can trump seniority during the frequent staffing cuts in public schools brought on by the expansion of charter schools. Michelle Rhee, appointed as the head of the DC schools by Mayor Adrian Fenty after he decided to take control of the schools from the elected school board in 2007, sent security staff with cardboard boxes to 266 teachers' doors one morning in 2009. Shocked teachers, many with tenure and supposedly safe scores on their recent evaluations, were told to pack up that instant and were escorted out of the building. The process of selecting the teachers to be fired was opaque, as it often was for the other 750 teachers fired during her three-year reign. At its core, though, was the "school reform" concept of using evaluation scores to justify firings of "ineffective" teachers. Resentment in high-poverty communities over this treatment of primarily black professionals (and, to be fair, a lot of illegal campaign funding) generated an enormous turnout that defeated Fenty in the election that fall, and led to Rhee's resignation.

When public school teachers talk about "the war on teachers," the scored evaluation process is the weapon they most have in mind. Charter schools use various evaluation scales as well, but they have little of the power or fear of the public examples. Nobody has the guarantee of a job in a charter school, not just for the next year, but for the next minute. Part of the ideology is that there is no tenure, no seniority, no job security, and no protection against immediate termination. The war on teachers has already been won there.

The evaluation process is a double-edged sword. One edge of the sword is the categories and subcategories of teaching skills that allow outside evaluators and the building's administrators to satisfy the district's desire to score as many people as possible low enough that they are always on tenterhooks, eligible for firing. One assistant principal told me that he thought there was an additional motivation for the clear instruction he received to low-ball teachers in the first evaluation one year: to make teachers eager to ingratiate themselves with the administrators for the next evaluation period by taking on extra tasks. The other edge of the sword is the recent drive to base a share of teachers' scores on their students' standardized test results.

The categories in the evaluations instrument are nothing more than the latest fads, which school reformers call "best practices" despite them never having been tested in practice for the statistical gods of validity and reliability. Validity in the case of establishing a "best practice" means that students whose teachers use a certain method to teach a skill will tend to have higher scores on a test of that skill than students whose teachers use a different method. Reliability in this case means that this result will be found for those teachers and methods when the study is repeated.

Both validity and reliability require that a sufficient number of teachers are selected randomly to make us sure, to a certain probability such as 95 percent, that the correlation between the method and the result could not have happened by chance. They also require that the students in the experiment be similar to the students in the school that would then use the method, in terms of important variables that affect learning style, such as age, actual grade level, social class, ethnicity, special education status, and, most importantly, the skills and motivation of their parents. Researchers don't actually have to match up kids like this. They can achieve the same effect by statistically controlling for these variables, although they rarely include the important assessment of parental skill and motivation.

Once the method has been established by these experiments as most likely being a "best practice," the evaluation instrument itself must meet the demands of the statistical gods. In this case validity means that teachers who score high tend to have students who score high, and reliability means both that an individual evaluator will score an individual teacher generally the same in repeated observations, and that different evaluators will rank a collection of teachers in roughly the same order. Again, sufficient numbers must be tested to rule out chance as the cause of any consistent findings.

As you can imagine, establishing validity and reliability for both methods and instruments is difficult in the complex world of human interaction. It is also expensive and time-consuming, since only by taking a larger sample size of both teachers and students can we strip away natural variations and get to the truth of the relationships we observe. Educational research is an art as much as a statistical science, because many choices must be made in structuring the experiment. School reformers duck all of this by doing little, if any, field-testing of "best practices" and evaluation instruments, and simply forging ahead in the name of urgency. DC school chief Kaya Henderson speaks of "trying to overcome 40 years of neglect in 15 minutes," although the administrators and teachers in the 40 years before her term probably didn't see themselves as neglecting anybody. Teachers face mysteriously altered or new instruments each year, instruments that they or their union have had little role in creating or adjusting, and simply lose faith in them as measures of their ability, or as tools to help them improve. The evaluation instruments remain, though, as career and morale-threatening games to be played.

The other edge of the evaluation sword is the growing practice of basing up to half of teachers' and administrators' scores on their evaluation instrument on their students' results on standardized tests. Many of these tests are of the state or district's own slapdash making, without pretense of validity and reliability. Most crude, and the easiest and so most popular to use, are the comparisons that form the basis of the "No Child Left Behind" penalties. In this method, each year's cohort is compared to the previous year's. For example, if 20 percent of last year's tenth graders at a particular school, or in a particular teacher's classroom, hit the score for a "proficient" rating in Geometry, and only 18 percent of this year's tenth graders do, then the school or the teacher is failing to make progress. Apparently nobody bothered to tell Congress before it passed the law that, statistically, this is absurd.

These are not the same students, and you have no idea how much any particular student rose or fell in their level after spending a year with a particular teacher. What you are measuring, as is always the case with standardized tests, is who came in the door that year, and not what they gained by being inside the door. Of course, Congress didn't show much regard for statistical advice anyway when it passed No Child, since its entire premise is that everybody in every subgroup will make progress every year so that after ten years they will all be above average. After the ten years of trying to ignore the definition of average, which means a mark which only half of a group attains, the Obama administration succumbed to reality and cancelled the penalties for being below average — but only for states that agreed to test-based teacher evaluations!

* * *

A new, more sophisticated development is the use of the tests to assess growth for individual students, in order to provide a class-average "value-added" score for each teacher that can be factored into their evaluation. The reformers' theory is that your impact as a teacher can be measured by comparing the amount a student's scores have changed during the year with the average of how students with similar characteristics in similar schools have changed in previous years. This is a theory that makes a lot of sense to statisticians, since it uses multiple regression to control for many of the important social drivers of test scores that were listed above, like income and ethnicity, although not tougher things to measure like parental skills. However, the average teacher and administrator cannot understand the workings of the models, and many districts have not made their data and their models available to interested statisticians, such as those employed by teachers' union, to check for the inevitable errors in the construction and interpretation of such systems.

Complicating the matter are two facts. First, average "value-added" scores tend not to vary too much between teachers. There can be a difference of a tenth of a grade level between two teachers, which has been calculated to be unlikely more than 95 percent of the time to be due to chance, and so we say that the claim that it is due to the teachers' impact is statistically significant. However, the tenth of a grade difference is not of policy significance, meaning that in the grand scheme of the challenges of high-poverty schools it doesn't make much difference the way that, say, an entire year's difference would. Second, an individual teacher's scores tend to bounce around a lot year to year, even with all the statistical controls. This is due to the "variance," a statistical term, meaning in this case the large percentage of difference in students' achievement that can't be explained by the measured variables. A class will have its own peculiar interaction of the personalities, absences, and previous and current experiences of the student, the teacher, and the school. Until the models bring down the variance by measuring and accounting for more of these variables and their interaction, "value-added" tests will still have significant problems with validity and reliability.

Assuming that they are scrubbed and improved in the coming years, and start to provide valid and reliable measures of teacher impact on standardized tests of grade level skills, what can we say about these "Holy

Grail" tests that are at supposed, at long last, to identify the good teachers, for rewards, and the bad teachers, for firing? This question cuts to the heart of our goals for high-poverty schools. What are we trying to achieve, and will firing consistently lower-scoring teachers help us achieve it?

The first thing to remember is that the tests are culturally biased, and that this is a good thing. The culture they are biased toward is the mainstream culture, and the goal of all the money we spend in high-poverty schools should clearly be to allow students to move into mainstream culture so they can earn a middle-class living. The testers have tried hard to remove superficial cultural bias, so there are less questions about golf courses and more about buses, but they can do nothing about the fact that perseverance at unrewarding and even discouraging tasks, reading for comprehension, exposure to and use of advanced Standard English vocabulary, and even concern with test results and so motivation for perseverance are all far higher in mainstream than in high-poverty culture, and in white and Asian than in black and Hispanic cultures, at all income levels.

What is the reason for the enduring gaps of about a standard deviation between low and high income categories, and between the black or Hispanic and the white or Asian groups in each of these income categories? You can see the gaps on any chart of scores broken down this way for the SAT, and all standardized tests throughout the school years are essentially proxies and preparation for the SAT. In the low-income category the average for the black and Hispanic groups on an individual SAT, like math, is 100 points, or one standard deviation, below the average for the white and Asian groups. The ethnic lines rise together, preserving the gap as they move to the middle and high income categories, by which point they are all 100 points higher. Hence, rich black kids score on average like poor white kids. The reason for the ethnic and income gaps is cultural in the deepest sense. We are measuring attachment to or alienation from the mainstream culture. Even to attach the word "bias" to tests based on mainstream modes is somewhat misleading in its negative connotation. In their essence the tests are trying to predict who can handle college, and the requirements for success are definitely in the mainstream mode.

When students score quite low due to a lack of perseverance, as high-poverty kids tend to by the time they are in middle school, there is not much more information than that to be gleaned from the tests. Recording their particular bubble choice can't really be analyzed for the reasoning inherent in making the choice, as it can be for students who are trying to fight their way through a problem. With high-poverty students you are primarily measuring perseverance on low-interest tasks, and secondarily measuring pure reading or decoding skills and reading comprehension. Students who run out of effort after a few questions are just guessing randomly, usually without even reading the questions. So if we could identify teachers who, in the midst of all the "noise" of cultural differences between high-poverty and mainstream culture, consistently raise the scores of their students, we would not necessarily know that they are particularly skilled at "teaching," that is at the art of presenting material in an engaging way and guiding students thoughtfully through it. Instead, we would more likely know that these teachers are particularly skilled at motivating some of their students to persevere more in class, or perhaps at silencing, isolating, or removing the unmotivated students so that the motivated can practice persevering.

Will filling a school with such teachers change the trajectory of the fraud I have been describing, in which half of the students entering the alien world of the college prep curriculum drop out and the other half are passed along to graduation despite failing to grasp the required material, or to work much at grasping it? Unfortunately, it won't make much difference. The reasons for the drop-out rate are deep and cultural, and the reasons for the phony graduations are deep and financial. None are addressed by employing only those teachers who motivate enough students enough to record a statistical achievement difference of a few tenths of a grade on average over other teachers.

First of all, it would take decades to increase significantly the share of high-performing teachers, since when you wash out low-performers you have to bring in new teachers, let them gain the few years experience needed to get a grasp of the profession, and then ferret out the high and low performers among them...and repeat and repeat. To short-circuit the process, schools would raid each other, like universities bidding for the limited pool of black professors, which of course doesn't expand the pool, but simply moves the fish around. Even as the percentage of high-performing teachers creeps up over time, though, we will still not have addressed the fundamental challenges of the trauma of race and poverty, family dysfunction, and financial and career incentives for administrators and politicians to pretend that the schools are working.

Teachers, both the survivors of the "value-added" test battle and the new recruits coming in to replace the ones who did not survive, would still be with the same alienated kids from the same dysfunctional families in classrooms that would still be segregated by the same barriers of race and class. Unless we provide a curriculum that reduces the alienation, a remediation program that separates disruptive and unprepared students from those ready to learn at grade level, and a program of support that reduces the dysfunction, teaching in high-poverty schools will remain largely what it is today. Good teachers will keep on taming the chaos of the unwilling enough to provide a space for the willing to work a bit more to advance toward the probably unattainable goal of college graduation. Potentially effective teachers will wash themselves out in frustration at their inability to tame the chaos of the unwilling or advance the work ethic and academic skills of the sometimes willing. And the gamers in both groups will keep on studying the evaluation rubrics and getting their raises.

* * *

Chapter 7. The Testing Class
No Administrator, Politician, Reformer, or Dollar Left Behind

It was the union's turn. During the three-day orientation in August 2010 for new teachers in the DC public schools, an hour had been granted to the leaders of the teachers' union. They were facing a serious challenge in an upcoming election because of the contract they had just negotiated, and the membership had ratified. The union had been in a weak position in those negotiations. Its public image had been damaged earlier in the decade when its president had been carted off to jail for stealing over $4 million of union dues. Its negotiating opponent, school chief Michelle Rhee, had been boosted by a 2008 Time magazine cover photo of her holding a broom (presumably to sweep out lazy teachers) and a documentary movie, "Waiting for Superman," that portrayed her as battling for urban children against selfish unionized teachers.

The union leadership had successfully promoted the contract to its members as a good deal: greater pay in return for accepting Rhee's complex new teacher evaluation plan, called IMPACT. However, the teachers were now experiencing buyers' remorse for accepting a plan that reduced tenure protection, perhaps reflecting the way the public mood had turned against Rhee. In just a few weeks, her unpopularity would lead to the surprising upset of Mayor Adrian Fenty in the mayoral primary. The leadership wanted to make a good impression on new teachers as it campaigned, it turned out unsuccessfully, for re-election itself. With the high turnover in DC's high-poverty schools, where about a third of teachers leave every year, the new teachers formed a sizeable voting bloc.

Out on the stage in front of the roughly 500 new teachers came the union's head of teacher support, a bubbly young black woman who strode the stage like a preacher working a revival. The teachers, most of them white and nearly all of them new to the profession, were largely mystified by her presentation and seemed uncertain about how to respond to it. "We are going to reach all our children so we can score four, four, four, all day long. And get paid, paid, paid the big bonus!" This was a reference to the top score on IMPACT, which would give its recipients the option of exchanging their seniority and tenure rights for a $25,000 salary boost, although very few of the eligible teachers in that category ever took the bait.

"And how are we going to do that? When we face our class, with kids who are way behind, and kids who are on grade level, what are we going to do?" She waited for a response but all she saw were puzzled faces. "That's right, we're going to diffrerentriate!" Now there was some buzzing, as teachers turned to each other, wondering if they had hear her right, and if there weren't a few too many r's in there. "Yes, diffrerentriate," she yelled again. "That's going to be our word of the year. Let's chant it all together, come on now, teachers: Diff-re-ren-triate, diff-re-ren-triate." For about a minute she clapped her hands on the beats and sashayed from one side of the stage to the other, imploring the crowd to chant along with her. A few teachers tried to join her, but she kept changing the r's around in the word, so sometimes it was differentrirate, sometimes diffrerentirate, so it was hard to know which mispronunciation to attempt.

"Yeah, whoo-hoo, teachers! All right!" And with that, the director of teacher support began to shout out instructions on how to score high in the seven categories for the IMPACT evaluation: "Category five, extend students' knowledge. How do we do that? Diffrerentriate!" The stunned teachers, who knew nothing about IMPACT and its categories or even its concept, had just been introduced to a professional subfield of which the director of teacher support is representative. It is a class, a movement, a cult, and a funding source all tied up into one. Its members include: district and building administrators; "professional developers" like our union presenter, who is replicated in central office staff and consultants with private and non-profit firms; curriculum planners and textbook writers and manufacturers; teacher evaluation and standardized test constructers and analyzers; governors, mayors and other elected officials and their staff; union busting groups and their lawyers; foundation staff and the philanthropists whose tax deductions they allocate; and charter school companies and operators.

It is best to describe all these people and groups by the common element that undergirds their plots and plans, the misuse of tests to demonstrate progress. They comprise the testing class. They took a licking in the DC union election later that fall, when despite our director of teacher support's energetic example the teachers angrily swept out the leadership that had negotiated the IMPACT contract, but they keep on ticking. Their control over publicly-funded schools is still almost absolute, as it has been for nearly 30 years, since politicians like the self-styled "First Lady of Arkansas" decided to take on the issue of "reforming" schools.

Hillary Rodham, as she was called then, led a highly-publicized and politically-popular drive to require a standardized test for teachers. She introduced the business analogies about testing products to achieve quality control that soon swept the nation's public schools, which justifies a constant political need to show "progress" with standardized tests and graduation rates of students, and credentials and ratings of teacher. Tiny cracks in the sea wall have appeared in the 2010s, as first parents and now teachers at middle-class schools have begun to say "enough, already," and encourage students to boycott standardized tests. High-poverty schools, though, are characterized by weak political involvement by parents and a corresponding untrammeled path for the testers. They were the first the first to receive the testers' wisdom, have been the most hampered by it, and probably will be the last to see it go.

* * *

The testing class is comprised of true believers, for whom progress is always being made and complete success is just around the corner, like the coming of the Messiah, if only the bad teachers and their union protectors would get out of the way. They believe that all students can perform well in the college prep curriculum that runs from pre-kindergarten to high school. If success doesn't come as predicted, which happens often as high-poverty schools continue to record pathetically low rates of proficiency despite being "turned around" with an administration of testers who only retain and hire teachers who follow their orders, various former administrators and teachers are blamed for having put the kids so far behind, and the predictions start again. The testers have their own holy buzzwords, like reform, accountability, no excuses, zip code doesn't matter, we now know what to do, high expectations, unbelievable progress (which always turns out on examination indeed not to be believable), aligned (as aligning instruction with standards, or aligning standards with tests), and, however pronounced, differentiate.

One of the testers' favorites is, "the research shows." The only problem is, if one asks for the research to see just what it shows, they can't provide it. For example, a "master teacher" told me after observing me to record an IMPACT score, "the research shows that you should break your period into four parts, starting with a silent work period when the students enter." I asked to see this research, so I could see how significant the improvement was when using this technique, how that improvement is measured, and whether the students in the research groups were similar enough to mine in terms of age, ability level, and social and family background to justify using the results to guide her choice of methods. All she could show me after three emails back and forth was a paragraph written by one of the testing class at the DC central administration that repeated the claim, without providing any details or references to any particular study or journal articles on it. Worse, the master teacher did not seem to understand the import of the question. She seemed to think that the fact that the claim was made by the central administration settled all questions about it.

The "diffrerentriate" incident came after an address to the new teachers by the doyenne of the testing class, Ms. Rhee. She had told her tall tale about raising her second-graders' test scores as a teacher in a high-poverty school in Baltimore into the 90th national percentile. To make the teachers feel better about some of the trials of the coming months, she did allow that before she saw the light of school reform she had been a horrible first-year Teach for America recruit, so unable to control the students that when she had to walk them down the hall to lunch she put duct tape over their mouths to keep them quiet. Rhee said with a self-deprecating laugh that she had put the tape on so firmly that when she took it off later it ripped the skin off the kids' lips, so they were bleeding and crying.

Rhee followed that story, which was supposed to show how bad teachers can be before they learn the trade, with one about how good teachers can be once they are following the school reform mandate. "Great teachers engage students. I've come across kids leaving a high school in a group in the middle of the day, and I ask them where they are going. They say they came to school for first period because the teacher was interesting, but were leaving now because the next teacher was not." When a group of the new teachers gathered in the coffee area later in the day, one told me she found this claim of Rhee's fully as bizarre and troubling as the "diffrerentriate" routine and the child abuse of ripping tape off mouths. Was the head of the schools saying that students could decide to leave school if they weren't entertained? How did they get out of the school, anyway? Why didn't she round the kids back up and get them back into class?

Rhee's implication was that the exodus was the teacher's fault and not an unacceptable avoidance of work by students. The students were portrayed as smart and logical for leaving a class, the teacher as problematic for being uninspiring. She never saw the teacher in question in action, but just accepted the students' opinion and their right to act on it. Similarly, in "Waiting for Superman," Rhee is filmed whispering to a young child during a lesson, asking if the teacher is good or not. The mystified child just sits there mute, not knowing whether to listen to the teacher's instructions or

Rhee's whispering, and perhaps not sure what to do with the concept that it is his role to judge if a teacher is good. The undercurrent of both Rhee's story about the exodus and her whispering to the young child is the testing class's certainty that everybody can recognize who the great teachers are, and that bad teachers are the reason for poor performance in high-poverty schools.

Add in the scene where Rhee gratuitously fires a principal on camera, and you can get a sense of why people on the front lines in high-poverty schools in Washington so often felt undercut and devalued by her. Rhee was, it should be noted, proud to be attacked for her lack of concern for the feelings, careers, mortgages, and lives of teachers, since it showed her fervent devotion to the children. In fact, after resigning her position in DC, she founded an organization whose name restates her position. She named it StudentsFirst, as if those who disagree with her somehow place teachers' selfish interests first. The organization funds candidates for state legislatures who are committed to breaking union protections for teachers and other workers and to backing the privatization of schools through public funding for charter schools and private school vouchers.

* * *

Most of the testing class lives in central administration, where the various departments of instruction, curriculum, and teacher and student evaluation are constantly meeting with outside consultants who help them make up new concepts that are known collectively as "best practices" for presenting a college prep curriculum in high-poverty schools. Nobody has ever actually seen these ideas rigorously tested in practice in enough classrooms to determine if they are indeed the best. The usual justification for the speed with which new approaches are implemented is the urgency of the situation. The thinking seems to be that what we're doing isn't working, so trying something new won't hurt, and might help. Of course, what we're doing is the result of the previous "best practice" that was foisted upon the weary and now wary teachers.

Best practices are delivered to the classroom teacher by a crucial subset of the testing class, the Professional Developers. At least once a month children are told to stay home, and all public and charter school teachers are subjected to "professional development" sessions on the latest evaluation instrument, curriculum mandate, or teaching technique. Particularly afflicted teachers might have an energetic administration that requires attendance at such sessions a few times each week, either before classes when you would prefer to be putting the final touches on your materials and plans, or after classes, when you would prefer to be reviewing and grading what happened, and calling guardians, so you can start thinking about how to follow up the next day. Actually, these things you prefer to do, you have to do, so to attend these extra professional development sessions you have to leave home earlier and come home later.

Every professional development session is similar: the Professional Developer has the staff introduce themselves, maybe with a cute little game, and then calls on them to take turns reading the lines off the PowerPoint presentation they have prepared. Let's say the Developer has been told to explain one of the categories of the teacher evaluation instrument, which is also a set of instructions on how to teach, whether or not the evaluator is in your room. The Developer will "unpack" the terse text, claim that "the research shows" that the idea works, describe the behaviors by the teacher that will result in a favorable score, and then divide up the teachers into groups for role-playing of the behaviors. Finally, the teachers will be asked to fill out a form about the way the session was taught. These data continue the never-ending cycle by giving the professional developer something to analyze and incorporate into the inevitable next session.

Each session is a little insult to the intelligence of the average five-year-old, and the stream of sessions throughout the year amount to death by a thousand cuts. Far more effective in improving teachers' skills would be for teachers to observe each other, and get together in the "PD" slots to discuss what they had seen. However, the PD time could not be set aside for that, because the constant introduction of new evaluation instruments and new curriculums requires, often by union contract, similarly constant explication to the teachers. The introduction of the Common Core college prep curriculum is a particularly rich gold mine for the Developers. Common Core is misnamed, since it is not a curriculum but rather a complex set of goals for each subject at each grade level. There will have to be new curriculums created, and explained to teachers, for all of this. Get ready for years of PowerPoints on the ins and outs, categories and subcategories, of these new curriculums, and how they "align" with various existing texts, tests, and best practices.

Another subset of the testing class that will find years of employment from Common Core is the Test Constructers. Despite the availability of a number of national achievement tests and the existence of a national curriculum map in Common Core, America's tradition of local control of education results in nearly all high-stakes tests being developed by state agencies or even school districts. State and district offices write these tests in collaboration with private companies and consultants. The process is surprisingly non-standardized, both between and within testing entities. It takes years and funds to standardize and then continue to standardize a test, like the SAT. The states, districts, and private companies do not have that kind of time and resources, and so sort of muddle their way through test construction with little thought to validation.

Definitions of what constitutes "proficiency" for a college prep curriculum, let alone the questions asked to determine it, vary by year and by entity, making the universal comparisons sought by the bureaucrats and politicians of the testing class impossible. The constructers get caught up in their construction, and are drawn toward increasingly difficult questions that less and less students can handle. The constructers see this in the results, which require them to push down the standard for proficiency each year, until students are proficient with scores of 35 percent right.

The DC tests are particularly slap-dash, because DC functions like a state, yet because of its small size cannot afford the staffing needed to write credible tests. The DC public schools only enroll about 50,000 students, down from 100,000 only 20 years ago primarily because charter schools have grown from zero to 40,000 students. School districts with the same number of students, like Syracuse or Louisville, would never think to write their own tests, but instead rely on state agencies with millions of students under their aegis. Yet the few test constructers in the DC central office have the same haughty certainty as the legion of SAT constructers.

At a meeting after the first pre-test early in one year, the constructers proudly told our math department that they had discovered a superior student among our 9th grade Algebra students. I laughed out loud at the name and told them that this was a student of mine who was border-line mentally retarded. She had about a 2nd-grade reading and math level, and had just filled in the bubbles on the pre-test at random, scoring so well only by laws of statistics, which require a normal distribution of scores from pure guessing. She was the one who happened to guess more answers correctly, out of the 200 who took that test. The constructers refused to believe my assessment, based on weeks of interaction and quizzes in which she had to show her work, and dismissed my point about the problem of interpreting the results of bubble tests with, "Well, take her to the race track with you, if she's that lucky."

I suppose they had to dismiss my point, because while "show your work" tests can be standardized, as on, for example, British high school completion and college entrance exams, they would then have to be graded by people rather than machines. The American testing system is a machine-based one, because it exists not to certify readiness for college, but to show progress so that the testers can claim that their reforms are working. To show progress requires multiple pre-tests throughout the year to familiarize students with the test environment and to identify "bubble kids" who are "on the bubble" because they are close to proficiency standards in the pre-tests. Machine grading of bubbled answers is the only cost-effective way to score multiple tests for millions of children.

Our math department at Johnson swore off talking to the DC test constructers after this first session, since they took our suggestion of reducing the number of items on the regular pre-tests from 23 to 12 and instead increased it from 23 to 43. This move was purely for the benefit of the testing class, since the more data there are to analyze, the more analysis there must be by the constructers. It could hardly have been for the benefit of our students, since they generally stopped trying after the first few problems. When our department administered the "end of course" exam the central office had written for 9th grade Algebra, though, we felt constrained to complain on behalf of the students.

The questions on the EOC were long and complex, which we expected from the pre-tests, but they were also shockingly disconnected from the material we had been told to teach. Some were just sloppy, and wrong both in their presentation and in the methods they required for an answer. A memo I sent to the test constructers after a number of requests for a meeting by our department were unsuccessful is excerpted here. The memo only analyzes the difficulties with the first three problems, which is probably all that most of our students actually attempted out of the 50 on the test. Despite a number of subsequent requests, there never was a meeting, or even a written response to the memo.

There are some overall problems with the End of Course test: most of our students are at 3rd to 7th grade skill levels, and testing them at the 9th grade level frustrates them quickly, especially with lengthy written introductions to many problems, which really tests reading levels as well. Using a multiple choice test rather than one where they show their work and find their own solution plays into this frustration, since it allows them to ignore or perhaps just glance at the problem, and just fill in the bubbles randomly or with little real effort to find the answer. However, I assume you are mandated to use this kind of test, so this memo concerns instead problems in the actual writing of the test.

I want to walk through the three questions that started the End of Course test, so you will see that they are (1) too complex to start with if you are trying to encourage students to get into the test and try it all, (2) not based on the standards or not based on the approved text, and (3) in one case, simply wrong. I think if you wrote the test with teachers, you could avoid such problems.

Question 1 concerns a system of equations. All the coefficients for the two linear equations that must be solved together are 2- or 3-digit and the total for each equation is 4 digits. This is unnecessarily daunting if your goal is to see who understands linear systems. You could achieve that knowledge with single-digit coefficients and 2-digit answers. If the question is designed to test familiarity with calculators, you could use simple operations rather than a systems problem.

- Be that as it may, our text and the standard tells students how to solve a system (we learn substitution and linear combination), but this question, according to the answer sheet, requires students to take each pair of values (for A, B, C, etc.) and simply substitute them in the sentences to see if they work. This is a gaming approach, not a mathematical approach, but the entire layout of the problem encourages a mathematical approach.
- I teach SAT math prep, and I specifically teach students NOT to start off on multiple choice problems by plugging in the answers in turn (because it takes a lot of time and does not require an understanding of the problem), unless they are stumped on finding a solution with their mathematical reasoning.
- Given the complexity of the coefficients and answers, it took me a few minutes and a lot of paper to set the problem up with one of our approved methods before entering it in the calculator.

Question 2 concerns a falling object, and provides a formula linking distance fallen, time fallen, and initial velocity, all in meters per second or second squared. In our text we have a different formula, which links HEIGHT (not distance fallen), time, and velocity, all in FEET. So, our students have learned to solve for height, and have not seen -4.9 as a measure for gravity — they have seen -9.8. Also, the problem is misstated, which caused me to take quite a few minutes to get the answer: "distance" fallen is a POSITIVE concept in mathematics (distance, we teach the students, is an absolute value, not a direction), so the problem does not come out right until you place a negative sign in front of the "d" in the equation.

- Finally, just as an aside, this question looks a lot like it wants to test knowledge of the quadratic formula, but in fact it is a substitution problem that does not require the QF. Most of our text's work on such problems is QF.

Question 3 concerns an annual three percent decrease in a town's population over a number of years. Our standard directed us to teach compound interest, rather than depreciation problems like this, and nearly all of the text's problems were compound interest. So, our students were taught to add an interest rate to 1 and compound the result, say $5,000 * (1.03)^10. This problem requires one to subtract the rate from 1, so is of the form 5,000*(.97)^10. Based on the standard and the text, I never taught this type of problem.

Incompetent high-stakes test construction is certainly not just the province of the public schools. Charter school systems usually link up with other charter systems to contract with private companies to construct their tests. At a workshop to familiarize math teachers with a new series of tests, I began noodling around with the first question on the 9th grade test. Longer and longer I worked on this question, which was intended to "align" with a teaching unit on solving a system of linear equations. It asked for a calculation of the total number of students that could be inferred from a set of subgroups, such as "15 are boys and from cities, 10 are girls and from rural areas, 25 in all are from cities..."

After ten minutes of trying, I raised my hand. "I can't get the very first problem. I don't know if it's because I am not using the right method or because there is not enough information. I do know that no child entering 9th grade will be any closer than me to picking the right method. Can anybody else get it?" Everybody, from the math teachers to the company's presenter (a former math teacher) to the actual test constructer (who happened to be present) worked on the problem for another ten minutes, without success. Then the test constructer went on-line to find his answer file, and gave us the answer. However, he could not tell us how one could get to the answer from the information, or even how to set up the information to test the various bubble answers to see which one worked. And this was just the first question on a test that was supposed to assess children's progress and teachers' effectiveness.

* * *

Nothing is a real "best practice" unless it has been turned into an acronym. The turn-around specialist hired as Johnson's principal in 2010 was a master of the acronym. Like many of today's principals, he had moved from high-poverty school to high-poverty school every few years over the previous decade. These principals can usually win a performance bonus in the tens of thousands of dollars in the first year in a new school by picking the low-hanging fruit, like intense test preparation for "bubble kids" identified in repeated pre-testing and attention to eligibility rules to remove weak students from the testing cohort. It also helps that random fluctuations in the abilities of the students in the tested grade, which in DC was 10th grade, mean that principal positions come open due to firings when a fluctuation is downward. There is a better than average chance that the next cohort in that grade will provide a fluctuation up the next year, back towards the average for the multi-year population in the neighborhood. Whatever its source, the first-year bonus comes in handy for moving expenses when, in the second year, the bump in test scores hits the inevitable plateau, and they need to move onto the next city. The pattern would prove out again at Johnson, where the principal resigned over low second-year scores, and moved to an army base high school.

The principal's office was identified by a giant banner reading "DDI — Data Driven Instruction." This is a favorite concept, and acronym, of the testers. The theory is that teachers can discover which students need "reteaching" on which concepts by reviewing the results of responses to individual questions on the regular pre-tests for the end of year, high-stakes test. Each wrong answer has a logic attached to it in the teacher's manual for the test, such as "choosing C indicates that the student thinks the square root of a number is half of it." Teachers are supposed to show each student who chose C that this is only true for the number 4, and then re-teach them the concept of square root. Of course, with a multiple choice test, especially one on which most students simply guess at most problems, it is dangerous to assume that an incorrect selection, or a correct selection for that matter, reveals anything other than randomness or exhaustion.

In any event, with dozens of questions, dozens of students, and four incorrect choices for each correct one, no human being could re-teach according to this model. At best, on the first few questions that the students might actually try on, the data show teachers what they already know from their weekly quizzes: which students are grasping the concept, and which ones aren't. The real purpose of all the pre-tests is to familiarize students with the coming test and test environment, so they can show the all-important progress that will keep the same principal and teachers on for another year, and give the central administration a set of scores from which to cherry-pick their own claims of district-wide progress.

I always thought of DDI as an instruction to teachers: "Don't Do It" unless it is an activity that will raises test scores. It also seems to serve as an instruction to administrators whose test scores in high-poverty schools are so resistant to true changes: "Do Do It" — cheat to make things look like they are improving. It's no coincidence that DDI was the favored slogan of the principal at the core of the Atlanta cheating scandal, where criminal investigators found that a "culture of fear, intimidation, and retaliation has infested the district, allowing cheating — at all levels — to go unchecked for years."

Another acronym favored by the Johnson principal and the "instructional coaches" (teachers taken out of the classroom and paid to help others teach and prepare for the tests with best practices) was SMART. The objectives for the day that were to be written on the board for students with another acronym in front of each one (SWBAT: Students Will Be Able To) had to be demonstrably specific, measurable, attainable, realistic, and timely if a teacher was to receive a strong IMPACT grade. The instructional coaches and their consultants would walk into a classroom during a lesson and, without asking permission, erase and rewrite the teacher's objectives to make them SMART. They would also encourage teachers to carry out lessons that could be designated as PBL. This stands for project-based learning, in which textbooks are put aside and a team of teachers of English, math, and science collaborate to develop a multi-week project, like preparing a report on the mineral and pollutant content of the local water supply. Teachers are expected to stay on track for the all-important pre-tests, of course, so they are instructed to integrate into the projects all the standards that happen to arise at that time in the curriculum, such as "students will be able to demonstrate an understanding of the three methods of finding the solution areas of sets of linear inequalities" and "students will be able to write a three-sentence paragraph using irony and the passive voice."

In the spring of one year, the principal had announced that Johnson would undertake an entire PBL curriculum the next fall. PBL, the principal explained, would motivate students by connecting the concepts students they were learning to "real-world" examples. By learning more eagerly and deeply, they would score better on the big test in the spring. The teachers didn't protest this unilateral decision, since they were used to such mandated changes, were already using real-world examples to teach standards (although not over a period of weeks and gathered under a single activity), and were looking forward to the part about putting away their textbooks. One of the "best practices" in school reform is that you teach a list of standards in order, and not the chapters in a textbook. As a result, teachers and students had already been bouncing all around their perfectly logically laid-out textbooks to find the standards, and an entire unnecessary industry has been developed to write cheat sheets "aligning" various textbooks with the latest order of teaching the standards.

What did concern some of the teachers was that the principal also announced that they would all stay at school throughout the summer, and be paid to practice teaching standards through PBL projects. The entering 300-student freshman class, he added, would attend the six-week session to gain familiarity with PBL concepts, so it would be like mandatory summer school teaching. Almost all the teachers took the extra money and the heavy hint of reward and penalty on the next year's teacher evaluations, cancelled whatever vacation plans they had made, and came in for the summer. The few teachers who did not come in for the summer were ostracized by the administration for not being "team players." However, since Johnson was an open admission school that needed lots of new students to survive, the principal could not make good on his threat that only students who came to the summer program would be admitted in the fall. Just a handful of the 300 promised freshmen materialized, so the teams of teachers were reduced to practicing their project-based lessons on each other. In the fall the team-based PBL experiment quickly faded away, since teachers had no extra time to meet for all the necessary joint planning. All that remained were the claims of PBL lessons being taught, dubiously generated by classroom, rather than team-wide activities.

PBL had fallen victim to the intense pressure that fall that was placed on the principal, and hence on the instructional coaches and the assistant principals and then the teachers, to improve test scores. The previous year had seen a slight rebound to a disastrously-low level of "proficiency" from a disastrously even-lower level the year before the principal came. Average math/English proficiency was now 20 percent, up from 15 percent. The principal had reached his "Safe Harbor" the previous year, but by the logic of No Child Left Behind, "Annual Yearly Progress" was now required. Of course, in some years before, proficiency had been in the 20s, so it was really just bouncing around based on the characteristics of the incoming class. Interestingly, the move to a new facility had permitted Johnson to take back in its 9th grade, which had been farmed out to a middle school during construction, so the tested kids in the coming year would ostensibly have the benefit of two years rather than one of the principal's program.

I wrote in Chapter 2 about the distortion of class sizes to favor the tested grade, and the "bubble kids" within it who pre-tests showed were close to proficiency. The record of each potential test-taker was scrutinized to find weak students who it could be argued did not fit the definition of an eligible student, although this repeated an effort with the previous cohort, and so would have little impact this time. There was also a distortion of the curriculum, with the tested grade shown and re-shown questions almost identical in format and content to those that would be on the DC-CAS. As the test came closer, nothing mattered to the administration but the testing cohort. An assistant principal entered one staff meeting with this clarifying statement: "If it's not about the test, I don't want to hear about it. Save your problems, because I won't be able to get to it anyway until the testing is over." Clearly, in this school, improved tests scores, not learning, guided nearly every administrative decision.

During the testing week, the principal actually cancelled all classes for non-testing grades, throwing the carefully-crafted semester curriculum plans he had demanded from all teachers into confusion, and told the students to stay home so as not to disturb the testers. When asked how the seniors could take a final exam including material that, as a result, they would have only one week on rather than the scheduled two, his response was, as always, "Just teach 'em, Doc." And it was all for nought. The required improvement over the previous cohort was not achieved, and the dreaded restructuring would be required. However, the rules were always murky and the waivers always negotiable. The principal told the staff that he had been given the choice of resigning or firing them all and rehiring a new "restructured" staff, and that he was falling on his sword for the good of the staff. The more resourceful members of the staff couldn't have cared less. Disheartened by the addition of the new chaos of the arbitrary demands of his intense testing regime to the usual chaos of a high-poverty school, they had been busy seeking positions at the district's admission high schools and even open enrollment schools, and a number of them deserted the sinking ship. The other teachers bemoaned their loss of potential bonuses because of the low scores but soldiered on with the next iteration of turn-around specialists. All that was left of the king-like principal who had dominated the staff meetings with his bluster, his preaching of the gospel, and the bizarre singing with which he accompanied his exhortations was his trademark claim, indeed an important one, about the success of the school, which he would repeat to all visitors: "No fires! Before I came here, students set 44 fires the previous year."

* * *

The principal occupies the highest level of the testers who actually pay the price for their belief that a strong dose of standardized tests will successfully guide students through a college prep curriculum. They are held accountable for the fluctuation of scores from year to year, and get bonuses when the fluctuation moves up and pink slips when the fluctuation moves down. To borrow from Tolstoy's dismissal of the impact of historical figures, they are like ants sitting on top of a log that is hurtling down a rushing river who think that their commands account for the bobbing up and down of the front of the log, and in this case are rewarded when it bobs up and punished when it bobs down. Exempted from riding the log and having their careers tied to its bobbing are all the curriculum planners, test developers, teacher evaluators, myriad consultants, top district staff, superintendents, school boards (and increasingly the mayors and city councils who have taken over their functions), and state and federal elected or appointed officials who legislate and then implement the testing regime. How do they evade responsibility? By having so many tests going on under them that they can pick out the ones that are bobbing up and talk only about them. They are always making progress.

With all the financial and career pressure for progress, sometimes, of course, the bobs up picked out by the top of the testing class are going to be the result of criminal fraud or cynical manipulation. Notorious examples from recent years include systematic schemes by teachers and administrators for telling children the answers, or erasing wrong answers and correcting them. In Atlanta and Washington, DC, auditors verified the schemes by studying the rate of erasures from wrong to right answers, which were up to ten times higher than normal, and could only have been achieved by adults changing students' worksheets. In Atlanta a police investigation showed that the superintendent and central staff had orchestrated the phony show of progress. Over 20 teachers, principals, and higher administrators pleaded guilty in the fraud, and 12 more will face trials. In addition, superintendent Beverly Hall will be tried when her health permits.

In Washington the teachers and principal of a middle school had received along with their cash bonuses fulsome praise from school chief Michelle Rhee that eerily presaged the coming disaster. As she has done with her now-discredited claim of lifting Baltimore ghetto kids to the 90th percentile as a teacher, Rhee cited the Noyes school's success as vindication against paternalistic racists who claim that poor black kids can't score like white middle class kids. She said that for these cynics, the results would seem "unbelievable." Unfortunately they were. The principal resigned as soon as the auditors began looking at the actual test sheets and spotting rates of erasures from wrong to right in excess of 10 times the typical rate. Despite ardent calls by the Washington Post, spurred by its pro-reform education columnist Jay Mathews, to investigate for criminal fraud, Rhee and her successor have managed to keep the scandal buried in the bureaucracy and out of the judicial system.

The real fraud, though, is not in the outright cheating but in the constant portrayal of progress by picking out, from all the minor changes that will accompany years of testing of multiple grades and subjects and schools, those that are bumps up, and calling them progress rather than random fluctuations and test effects. Year after year, in city after city, and at the state and federal level, the testers release grand claims based on these bumps that would be laughed out of an introductory statistics course. Yet instead of laughing, the media reproduce them uncritically, giving the desired but deeply fraudulent impression of constant progress.

Consider this (of course) unpublished submission to the Washington Post, whose editorial page's ardent backing of school reform explains in part why it was so eager to catch the "bad apples" at Noyes middle school who were discrediting the movement. Indeed, the Post has been at pains to note that that the district-wide results it picks to cite could not have been much affected by a single school's cheating. In the editorial that led to this letter, the Post had cited the upward movement of fourth grade scores on a national test over a few years as proof that school reform was working.

The Post had failed to note that over this same period there had been a significant increase in the number of white, upper-class students in elementary schools on the white side of town, just as the number of poor black students was falling because of the drain of charter schools. Any upward trend in scores would certainly be related to the upward trend in the income and orientation toward school of the families of fourth graders. With just a smidgen of research, a similar letter could have been written in almost every case of claimed progress by the reformers over the past 30 years, from Governor George W. Bush's "Texas Test Miracle," where graduation rates soared by redefinition, to the slick brochures of every charter system on the public dollar today, in which motivational differences between charter and public school families are conveniently ignored, and differences between some of their children's test scores are highlighted.

Here is the submission:

It would be nice to believe, as the Post editorialized about former D.C. school chief Michelle Rhee (January 11, 2013), that "D.C. students made significant progress during her tenure as measured by the National Assessment of Educational Progress." But it's just not possible to say so.

Ms. Rhee was in charge for three years. Even if DCPS had a legitimate testing protocol that could reflect ability and knowledge for the same students over her three years — and comparing different cohorts of children at the same grade level, as the NAEP does, certainly is not that — most of Ms. Rhee's changes would have taken a number of years to percolate through the system, and we would just be seeing their effect today.

Anyone who has administered DC's various standardized tests in our high-poverty, open-admission schools knows that they are almost a form of child abuse. They take groups of students who have massive attendance, reading, and effort problems and on average are many years below grade level, and force them to read lengthy questions that are all at grade level and above. Most of these students are helpless before these tests, and don't even try.

Then school officials mine through a variety of test scores for a number of grade levels and pick out a few positive trends to claim success while ignoring the rest of the data, never running checks for the statistical significance or random likelihood of such variations. Even if there are significant trends, they will almost certainly be due to demographic changes in the cohorts. Is the new cohort poorer or richer, whiter, more Asian, more Black, or more Hispanic, more the product of college-educated families, more stripped of involved parents who can navigate applications to charter and admission schools, or more burdened by students forced out of charter and admission schools for attendance, academic, and behavior problems? Those are the sorts of questions that determine nearly all the direction of the average scores.

Why do I say this? Because, as shown by the College Board results over decades, standardized test scores in America are themselves largely determined, at the macro level, by these demographics, so changes in averages will be as well. That is why standardized tests were originally designed for the individual, to see changes over time, and make little sense for assessing changes in group and school cohorts.

It is extremely hard, unfortunately, to say "what works" for our core public school student, who is challenged by poverty and medical deficits and grows up in a household that will almost always be led by a single female with low educational attainment, particularly when the lingering effects of slavery, segregation, and violence are factored in. You can't go by cohort test comparisons. And you certainly can't go by graduation rates: those are fraudulent from the get-go, thanks in DC to Ms. Rhee's "credit recovery" scheme, where thousands of students who blew off attending and trying in class take phony after-school courses and graduate in near-ignorance.

In my experience as a teacher, it is best to forget the macro level and focus on one kid at a time, whether they are in jail or out, pregnant or not, troubled at home or not, and take them forward. We need to stop the standardization, value the teachers, and let them try to reach kids where they are, not where we are pretending they are. "School reform" standardization and demands for "progress" in a few quantifiable subjects for students who face a host of social challenges are closing off the path to improvement that is the dream of American public education. You may notice that no private school voluntarily adopts the crazy fads and gyrations of "school reform." Wonder why.

Perhaps the worst consequence of all the focus on the college prep tests and their results is that the attention of educators and politicians alike is diverted from the real challenges of preparing high-poverty students for a middle-class life, and from potential solutions to these challenges. At the building level, this is shown in the Johnson assistant principal's warning to the teachers that all other matters would have to wait until the tests were over. At the level of superintendents and politicians, it is illustrated by the approach that is taken to the attendance crisis. High-poverty middle and high schools are likely to have at least a third of students absent on a given day, and up to three-quarters of students missing an average of two days per week. Virtually no learning by anybody can take place in such a disrupted classroom environment. Solutions like those offered in 2013 by DC chancellor Kaya Henderson and DC city council member David Catania focus on the "how" of tracking them down and bringing them into school, and not the "why" of the reasons for their absence.

The "how" is always a combination of more personnel to go find students at their houses and more legal threats to their guardians, who are often at the doors the truant officers are knocking on, lying to them about their children's whereabouts. The only child I ever saw dragged in to school other than for a high-stakes testing day remained so angry and uncooperative throughout the day that I ended up wishing they had left her at home. We need to ask why this child and at least half of all high-poverty students want to skip and skip and skip school. After all, school is warm on the cold days, and cool on the hot days. There's free food and all your friends, the excitement of the social scene, the drama of fights, and the chance to score dope and sex if you are so inclined. Most important, all those security guards, teachers, and administrators make going to school far safer than being at home or on the street.

The "Goon Squad" discipline aides and the security guards at Johnson could tell teachers with confidence which of the "l'il gangsters" who acted out in school were "hard" and could actually back up their tough school demeanor on the street, and which were "soft" and would never dare call out students or adults there the way they did at school. The soft kids knew they would be protected from retaliation while at school, and even the hard ones should have enjoyed a break from the dangers of the neighborhood. So why don't they want it?

* * *

Those of us who work with high-poverty kids know why there are so many absences. The problem is in the classroom curriculum, not the school itself, which explains why many students come to school, and then wander the hidden nooks and crannies of the halls during classes. The students who skip are typically years behind academically, with no means or hope of catching up. Questions, quizzes, and tests on the required college prep material are downright embarrassing even to the hard kids who say they don't care. To avoid the embarrassment, the sense of shame and low worth, high-poverty students implicitly conspire to disrupt class with clowning, talking, or if necessary fighting, anything to avoid more attention to their deficits. And if they haven't been suspended and relieved of the problem by school authorities, they will often relieve themselves of it, and skip school.

Of course, students fall farther behind as a result of skipping, but few think they will get much out of school anyway, whether or not they graduate. And why do they think that? Because they are street-smart. They can look around their neighborhood and see the graduates right next to the drop-outs and even most of those who tried college for a brief time, all wasting away their young adulthoods. The college prep curriculum is so irrelevant to their past, present, and future that they see no need to engage and be regularly reminded of their failings. They skip.

The true believers in the testing class respond to the core cause of skipping, which is students being years behind, by pressing for more of the same to promote a rapid improvement in their grade level and their connection to the school. DC school chief Kaya Henderson has the experience and the intelligence to identify the cause perfectly. She has told reporters that the core reason for students to skip high school classes is because they are hopelessly behind grade level and tired of being failures every day. Unfortunately, she is so busy gaming the tests in her college prep, standardized test curriculum that there appears to be no time for her to reflect on its failure. Her solution is still to push teachers to make up the years as fast as possible, even while the students are in the grade-level courses.

Henderson told me in a meeting in 2012 that, "We have some teachers who take high-school kids from 3rd to 7th grade level in a year." I agreed, and said I had seen that kind of growth in some of my kids, but that with their new 7th grade skills they still couldn't pass 10th grade geometry. She surprised me by agreeing with that, and for just a second I saw a flicker of hesitancy in her usual hard-charging style that might let us talk about alternatives to the college prep curriculum. The moment quickly passed, though, and Henderson reverted to the campaign mode of school reform: "We need teachers and principals, and we need to develop and support them, who can get kids excited about coming to school, and who have high expectations for the children." Here it is again, the school reform creed: absenteeism, like all that is dysfunctional in high-poverty schools, must come from teachers' failings, rather than from the fundamental mismatch between the black culture of poverty and the testing class's college prep orientation.

* * *

The testing disaster that has been visited on high-poverty schools over the past 30 years is in large part a reflection of white middle and upper-class America's complex relationship with the black underclass. The members of the testing class, and the white voters who respond to their goals and claims at the polls, want to help the black poor, but don't want to live too near them, or send their kids to school with them. They know that the black poor deserve a break because of slavery and segregation, but are not about to explore integration, reparations, or targeted employment as recompense. On one hand, as Americans with a creed of equal opportunity and fairness, they sense, as George Bush has said, the "soft bigotry of low expectations" in any suggestion that the black poor cannot attain the same success as upper and middle class children. On the other hand, they sense that Lyndon Johnson's 1965 analogy about blacks being well behind the white starting line in the race of life is still legitimate for the black poor, who are indeed segregated "by zip code" in all aspects of American life and lack all the things that middle and upper class parents make sure their children bring to and use to support their college prep schooling.

The result is a college prep curriculum for a group in which few will attend, let alone complete, college. President Obama tells us constantly that everybody has to go to college, that it is the gateway to good jobs and a good life. Yet only about half of the black underclass graduates from high school, a quarter attends four-year colleges, and maybe ten percent receives a bachelor's degree. The tension is evident in the ponderings of DC school chief Henderson. She agreed in a discussion with me that I was probably right to judge that none of the Johnson graduates could survive at the middle-tier university I had taught at, and she has mused to reporters that vocational programs for the black poor might bring chronically-absent students back into school. However, she still says that vocational programs for the black poor carry "the danger of denying them the ability to expand their horizons."

So the universal college prep curriculum lives on, enforced by tests that constantly show that just a fraction of students are "proficient" at absorbing it. The sadness of this situation was brought home to me the day the students in Johnson's 10th grade geometry classes visited a training center run by the brick masons' union. During the semester my classes had taken part in a fairly chaotic but well-intentioned weekly math sessions led by a group of architects, masons, and contractors. These expert volunteers came in with a grand scheme for the students to plan a neighborhood sports stadium, construct a scale model in clay, and then prepare a presentation for a city-wide competition at a downtown banquet and awards ceremony for students and parents.

This plan, quite appropriate for a middle-class school, had to be dramatically reduced in scope because of the alienated clientele. The same few students who tried to work in class also tried to work in the project sessions, and the many who tried to avoid work and disrupt class did the same. The resulting model was largely prepared by the teachers, and not a single student, let alone parent, would venture out across the river to the banquet. However, on the day of the visit to the brick masons, the students matched and probably exceeded the performance of middle class kids.

The task was to build a wall in small groups. To do this, students had to attend carefully and mimic and practice mixing mud, apply it to a charted system of bricks, and level the bricks to perfection. None of these tasks was easy, and all repeatedly brought the frustration of admitting error, the very things that rule out progress for most of the students in their regular college prep math classes. Shalonda and "May'vonn" were typical in their shocking changes in persona. Shalonda was the usually moody, often stormy girl we met in Chapter 3 who generally threw up her hands and threw down her pencil after a minute of class work. May'vonn was a personable clown whose booming voice would disrupt the class constantly as he joked instead of worked, but he was hard to punish because he was just so funny and nice about it. Both tested at the early elementary math level. Yet with their trowels and towels, suddenly unconcerned with their fancy clothes as they splattered them with the mud, they eagerly led their groups through the mission, cajoling and correcting others. They rapidly replicated a number of challenging charts, and then begged to be allowed to build more walls and gates, passing up the promised snack in favor of more work.

What was going on here? How had the pathetic college prep students become the star brick masons? Just by being given work that suited their skills and interests. By the way, a union brick mason makes more money than most college professors. That is a lesson for the testing class to ponder.

Chapter 8. The Sports Trap for the Poor Black Student

OK, write down your sport, the position you play, and two of the colleges you'd like to play at. Then let's talk about grade point average, SAT scores, and the business of getting a scholarship. And make no mistake about it, sports may be a game you love but sports scholarships are a business you have to master.

"Brianna James," former college hurdler, former middle school teacher, and current assistant director of an education think-tank, was speaking to 40 varsity athletes at the high-poverty Johnson high school in the District of Columbia on an October afternoon. As the athletes' tutor for the SATs, I had invited her to lead a session on how to win a college scholarship. Brianna was speaking during a required pre-practice, after-school study hall, but only about half of the football and boys' and girls' basketball teams' players were present. The coaches certainly weren't, and the behavior reflected that. It was like the regular class periods at Johnson: most of the kids were in constant conversation, calling out "jones" to each other or immediately riffing and joking on Brianna's statements, massively resisting benefiting from either her knowledge or their own focus.

Having taught in a high-poverty school, Brianna was not thrown off task. She knew how to rally enough attention to get a few main points across to most of the students. First she asked me to remove a couple of girls from the basketball team who were egregious in their chatter. Her teaching radar had picked precisely the next two to be dismissed from the team for disruption, who would then drop out and not need a college talk anyway. Then she called on individual students to read off their answers, which encouraged others to listen a bit.

After a few students read off their college choices, accompanied by cheers of support for favorite ones, Brianna dropped a shocker: "I've got news for you. You're all writing down the colleges everybody knows, because they are in major conferences and are on TV, and win all the time. In reality your best bet for a scholarship will be with colleges nobody knows that are in small conferences, are hardly ever on TV, and have losing records. The last place team in a small conference needs just as many players as LSU and Alabama football, and Georgetown and Syracuse basketball. While you're waiting for the big shots to come to you, you have to make a list of the small shots, and call them and go see them, and generally never stop bothering them until you close the deal. Sell yourself as an academic sure thing that they'll have five years to turn into a better athlete."

Deal? Sell? That grabbed the kids' attention. What does dealing and selling have to do with getting a college scholarship? Doesn't the famous coach seek you out after watching game videos, and offer you a free education at your mother's coffee table, manfully promising her that they will make sure you get your degree? For probably 95 percent of all college athletes, there is nothing like that movie scene. Coaches are educators, but they are also in a business, which is the business of winning so they can keep their jobs. They have only one commodity to sell, which is their limited number of scholarships. They prefer to give a prospect a half-scholarship, or even a quarter of one, if they can get him or her to accept it. Very few colleges offer an upfront guarantee of a full scholarship for the four undergraduate years and the frequently used extra, "red-shirt" year in which athletes can practice with but not compete with their teams. As a result, athletes who get hurt, perform worse than expected, or get cut from the team often lose their "rides."

The awarding of scholarships by the year is the hallmark and the shame of college athletics. This is the attribute that best reveals sports as a business for the benefit of the college rather than an educational venture for the good of the student. Low-income athletes who lose their athletic scholarships almost never graduate. The loan-heavy financial aid packages offered by their colleges at that point compare poorly with the debt-free sports deals they have been enjoying, which include room and board, book money, summer jobs, and lately even living allowances. More importantly, these students' identity has been as an athlete, their friends are athletes, and their academic advisers are in the athletic department. Cut off from all that, they invariably wither and flee.

During the session it became clear that virtually none of the student-athletes, all of whom expected to win college scholarships for their sports skills, knew their grade point average (GPA), or how to calculate one.

Brianna encouraged them to change that: "Not only should you know your current GPA, which is the first thing recruiters will ask you about, but you should keep a running tally of your estimated grades in your current courses, so you can factor those into your expected GPA." I kept to myself what seemed obvious: most student-athletes who were this far into their secondary schooling and didn't know their GPA, let alone how to calculate it, were either not going to be eligible for a scholarship, or not going to be motivated enough to take advantage of one.

After reviewing the basics of how to calculate a GPA on a scale from 0 to 4 from a set of grades, and extracting a soon-broken promise that each student would confirm it with their guidance counselor in the next week, Brianna turned to SAT (or ACT) scores. The National Collegiate Athletic Association (NCAA) combines these with GPA on a sliding scale to determine eligibility to play on a freshman scholarships for the 350 Division I colleges. These are generally the larger colleges, with the resources to sponsor a number of sports and a lot of scholarships.

Brianna explained that the sliding scale is designed to identify students who probably can handle college level work, and to exclude those who probably can't. Students can balance off weak tests with strong grades, or weak grades with strong tests, but being weak on both will put them below the cut-off marks. For example, a student scoring the average 1,000 on the 1,600-point SAT only needs a C average, a GPA of 2, to be eligible for a freshman scholarship. A score of 600 on the SAT (on which, for some obscure historical reason, you receive 400 points just for showing up), which is in the bottom three percent and is more typical for high-poverty students than the 1,000 point average, must be offset by an average of at least a B, which is a GPA of 3. A similar approach, but with slightly different targets, is taken by the 280 small colleges in Division II and the 430 small colleges in the National Association of Intercollegiate Athletics. In D-II you need a C average and an 800 on your SAT, which is the 16th percentile. In the NAIA you need two of these three: a C average, an SAT of 860, which is the 24th percentile, or being in the top half of your class.

With NCAA penalties starting to be imposed on colleges for low rates of athletes graduating or staying on pace to graduate, many college coaches and administrators have clauses in their contracts about on-pace and graduation rates. They have less and less interest in admitting unproven students who require high maintenance to stay on pace for graduation, like personal tutors who guide and at times effectively write their papers and special, no-show, "independent study" courses. Only the few financial giants whose sports payoffs cover their expenses and then some can afford to maintain the expensive systems needed to keep weak and disinterested students on pace. In nearly all situations coaches prefer the stronger student who will boost their academic statistics over the weaker one who doesn't make it to the second semester and brings down the graduation rate. This focus on academic strength surprised the Johnson students, most of whom saw athletic success as a way to avoid doing much work in their courses.

The 440 Colleges in Division III don't technically offer athletic scholarships, but do so in effect by offering admission based on a coach's recommendation, and then negotiating a regular package of financial aid. So, most of the preceding discussion also applies to students who want to attend them. In particular, a student's GPA and SATs play just as great a role in admission decisions in Division III as in Divisions I and II. These coaches too are concerned about academic progress, and they have a lot less resources to throw at the problem than the big sports powers in Division I. The Ivy League has similar rules to Division III, but very few athletes from high-poverty schools can survive academically and socially in the Ivies, so very few are admitted.

Community and junior colleges, which is where many kids from high-poverty schools start when they can't achieve college eligibility, are not constrained by NCAA rules. The four-year Historically Black Colleges and Universities (HBCUs) that take nearly half of black undergraduates are spread throughout the NCAA divisions and the NAIA, but they seem to find ways to bring higher-risk athletes to campus, just as it is often their mission to bring in higher-risk students in general. They offer non-athletic scholarships for the first year to student-athletes who are not eligible for athletic one, and then review their academic progress before offering athletic scholarships in subsequent years. Still, both the two-year colleges and the HBCUs, like all colleges, favor the academically prepared over the weak when recruiting athletes.

* * *

All the 40 students in the room and the 40 more who had skipped the session had devoted untold hours to their sport with the vague sense, fueled by the improbable tale of the Johnson quarterback who rode his arm all the way through to millions of dollars in the National Football League, of using it to build their adult lives. Only about ten of these 80 would be offered an initial full ride to college. The irony is that many of these lottery winners would have had a greater chance of a full scholarship, and a four-year one at that, if they had gone the purely academic route and taken one of the scholarships that have proliferated for the young, black, and not even gifted but at least perseverant. Many of the lottery losers could have been academic winners as well, if they had put their untold hours into that arena instead of sports.

That is not to say that there are not success stories solely dependent on sports scholarships. Consider Roger Barbee, who was profiled previously as the sterling private school teacher who became unwanted by the public school administration in the rural county to which he had retired. He will tell you that he would never have been able to escape his Appalachian culture for a decent college and his rewarding career without his wrestling scholarship to a small North Carolina school. Or take NFL superstar tackle Michael Oher, the subject of the book and movie *The Blind Side*. Within two years of taking the field at a Memphis private school as a homeless scholarship student, he was on his way to the University of Mississippi with a full ride. And you'll meet a number of success stories from my years at Johnson High School shortly. The numbers, though, greatly favor the academic track. Being adopted by a white family that can afford a full-time tutor to move to college with you is hardly a plan for the masses.

Most of Johnson's scholarship winners came from the girls' basketball team, whose coach over the previous decade had built a powerhouse by enrolling girls from other schools. The coach was not a teacher at the school but rather a basketball guru who wore a variety of hats in the youth league and college recruiting worlds. When he left in a dispute with the administration later that year, the program dissolved as the girls transferred *en masse* to a small private school known for its strong basketball teams. The coach dominated the girls' lives, which explains why all his athletes came to every SAT tutoring session that fall, while all the boys on the basketball and football teams soon drifted away. His team routinely won its city games, and even the championship, by tripling opponents' scores.

The girls were often excused from classes to fly to other states to play in high-profile tournaments, where they would log onto the hotel computer in the lobby, checking updates to their ratings on basketball websites that college coaches scour for leads. These trips were funded by the tournaments, which must have some financial backing from somebody with an interest in the college game, like universities, agents, or shoe companies. The trips contrasted with the two or three lengthy bus trips the football team would take each season to play non-league games in Ohio, Pennsylvania, and deep Virginia. For half of the gate receipts of a packed house, which funded the program for the rest of the year, Johnson's outclassed team would suffer 40-point defeats to powerful programs that needed an extra game and an extra win.

"La-Niece Taylor" was anybody's definition of a hopeless case — homeless, absent, angry, in legal trouble, and years behind in academics and behavior — when she was convinced to play basketball for Johnson High School in 2008. At 6' 7" and about 250 pounds, her massive and athletic presence at center lifted Johnson to the city championship, and a lengthy profile of her in the local newspaper announced her scholarship offer from one of the top college programs. It turned out to be a long road there for La-Niece, but she eventually made it — sort of. When a weak student is grandly recruited and dramatically offered a scholarship by a Division I university, it is invariably an overbooking, like an airline selling more seats than it has in order to account for no-shows. The offer is made contingent on improvement in grades and SAT scores, and the coaches are correctly playing the odds that few of these students can become eligible.

Despite some overly-generous grades, La-Niece's final SAT scores made it clear that she could not handle the work as a freshman at the university, so her scholarship was put on ice. Someone, probably on the coaching staff, arranged a scholarship for her at a community college in Florida. Room and board must have been a welcome relief for a girl with her past, and she took full advantage of the opportunity. She played well, received her associate's degree, and went on to a small state college, where she averaged two points per game as a substitute and at least got on the court during a game at her original university. Given her initial educational deficit, La-Niece may never be able to get a Ph.D. in biochemistry, but her sociology major in college has given her a shot at a middle class job in social services.

Another Johnson student followed the same trajectory as La-Niece, with her Division I scholarship being put on ice while she labored in a Florida community college. The difference was that "Bahbi" (pronounced "Bobby") had all the tools she needed to win a four-year academic scholarship from a Division I college. In our pre-calculus class she would quickly grasp concepts and then explain them to her seatmates, who were usually her teammates. However, she did little homework and would often plead depression to avoid the class assignments she needed to change her conceptual grasp into a working knowledge. It is not accurate to say that Bahbi's hours, indeed years, of practice and travel for basketball forced her to skimp on her academics. High school athletes have lots of study hall time before practices and on trips that she could have used to stay current with her assignments. It was simply that Bahbi had always seen basketball as her ticket to college, and didn't feel the need to do much academic work, in or out of class.

Another lottery winner was "Don," who was in Bahbi's pre-calculus class after transferring to Johnson for his senior year from a mostly-white Catholic academic and sports powerhouse. A disproportionate number of top college prospects come out of private and Catholic schools, which spot and snag them early. Don had come to the attention of the coaches at the Catholic school while starring at safety on his all-black youth football team in 9th grade, and his mother had bargained for a half-scholarship. He responded to the academic culture around him and became as solid a student as someone from his weak middle school could be. However, Don was not satisfied with his playing time at the Catholic school. Although the level of play is better and the support system for helping students find athletic scholarship's is much better organized in the Catholic league than in the DC league, he thought he would generate more interest from college programs by being a starting player at Johnson.

Technically, as a public school, Johnson cannot recruit players. Practically, that is what all the coaches and their assistants do. The dozen or so position coaches it takes to run a football program and the half dozen aides typically associated with a basketball program are volunteers drawn from alumni or community sports activists. They haunt the youth leagues and middle school circuit, keeping their eyes and ears open for opportunities to talk with the players and coaches. It is particularly hard to field a winning football team, or any football team, for that matter, in most high-poverty schools. Perhaps 50 players are needed, yet declining enrollments and drop-outs constantly reduce the pool. Most school districts require a "C" average for eligibility and instruct teachers to record an automatic "F" if a student has ten unexcused absences in a quarter. If a college prep curriculum were honestly graded and rules about absences were faithfully followed, few coaches would be able to field a team.

Like Tour de France doctors manipulating their drug-aided riders' hormone and blood-oxygen levels to keep them under the trigger points used to establish cheating, coaches follow their athletes' GPAs closely, and try to manipulate them to keep them on the field. As every grading period winds down, the coaches appear at the classroom doors, with their players in tow, and ask teachers to "work with" the students and accept "extra credit" work to boost their grades. They offer explanations to excuse their absences. If teachers won't cooperate, some coaches encourage guardians to explore special education designation. The rules keep changing in this area, and simply being in special education is usually no longer an automatic waiver for eligibility in most districts, as it has been in the past. In general, though, it is still much easier to generate passing grades for a special education student than a mainstream one. And when all else fails, the coaches recruit, especially students who can maintain eligibility on their own.

The efforts to field a team can get comical in Washington, DC. As the season winds down every year, losing football coaches get revenge by reporting recruiting violations of winning coaches, to get their teams knocked out of the playoffs. In DC the city championship game is usually a legal and administrative circus, with the winners of the two divisions being replaced by the second place teams because of charges that the winners had players who actually lived outside the district but had been illegally enrolled under a DC address. The second-place coaches who make the charges only know because they lost the recruitment battles for the athletes in question. They usually wait until the last minute, so that the third-place team doesn't have time to challenge their own athletes' eligibility.

However it happened, Don transferred to Johnson with the understanding that he would be the starter at his position, safety. And he was. In the pre-calculus class Don stood out immediately as having the most affinity for the subject, and the best organization of his work and the best work ethic. A senior, he tested at the 9th grade level, which was the highest of all the students, and he was one of only three students of the initial 38 to have the first homework completed, neatly laid out in his binder, the next day. It was all downhill from there.

Don realized that hardly anybody else in the class, and none of the top athletes, were doing much homework or class work or worrying about their grades, and he soon fell to the norm, just as he had risen to it at the Catholic school. His play on the field went well, but as his recruiting status rose his impeccable behavior began to deteriorate, way past the lackadaisical resistance of the typical surviving seniors, right down to the wild resistance of the half of freshmen who will drop out long before becoming seniors. There were a few plateaus and rises along the way down simply because Don liked the way math worked and liked showing the other students that he was way ahead of them. In November, though, he accepted a full ride to a Big 12 university, a rare event for the Johnson program, and descended to the "Get the (expletive) out my face" level when told to stop talking and start working.

I had to have Don removed from class by the security guards, and then I met with his coach and his mother. His mother was mystified, but Coach Tully came to the point immediately, as was his style: "The offer went to his head. Big head. Gotta knock it off him. Tell him the next time he's put out of class he's getting an F for the course, and I'll call his new college coach and break the news." Don rallied for the final exam, scoring an A when the next highest grade was a D. He kept his scholarship, and went on to play and study in the Big 12. If he had focused only on academics, he could have had his pick of colleges at that level under the many programs set aside for the young, gifted, black and poor. Admittedly, though, it was his football prowess that first put Don in the Catholic school environment where he could show his academic potential.

"Markus Green," the only Johnson player to win the Division I lottery the year before, was like La-Niece in talent, but not trauma. His mother ran a warm but tight ship and he was a pleasant, cooperative soul, but he had very limited academic potential. His strength was in his demeanor and behavior. Markus was invariably pleasant and punctual, and he was the only football player of the many who started who came to and worked hard in an SAT prep session every lunchtime in my room. His decent grades were more a measure of relief at good behavior than of his grasp of the material, and while he improved his SAT math score by a remarkable 150 points after learning some testing techniques in our sessions like "reading backwards" so you know what you're looking for in a question ("how far does he have to go?) before you read the details ("John and three of his friends are on a trip..."), his SAT scores were still so low that some Atlantic Coast Conference schools turned him down as too weak to do the work. But one, Virginia Tech, took a chance on him, and he gained athletic and academic strength in his "red-shirt" freshman year and became a starter at tight end.

Most of the Johnson athletes who receive a sports scholarship will never set foot in a four-year college, other than the academically weakest of the HBCUs. Unlike the top tier of HBCUs, like Morehouse, Spelman, North Carolina A and T, and Howard, the weaker schools often resemble the high-poverty high schools the students just left: open admission, lack of work ethic, easy grades, and still staggeringly-low graduation rates. Many students spend their first year in remedial, non-degree courses. "James," a muscular Goon Squad warrior, had been a skinny star end at Johnson when he won a football scholarship to an HBCU. He graduated from that college. Most of the Johnson athletes who followed his example did not. "DeMarius," an all-conference football lineman and a hard-working student in my pre-calculus class who was successful by Johnson standards, found that his weak SATs limited his sports scholarships to HBCUs. These schools lack the expensive support system for athletes of the wealthier Division I schools. DeMarius had to drop off the football team, and so lost his partial scholarship, because he found he could not keep up with both his school work and the twice-daily, tiring practices. His family could not afford a laptop computer, and he fell behind in his courses because he had to wait hours to borrow one from the library each time he had homework. His grades suffered, and then his family fell behind on the increased tuition payments. DeMarius was back in DC within the year, unable to transfer to another school because the college refuses to release his transcript until the debt is paid.

A DC football coach made the classic argument about sports keeping kids in school and out of trouble hilariously clear in a 2010 newspaper interview: "These are big kids, I mean big kids. You want them roaming the neighborhood, robbing and thieving, and smashing you, or do you want them smashing each other on the field?" There is no doubt that sports keeps some high-poverty kids in school, but there are a number of holes in the coach's argument. First, most kids who are running with a gang won't last on a team because they don't have the discipline needed to come to practice regularly or to help coaches arrange enough special assignments with teachers to remain eligible. Second, any kid who is with a gang won't stop just because he is on a team. Practice only runs until six p.m., and there are lots of deadly hours left before morning.

A corollary argument in favor of sports is that it increases graduation rates. However, the kids most at risk for dropping out have years of barely measurable GPAs, because of absences and acting out, and only make it out of middle school through social promotion. Even if coaches prevail upon teachers to boost their grades to the acceptable minimum, like the gang members they will lack the discipline needed to stick with most teams. Coaches generally insist on players coming to practice and following instructions once there, without drama. At Johnson, some kids who would dominate the annual staff–student basketball or flag football games didn't even bother trying out for the teams, because they knew their academic and discipline problems would make it impossible to gain or retain a spot.

Special education status does permit some DC students with abysmal academic records to play, in the recent past through a blanket waiver from the C, or 2.0, standard for eligibility and at present through teachers tending to grade special educations kids on effort more than on achievement. This doesn't necessarily lead to graduation. The Washington Post looked into the background of James Richardson, the Ballou high school running back who starred in the 2003 city championship game and was then gunned down in the school cafeteria three months later. It discovered that he had been registered as a special education student at the suggestion of a football coach, because that kept him eligible despite his years of failing grades.

* * *

What awaits athletes from high-poverty schools if they win the college scholarship lottery? Most will lose their scholarship after a couple of years of play and drop out, due to injury or their inability to keep up with even the minimal academic requirements for heavily-tutored courses in athletic disciplines. Some of those who can stay healthy and manage passing grades in these weak courses may actually obtain a degree. But did even they really win?

Dexter Manley was a popular figure on the Washington, DC, sports scene in the 1980s. He played for Washington's professional football team, and he was a tough lineman with a talent for outrageous statements. As civil rights historian Taylor Branch describes in a 2011 Atlantic article, "The Shame of College Sports," in 1989, after he had been banned by the NFL for repeatedly being caught using illegal drugs, Manley testified before Congress that he could not read when he was in college. How could somehow who, even after years of tutoring at a famed Washington school for the learning disabled, still struggled to sound out his prepared statement, have remained eligible for four years at Oklahoma State University? How many professional educators had to violate their ethical duties and collude, from his Houston junior high school to his Stillwater college, to maintain the fiction that Manley was a legitimate student?

Manley's two head coaches at Oklahoma State later worked in the NFL. That is appropriate, because Division I college programs comprise a farm system for the NFL. One was Jim Stanley, who became director of player personnel for the Arizona Cardinals, and the other was Jimmy Johnson, who became head coach of the Dallas Cowboys and the Miami Dolphins and is now a television commentator. Under their leadership Manley stayed eligible despite earning barely more than half of the required credits over his four years. These coaches were famous and highly-paid. During their tenure the university improved its alumni fundraising by hundreds of millions of dollars as it began moving to a higher profile in football and began to challenge its long-time dominator, the University of Oklahoma.

Oklahoma at the time was being led on a wild and successful coaching ride by Barry Switzer, who turned aside the advice of his sage friend Penn State coach Joe Paterno and wrote a book in 1990 describing the systematic violations of recruiting, "pay for play," and the academic rules he oversaw. That's the same Joe Paterno whose reputation for wisdom and propriety came crashing down along with his statue outside the Penn State stadium when he and the university's president were fired in 2011 for failing to investigate a report of child sexual abuse ten years earlier.

As the connections from the Dexter Manley case show, the corruption of academics by college sports is legion, from the first identification of a prospect in the early teens through the usual end, which is being cut from a college team for a combination of injury and academic disaster after a couple of years, and losing your scholarship. So let's just say it: the revenue sports of football and men's basketball are all about the Benjamins, not the Socrates. As the dominant players in the business they have infected the non-revenue college sports and even high school sports, which comprise their farm club feeder system, with their view of academics as an impediment and athletes as cogs in the wheels that run an institution's high-profile winning "program."

With billions of dollars of television revenue riding on getting into the basketball or football final four, along with decades of fund-raising good will and a raised profile to compete for students thrown in for even lesser levels of athletic success, there are no professional ethics in college sports other than Oakland raiders owner Al Davis's motto from professional football: "Just win, baby." It's silly to pretend otherwise, and it's like shooting ducks in a barrel to find examples. College sports as organized today have nothing to do with the purpose of college, only the business of college. We can blame Harvard and Yale for bringing in the first football "ringers" as temporary students to win The Game in the early 1900s. We can blame college presidents today who allow their coaches to earn more than them. We can blame ourselves for watching and cheering nonetheless. Or we can stop blaming and start standing up for poor, black athletes by ending athletic scholarships and encouraging them to pursue academic ones.

* * *

When Georgetown basketball coach John Thompson joked that Patrick Ewing made him a great coach, he might have added that Michael Graham made him a champion. Thompson knew the mean streets of DC from his youth. He showed that once by calling drug boss Rayful Edmonds into his office to ask him to stop socializing with his players. He had no illusions about what type of student he was getting when he prevailed on his president to override his admissions department and offer a scholarship to Michael Graham, a six feet nine inch, 270 pound, 20-year-old freshman. It is doubtful that Georgetown had ever admitted anybody from Spingarn, Graham's high-poverty DC high school, where he had starred in basketball, not academics. The intense tutoring program Thompson had developed for students like Ewing could certainly keep Graham eligible for at least one season before his academic and effort deficits in the classroom derailed him.

And what a season it was. Graham took on the role of intimidator on the all-black team on a mostly-white campus, taking Thompson's "us against them" image to national prominence. He glowered at and shoved aside opponents, white and black alike, taunting and scuffling like he was on a DC playground, and freed the less-physical Ewing to focus on scoring. In the NCAA tournament Graham simply ran over an opposing player on his way back down the court after an aggressive rebound and thunderous dunk, setting the team's tone for the tournament. Within weeks of Georgetown's victory in the championship game, he was gone from the campus for "academic reasons." The university administration knew that Michael Graham had no more business being in a college classroom than Thompson's forward who spoke French and Wolof, but not English, and was awarded a gentlemen's "C" in a history course he rarely came to because of practice and travel for games, and couldn't understand anyway when he came.

- Or Richie Parker, the New York City basketball star recruited by George Washington University in 1995 despite being charged with rape, an error that president Stephen Trachtenberg tried to rectify by admitting the victim as well.

- Or Andrew Gaze, a 23-year-old professional basketball star in Australia who played a season at Seton Hall in 1988 without attending many classes, and then decamped back down under.
- Or football legend Herschel Walker, who was guided through three seasons of eligibility at the University of Georgia despite suffering from multiple personality disorder, while Jan Kemp, the coordinator of the remediation program who worked with Walker and reported the fraudulent raising of grades to maintain football players' eligibility, was hounded out. She later won a lawsuit and was reinstated.
- Or football and basketball star Julius Peppers, whose transcript at the University of North Carolina was leaked to the press during the criminal investigation of "independent study" credits for athletes. It showed that he remained barely eligible only by taking bizarre sports-named courses and the no-show, no-write, independent study courses that nearly 1,500 athletes took in the department of African and Afro-American studies. An independent review commissioned by the university described the operation as a "shadow curriculum" consisting of "phantom classes." Jan Boxill, an academic counselor who submitted athletes' pathetic, plagiarized papers and requested grades that would keep them eligible, later became the director of an ethics program at UNC.
- Or feel-good movie subject Michael Oher, who had to bring his own tutor with him to the University of Mississippi so as not to be blindsided by course requirements.
- Or the "fifth-year" players who are in graduate school, often at new universities, because they have actually graduated in four years and have a year of eligibility left because they took a one-year "red-shirt" injury break from sports.
- Or the grown men, like the 28-year-old quarterback Chris Wienke of Florida State, who had a professional career in baseball but remained eligible for four years in a different sport, or the 30-year-old wrestler on the American University squad who came to college after ten years as a Navy SEAL.
- Or most of the hundreds of professional athletes America watches on its television on college football and basketball game days and nights, which now run just about throughout the week on major networks as well as profitable special ones, like the Southeastern Conference and Texas Longhorn networks.

This is the entertainment and fund-raising system that sports in high-poverty schools are feeding in the best of circumstances, when everything goes according to plan. The system is fundamentally incompatible with the educational purpose of higher education, and proves it by consistently sacrificing the interests of the student-athletes and seizing their scholarships for review each year. And everything rarely goes according to plan. Interscholastic sports at high-poverty schools are fraudulent not just for feeding their fraudulent college masters. With their banners, bands, cheerleaders, games, homecoming ceremonies, trophies, and picture spreads in the newspaper these schools mimic the mainstream schools, and fool the community and the students into thinking that they are just like them.

Interscholastic sports mask the tragedy of high-poverty schools' disastrous college prep academic programs, which if honestly assessed would leave too few students to field any teams. They distract students, both athletes and others, who could win academic scholarships, for four years and not one at a time, and they displace important subjects like art, music, dance, and drama that have been axed from high-poverty schools because of the relentless focus on subjects that can be assessed with the high-stakes standardized tests. They can only be offered as after-school clubs. Providing community bonding and entertainment through attendance at football and basketball games is a luxury that these schools can't afford. It may be great for the community and the school system's popularity, as it is for colleges, but it's not great for the athletes.

High-poverty schools should stay away from the sports scholarship hunt, turn their interscholastic programs into intramural ones, and put the savings into their arts programs. You can actually major in college in art, dance, music, and theater, and there are careers in all of them. There is no major, and at best an unlikely and short career, in playing sports. I love sports, we all love sports, and they are good for kids and adults to play. But the unique American tradition of competitive athletics as a definitional part of the high school and college environment is a net negative for the principal enterprise of the high-poverty high school: preparing kids for success in the middle class. The cost–benefit ratio for students and for schools is well on the side of time spent on academics rather than on competitive athletics.

* * *

Chapter 9. Charter Schools: More of the Same

Diane Ravitch has written the book, as they say, on charter schools. Her definitive, even-handed review is called *Reign of Error*, and in it the former H. W. Bush education official and school-reform turncoat makes three things very clear: there is tremendous variety in these schools, their rapid growth has not improved the fundamental trajectory of their high-poverty students, and they are here to stay.

Charter schools are publicly-funded private schools. The typical state or local charter law creates an entity, a board of some sort, that grants a "charter" to virtually anybody who has formed a for-profit or non-profit educational corporation. The chartering entity develops standards for renewing charters after the corporations have been in operation for a few years, but it has little basis to deny an initial application, because there is no track record. Indeed, the fundamental reason for the chartering board's existence is to promote experiments to find out which ones work. Once chartered, the corporation starts recruiting parents to enroll their students, and receives roughly the same amount of money for each student that various governmental offices would otherwise have dispensed to the students' public schools. Charters are a multi-billion dollar business and are currently hailed by financial analysts as lucrative opportunities. Given the healthy salaries and consulting fees that charter operators pay their founders and leaders, there is little "non-profit" even about the non-profits.

Ravitch notes the irony that when charter schools started in the 1980s, well before the college-prep testing movement took off, they were intended to act in partnership with public schools. The original charter schools were given flexibility from the college prep curriculum so they could use innovative approaches to engage hard-to-reach kids. A few did focus on preparation for college, but these were selective schools for high-performing students who were bored by the standard fare. The explosion of charter schools only came in the 2000s with the growth of multi-school and multi-city systems whose operators promised to take any and all poor children into a "school reform" setting and break their family's cycle of poverty by delivering college-ready high school graduates. This charter setting usually includes an end to teacher rights in the classroom and in employment, a longer school day and year, regimented teaching and discipline, "no excuses" for the challenges of poverty, and even more intense pressure than in public schools to raise standardized test scores and cherry-pick a few to claim stunning progress.

Far from being partners, the "system" schools were now intended to be competitors with public schools. Their operators claimed that they would either quickly goad the public schools into mimicking the charter setting and supposed successes, or eventually force them to do so by bleeding them of children and their public funding. Philanthropic foundations, investors, and politicians frustrated with the dismal outcomes in high-poverty public schools found the college-ready, poverty-busting promises made by the charter operators irresistible. Without quite admitting that they didn't believe the perpetual flow of good news on tests, dropouts, and graduation rates being publicized for the public school reforms they had been backing for over a decade, these funding sources shifted the bulk of their largesse to the charter operators, adding it to the substantial per-student payment the charters received from public funds.

Today charters enroll nearly half of the public school children in Washington, DC, and all of them in New Orleans. They have enough political clout to stare down the mayor of New York in a cost-sharing dispute. Charters are a permanent fact of life in every state legislature and every big city. They are beloved and embraced by Democratic and Republican politicians alike, who shower the sort of exceptions and creative funding channels on them that they usually reserve at the state level for incoming corporations and at the federal level for aid to Israel.

This chapter will show that charter schools are largely redundant to what can be achieved in the public schools, and so are generally unnecessary and unsuccessful, even in their own terms. The exceptions tend to be schools that hold to the original intentions of the charter schools, which were flexibility and selectivity. The charter school funding network has yet to reach this conclusion, but when the mismatch of claims of progress and the reality of continuing educational failure becomes clearer in a few years, charters will face the same wave of closures that they have forced on high-poverty public schools. One hopes that at that time the funders and politicians will realize that the problem is the college-prep testing model itself, and not its mode of implementation in high-poverty communities.

Charter schools now fall into three main categories: those that are selective, those that are part of a "school reform" system, and those based on their founders' singular approach, such as Afro-centrism, single-sex education, military values, hotel management, or classics.

Selective schools

In a sense, all charter schools are selective. They naturally select the most capable and committed guardians in a high-poverty community. This is because it takes significantly more effort and initiative for guardians to seek out a charter school and register their child than it takes to continue the child's enrollment in their assigned neighborhood school. In addition, charter schools are more insistent than public schools that guardians, once their child is at the school, perform school-related tasks like signing homework and coming to meetings. Guardians who fail to perform these tasks can feel pressure that leads them to withdraw their child. Finally, charter schools are freer than public schools to encourage lackadaisical or disruptive students to transfer to other schools or, in extreme cases, expel them. These are the realities behind the charge that charter schools "cream" the most functional families and students off the top of the pool, and behind the difficulty of comparing academic outcomes between charter and public schools.

Some of the original charter schools and a few of the newer ones go beyond this natural selectivity and make no bones about being exclusively for cooperative families and students. In this, they function like "application" public schools. Thurgood Marshall high school, located "across the river" in a section of Washington, DC, that is entirely black and poor, is a charter school established in 1998 by some lawyers at a prominent firm on the "government side" of the Anacostia. Benjamin Banneker high school, located next door to historically-black Howard University, is a DC "admission" public school established in 1996. The two schools draw their students from the same demographic pool as DC's chaotic neighborhood public schools: black, poor, a single parent without a high school degree, and not a book in the house. Yet in both schools, students work quietly throughout a class period, watching the teacher and raising their hands to ask questions. In both schools, the students come in with their homework done, often as a result of calling their teacher at night for help. In both schools the hallways and lunchroom are orderly and calm. In both schools nearly everybody who graduates wins a college scholarship, and there are intense support services throughout the undergraduate years to help keep them on track.

The reason for these striking similarities is simply that both schools mean what they say in the posters in the classrooms, the ones that list the rules and promise disciplinary consequences up to expulsion for violating them. These posters appear in every other public and charter school classroom in DC, but the kids there know that they are usually just for show. If they expelled you for talking or not doing homework, who would be left? At Marshall and Banneker, though, the threat is real. There is a long waiting list of families who want in, and if you don't want to follow the rules and do the work, you are quickly invited to head back to your neighborhood school. As in all application schools, the only students remaining are those who have enough of a work ethic to behave and succeed. They comprise a low and no-income group that has escaped the ravages of the post-traumatic slave and currently-traumatized segregation syndromes.

The public school, Banneker, is a classic application school. Students submit their transcripts when they apply, and the school chooses the ones it thinks are best suited to the academic and behavioral rigor. The choices are confirmed in an intense summer session and placement exams. The charter school, Marshall, has to be trickier about its admissions policy, which by law must be an open rather than a selective one, but it achieves much the same purpose by counseling prospective guardians about the challenges of the school and the likelihood of a student "not being a good fit." Marshall's caution is due to a deal with the devil the charter school movement made with governments to gain access to the large-scale funding of recent years. Contrary to the original charter concept, public funding for charters is now contingent on the charters being more of the same by showing "progress" on high-stakes tests and by serving all potential students, whether or not they seem prepared for the school's demands.

As a result, charters have lost their untrammeled ability to shape their curriculum and choose their students. They must enroll students by a lottery, and they face pressure to increase their share of special education and emotionally disturbed students and non-English speakers. So, there are some legal gymnastics involved in a school like Marshall enrolling and maintaining the students it feels can succeed while convincing the guardians of those it thinks cannot succeed to withdraw their application or, if their children are already students, to withdraw them from the school. Fortunately for Marshall the lawyers who sponsor the school are exceptionally good at legal gymnastics. Time will tell if the lawyers will be as good at Rocketship, the purposely high-flying college-prep school system that has recently expanded its program from San Jose to DC, and has promised to take all comers.

For now, the warnings on the posters are still real at Marshall. Students who "don't believe the rules apply to them," as an administrator puts it, will find themselves in a meeting with administrators and a guardian in which withdrawal is suggested. If the suggestion is rejected, disciplinary reports can usually be found to justify expulsion, and the suggestion is then often accepted as the better alternative. The warnings are real at Banneker, too, whose administrators are in an even stronger position, since it does not admit by lottery, and can simply send students back to their neighborhood schools at any time.

Like most urban systems, DC's has a number of application high schools. In addition to Banneker, high schools that do not draw from neighborhood boundaries include the long-standing Duke Ellington School of the Arts, whose student body is largely black and terrifyingly talented, the more recent Columbia Heights school, which is largely Hispanic, and the most integrated high school in the District of Columbia, School Without Walls, which started as an internship-oriented safety valve for a handful of talented students who chafed at school discipline but has evolved into a 600-student academic school, with walls.

These application schools hire their own staff, and maintain focus and discipline by selecting less than half of their applicants and keeping a strong waiting list so they can replace the few kids who turn out to be a "poor fit." The one neighborhood high school in the white part of town enrolls lots of "out-of-boundary" students, and achieves the same effect by being able to send them back to their neighborhood schools for misbehavior. So, selective charter schools like Marshall appear to be redundant, because they can be replicated within the system.

System schools

At the core of the charter school movement today are the corporations that run a system of schools and promise success for poor children in a college-prep, school reform setting. The schools of the different systems are more alike than they are different. Their leaders all share the school reform ideology that relentless teaching to the test can overcome poverty. This, of course, is also the ideology of their public school counterparts, but they further believe that the public schools are failing to achieve that dream because they are constrained by union protection for bad teachers. System schools are driven by this belief to expand as fast as possible so they can save as many students as possible from the disaster of public school. This drive to expand dovetails nicely with the funding base, public and private, that system schools share. Every student brings in over $10,000 in public revenue, and special education students bring far more, since special state and especially federal funding is attached to each one. Foundations and philanthropists favor big things that make a big impact, and are drawn to the "game-changing" promises that charter systems make. The educational landscape is littered with failed experiments that were backed to the hilt by the founders of such firms as Facebook, Microsoft, Wal-Mart, and the GAP.

The ideology of salvation and the financial interest in growth combine to favor the recruitment and retention of any and all students, including the academically weak and the disruptive. Claims by their opponents that system schools purposely "cream" the best students off the top of the pool to improve their test scores are generally false. There is certainly an unintentional creaming of the most functional families inherent in the charter model, because they are the indeed the ones who are able and willing to undertake the hassle of enrolling in a new school, leaving the public schools with families that lack the wherewithal to do so. But the system schools truly want them all. They are constantly taking over vacant public schools, sometimes floor by floor, coexisting with a public school as its enrollment dwindles before it is closed, and they are constantly building new buildings that need to be filled with students. Once children are enrolled, system schools are as reluctant as public schools to lose them. Unlike selective charters, they don't mean it when their posters threaten expulsion. They develop complex discipline rules replete with meetings and threats, but the threats are rarely carried out, leaving the same sort of constant disruption of more serious students that exists in the public schools.

The belief that the public schools are sandbagged by union protection of teachers is expressed in the universal insistence of system schools that the laws governing them allow them to hire and fire under the legal term "at will." Unions would never stand for the practices of system schools that believe "we know what to do" to improve the test performance of poor children, and tell teachers exactly how to put these "best practices" into operation, day by day, indeed minute by minute, in a way that is far more intense than in most public schools. Ignoring the realities of frequent disruption, low achievement, and lower effort, supervisors demand lesson plans that are scripted down to the minute and cover in a purportedly logical sequence the skills that will be included on the high-stakes tests that measure the system's impact. Teachers are shamed into compliance with public posting of test results, threats of termination, and perhaps most importantly, daily pressure by supervisors, who are themselves under similar pressure from the system's leaders.

The constant planning, observation, filming, and reviewing of results that is promised by school reformers in the public schools is actually carried out, aggressively, in the system schools. Teachers have so many extra duties and hours assigned to them before, during, and after school that they end up planning and grading in the evening and on weekends, effectively working an 80-hour week. If a promised lesson plan is not emailed at an agreed-upon time, such as noon on Sunday, a supervisor's email of remonstration will shortly appear. When the plan is submitted, a supervisor's email with demanded changes will shortly appear. There is no appeal, no union or association process for a grievance against a supervisor's actions or judgments or demands, as there is in the public schools. System schools for a teacher are like a test-mad public school on steroids, with no union protection to soften the wild blows of the desperate administration.

In such a setting, it is no wonder that system schools are also alike in favoring the use of young, malleable teachers from non-traditional programs like Teach for America. They hand young people with no teaching experience the hardest population in America to motivate, and tell them to make up their students' multi-year deficits as fast as possible while also maintaining a grade-level curriculum for the frequent pre-tests leading up to the career and school-defining high stakes tests at the end of the year. It is no wonder that there is an even higher turnover of teachers in system schools than in high-poverty public schools.

The archetype of a charter system, and one of the largest systems, is the KIPP (Knowledge is Power Program) corporation, which was founded by two Teach for America middle school teachers in the early 1990s, but now includes hundreds of schools at all levels. KIPP's founders very bravely allowed Jay Mathews, the Washington Post's education columnist, to dig deep into its history and operations for his 2009 book, "Work Hard, Be Nice." Mathews' book is generally laudatory, and positively exuberant in reporting the usual sky-rocketing test scores. On a close reading, though, it does not contradict Diane Ravitch's conclusion that no system of charter schools has a better record on standardized tests than public schools when serving an entire population, because the income and education levels of parents are still the primary drivers of average outcomes. Mathews focuses on how KIPP coaxes improved test scores and social outcomes out of the part of the middle school general population that comes to and sticks with the KIPP approach.

Given KIPP's 37 percent withdrawal rate over four years in its middle schools and the 40 percent rate in its DC high school, this part turns out to be smaller than reformers had hoped, or acknowledge. It should be noted that this level of attrition is not atypical for high-poverty populations in any school. Poor students not only have more academic weaknesses than middle-class ones. Their families also have their lives disrupted by employment, financial, judicial, and other complications far more frequently, and are often on the move to other cities and states.

Courage was required for KIPP to bring Mathews into its bosom because he has a track record of contradicting the claims of his subjects, even those he admires. He has relentlessly criticized the DC public schools for feeble and self-serving "inquiries" into test-correction scandals, even as he has hailed the purported success of DC's school reforms. Similarly, he lauded the achievements of the late Jaime Escalante, a calculus teacher in East Los Angeles in the 1970s and 1980s who was the subject of the movie "Stand and Deliver," even as he debunked two claims that have burnished his legend.

Mathews' book traces Escalante's success in preparing students for the AP calculus exam to both his promotion of *ganas* (desire) in his students, and his standing up to his early principals and eventually finding one who would allow him to exclude from his regular math classrooms, let alone from his voluntary, extra-time calculus program, the large number of students who would not do homework. Escalante's calculus stars were a self-selected, voluntary group rather than, as portrayed in the movie, just a regular class of high-poverty students. More dramatically, Mathews cracked the mystery of the Advanced Placement cheating incident that makes the AP people look like such unreconstructed racists and classists in "Stand and Deliver." The students eventually admitted to Mathews that they had cheated. They claimed to have copied each others' work and so arrived at the same illogical answer on just one problem, but even if the AP's computerized checking programs had discovered just this one statistical anomaly, the AP would have no choice but to throw out all their tests.

Many of Escalante's students passed the retest, and hundreds of them passed the AP exam in subsequent years, so he had proved his point. On examination, though, the fact that his point is actually quite unremarkable has implications for the claims of dramatic progress by KIPP and similar systems. In his book on KIPP, Mathews often beats forcefully on a straw man, reporting increases in test scores to "prove the skeptics wrong" and deal yet another "blow to the assumption that low-income children couldn't learn very much, no matter how hard they tried." In fact, educators know full well that some poor children can escape the damage of poverty and achieve without limit. They also know that most poor children cannot. It is hardly surprising that out of a mass of poor students from challenged families Escalante could identify a few who were highly-motivated enough to volunteer for special sessions and work hard enough to grasp calculus, or at least its methods. The trick is to expand this achievement to include the mass, who are decidedly not highly-motivated and who definitely will not voluntarily come in regularly for before-school and Saturday classes.

For a few years, the pride and the power of the example of Escalante's core of achievers attracted a larger number of students into the calculus program and on to success on the exam. Soon after Escalante left because of conflicts with administrators, though, the program fell apart. Mathews' discoveries do not seem to have dimmed the appeal of the morality tale, false as it is, in which a great teacher got everybody to learn calculus, even if racist testers didn't believe the results. Like college students reviewing claims of the horrific health effects of chromium VI in water made in the Oscar-winning movie *Erin Brockovitch*, which turn out to be nil, people who hear of Mathews' findings are prone to say: "But they wouldn't have said so in the movie if it wasn't true."

Mathews' wrote his book on KIPP when the only system-wide claim about its impact on test scores was a posting by its founders in the 2007 KIPP Report Card. The posting stated that after three years KIPP students were on average 1.1 standard deviations ahead of their non-KIPP peers in math and .8 standard deviations in reading, both on nationally-normed tests. These are strong results. A standard deviation is a statistical calculation of the typical difference between the scores of test-takers. To use an example that will be all too painfully clear to readers who have ever, or whose children have ever, applied to college, an improvement of one standard deviation would be like going from 500 to almost 600 on an 800-point SAT test, which would move you from the 50th percentile of all test-takers to the 84th percentile. (This size of this effect depends on where you start on the Normal curve. Because of the "bell" shape of the Normal distribution of test results, moving up another standard deviation, from 600 to 700 on the SAT, would only result in a 13 percentile increase, to the 97th percentile.) That's a big jump, and one that the expensive SAT prep programs would be proud to cite as an average effect.

Perhaps judging that standard deviations were no way to communicate with the general public, Mathews used in his book a more digestible version of KIPP's remarkable results. He stated that after three years KIPP students in 28 middle schools had gone on average from the 34th to the 58th percentile in reading, and from the 44th to the 83rd in math. These are consistent with the standard deviations cited in the 2007 KIPP report card. Mathews claims that "gains that great for that many low-income children in one program have never happened before." He also randomly tosses in claims of ten percent annual growth, "in all categories" for a group of eight new principals, generally "soaring" test scores for a KIPP ally, and even, reminiscent of Michelle Rhee's phony record in a Baltimore classroom, a 60 percentage point, one-year gain in a particular KIPP school.

This is all standard school reform fare, and Mathews, of course, had no way to verify any of these claims, nor did KIPP provide any methodology to allow an assessment of the appropriateness of the peer groups with which KIPP students were compared. The starting point for KIPP's students was in some ways as striking as their ending point. The average score for poor urban children like KIPP's on a test given to all students in America test is usually at least a standard deviation below the mean, at about the 16th percentile. That KIPP's students came out of 4th grade from public schools scoring at the 34th percentile in reading and 44th in math shows that some "creaming" was occurring in their recruitment.

After 15 years of operation, KIPP used a grant to hire the research firm Mathematica to conduct a study that would correct some of the obvious biases in its and Mathews' earlier claims. For example, those earlier claims had included in KIPP results only the scores of students who had remained in the school for all three years, and so tended to measure students KIPP had reached successfully rather than those it had not. The new study, published in 2013, more appropriately included in KIPP's scores all the students who had ever been in the KIPP system, even if they had left. It then compared the KIPP sample with a control group of similarly-achieving and similarly-poor students in the nearby public schools, using a complex matching technique. The comparison was weakened by the previously-mentioned high mobility of poor families. Mathematica was often forced to "impute" yearly scores for departed and control group students as their families dropped out of contact or disappeared from the jurisdiction, or the students repeated grades at different rates.

The Mathematica study found far smaller gains than in KIPP's 2007 claim. The average benefit for KIPP students over four years were .36 standard deviations for math and .21 standard deviations for reading, compared to the average for schools in the locality of each KIPP school. These gains are about one-third and one-quarter the size of those claimed in the 2007 study. For our SAT example, the overall result would be like an increase from 500 to roughly 528. In addition, these scores were on "jurisdiction" tests in high-poverty cities, which are not as rigorous as the previously-claimed national tests. The Mathematica results have statistical significance, meaning that we can be at least 95 percent sure that they did not occur by chance. However, the small differentials between KIPP and the matching control group imply that the educational significance of the KIPP effect is not very important. A couple of month's advantage is hardly justification for either KIPP's grandiose claims or for four years of its extraordinary funding level. Perhaps KIPP was more successful than the public schools on important variables that are difficult to measure, like keeping kids alive and keeping them moving forward in a positive frame of mind, but those are not the ones on which KIPP hangs its claims, or its curriculum.

Ironically, the new study still fails to address what it says was its biggest fear, and what was probably the biggest problem with the 2007 comparisons. By controlling only for students' previous achievement and income, the new study still does not account for the higher motivation, discipline, and other achievement-increasing factors in the families who enrolled their students in KIPP compared to the families who did not respond to KIPP's well-publicized and aggressive recruitment outreach. Mathematica tried to take these crucial variables into account by comparing KIPP results with those of students whose families had applied for KIPP but were excluded by a lottery, but because so few schools had enough applicants to require a lottery, the sample of such families was too small and too scattered to be statistically valid. In a breach of statistical protocol and simple logic, Mathematica bizarrely followed this explicit warning by frequently going ahead anyway and interpreting the results from the winning and losing lottery results as confirmation of the results found through the use of the matching control group.

The small effect shown in the KIPP results should not surprise anyone who has seen first-hand the role of poverty, race, and culture in shaping students and their school environment. And it does not argue against the original charter school concept, which was to help public schools by taking on harder-to-reach kids with innovative programs, or the current one, which is to force public schools to improve by competing for their funding base. It simply recognizes that system schools are no panacea, because there actually is no college prep, high-stakes test-based panacea. At the heart of any claims to the contrary, like those in the Atlanta or DC public schools reviewed earlier, or the massive gains reported by Mathews for KIPP, will always be the unethical fraud of unfair comparisons, the creative "gaming" of the testing system identified by former Congressman George Miller, who was in on the creation of No Child, or the illegal fraud of outright cheating and lying.

KIPP is the Cadillac of charter systems. Its fundraising, from its original connection with the founders of the Gap clothing line to the billion dollars it has generated from foundations in addition to all the public per-pupil funding it receives, is legendary. Other charter systems mimic its methods, but they cannot mimic its funding. As a result, the high turnover of shell-shocked and exhausted teachers at KIPP is even higher in most other systems. Teachers at most system schools have many hours more duty than at public school, and much of it feels like babysitting that simply saves the system money by substituting teachers for supervisory staff. In the Friendship charter system of Washington, DC, and Baltimore, teachers work straight through for eight and a half hours each day, so they must come in early and stay late to set up the classroom for the next round. Additional planning and grading must be done at home, in the evenings and weekends, easily adding up to another three hours daily and a 65-hour week. Teachers are expected to coach or offer an after-school activity for little or no extra compensation, so the 65 hours can become 80 in a hurry.

Friendship's teachers start their day by standing in the cafeteria for half an hour before school, supervising a few tables of students, wheeling around a trash can to collect their breakfast residue, shushing students as an administrator with a microphone counts down to silence for the morning announcements, and writing down the names of the many students who persist in talking so that these "public space" disruptions can be registered for an automatic after-school detention. Then students are then placed in a homeroom for half an hour, and the teacher must offer activities and discussions about the day's news.

During the academic portion of the day, the teachers have three teaching periods and one planning period, each 80 minutes long. The planning periods, though, are often denied to the teacher, since they are coordinated by subject, which allows the administration to schedule department meetings for "professional development" and group planning a few times each week. Other planning periods are taken up with regularly-scheduled meetings in which various levels of administrators modify teachers' lesson plans and pressure them to improve test scores and grades, or with "restorative circles" in which a guardian or a disruptive student comes in for a meeting with the teacher, the student, and an administrator.

One devious use of the planning period is the requirement to "cover" other teachers' classes in their absence. Teachers who know that they have a medical appointment, or that they are going to use one of the personal days provided in their contract, are told to find other teachers to "cover" their classes, using material and instructions they leave behind. This saves Friendship the cost of hiring a substitute, but negates the contract's promise of time off for personal business like medical appointments, since to get other teachers to cover for you, you have to give up your planning periods to cover for them when they are on leave.

Teachers must call a guardian as soon as they issue a "classroom space" disciplinary report and have a student removed for disruption. As a result, the 40-minute lunch break for teachers consists of supervising tables and hauling trash cans in the cafeteria while trying to find working numbers and reaching or leaving messages for guardians. After classes are over, teachers are assigned two extra periods of about an hour each. In the first of these periods teachers are given another class, called a club, but with a pre-planned curriculum from which students write papers that must be graded for academic credit. For example, a "film club" class requires students to write responses to questions about a film they are watching in installments.

By this time of the day, few students are focused, and the clubs tend to be chaotic, yet the teacher is pressured as much as in the academic classes to make students do a modicum of work and record passing grades. In the final period, teachers remain in their rooms to tutor students who have recorded poor results of classroom quizzes or system-wide tests, or have disrupted class and been removed earlier in the day. This period is technically after the school day has ended for students, so most students skip their required attendance, setting off a new round of referrals and phone calls. In theory, a student who misses a required tutoring session will be taken into detention before the end of "club" classes the next day, and can be picked up by the teacher for classroom work. However, those students can easily evade the dragnet, and will do little work, extremely slowly, if dragged into the classroom.

Friendship tries to recruit and retain as many students as possible, so such cases do not result in expulsion or encouragement to leave, as they would at a selective charter school. Numerous extreme disruptions, over months and even years, of administrators' duties and "public spaces" rather than of the classroom are required before the principal decides to expel a student. As a result, the day after a dramatic classroom disruption starts just like the day before, with the disruptive students entering class, loud and proud. "I'll be back tomorrow," is a favorite line that students throw over their shoulder at the class as a security guard escorts them out of the room toward the "focus room" for miscreants. Sometimes the pledge is redeemed even sooner, with students strolling back into class within a half hour, after a heart-to-heart talk with an administrator. In the rare case that a teacher is given an "honors" class of well-behaved high-achievers, life is grand and the time is devoted to actual teaching rather than the usual coaxing, controlling, and drama. Most of these classes, though, are offered before school, and teachers are pressured to take them with no extra compensation.

Teachers often run screaming from the public schools to the charters, to avoid what they see as a battle between teachers and the demands of the school reform administration. But if they have run to a system school like a KIPP or Friendship school, they soon realize that they have run straight into a full-fledged war on teachers. The ideology of the charter system requires that the inevitable failure to turn all poor children into college-ready scholars be seen as the teacher's fault. After all, it can't be the charter school's curriculum and methods that are at fault, because those consist of "best practices" that superior teachers have used to eliminate the effects of poverty in three years. And it can't be the administrators who are at fault, because they are properly data-driven and accept "no excuses" from their teachers. So, if the students are still far behind after years in the system, it must be because they didn't have enough superior teachers, which provides all the more urgency for a vigorous separating of the wheat from the chaff in the current teaching corps. Raise the scores or leave, is the message that is clearly delivered to teachers in the system schools.

The problem with this logic is in its assumption that there is some fault to be discovered somewhere in the schools that will explain the historically poor performance of black poor children in a college-prep curriculum. Once this decision is made to ignore the realities of the students' lives and backgrounds in planning their program, the war on teachers is predictable. Their constant turnover, long before they can develop the feel for the classroom and for kids that a career teacher rises to after many years, ensures that the cycle of blame and shame for teachers will start again, feeding the cycle of frustration and failure for students. The system schools make the boldest promises in the charter world, but they deliver the least.

"Vision" schools

A final category of charter schools is comprised of numerous, small, "one-off" schools that follow their founders' singular approach. An entrepreneurial soul, determined to help poor children achieve middle-class success, will decide that what kids need to be successful is a sense of pride in African-American, American Indian, or Hispanic culture, or the discipline of military life, or the end of gender distractions through single-sex education, or a trade, like hotel management or plumbing, or a deep sense of wonder and powerful reasoning, which can be gained by studying Latin and the classic works of philosophy, or courses based on a community-oriented internship. Many such schools are chartered, but few are re-chartered. As is the case in general for start-up small businesses, a few of these low-budget, experimental schools grow into something large and successful, but most disappear within a few years. Vision schools seem to be particularly prone to descending into chaotic administration, weak performance, and possible fraud.

Their concept, though, is often sound, and given where the students are is almost always worth trying. The charter schools that offer vocational degrees are clearly filling a demand that has gone purposely unfilled in high-poverty urban communities in recent decades by public and system charter schools, and indeed by the entire school reform movement. From presidents down to principals there has been a silly insistence, which drives the school reform, college-prep curriculum, that a four-year college degree is the holy grail for poor students. With 50 percent of poor students dropping out of high school and the remainder being years behind in academic achievement and effort, success in college is extremely unlikely for most of them.

The goal of the vocational charters is for graduates to be able to step into starting positions as carpenters, electricians, plumbers, masons, experts in refrigeration and air conditioning, carpeting, tiling, and flooring, cosmetologists, computer technicians, nurse's aides, and carpenters. School reformers and colleges claim that a college degree is "worth it" financially, because college graduates have higher average salaries than high-school graduates, but that is a misleading comparison between young people from the middle and lower socio-economic classes. The fields listed above for vocational school graduates often pay as well to start, and certainly throughout a career, as positions filled by holders of bachelors' degrees.

Vocational programs have a curriculum that is inconsistent with the school reform laws that demand test progress on a college prep curriculum for all public school students. Until public schools can engineer a waiver process for vocational students, charter schools will provide the best setting for these programs. Unfortunately, chartering boards are generally moving in the wrong direction as well, demanding that vision schools show progress on college prep tests, just like selective and system schools. It is worth noting that in rural public school districts, where vocational programs have been entrenched for decades and are the first choice for generations within many families, school reform demands and weak results on academic tests have generally been unable to dislodge these popular programs. The rural vocational students usually spend half of their day at their home high school, taking a more life-oriented and less college-oriented academic curriculum and degree. The other half of the day is spent at a top-notch, multi-district vocational training center. The high quality of previous graduates usually guarantees a graduate an apprenticeship at a local business that can blossom into a life-long career.

One entrepreneur in the category of vision schools has undertaken an experiment that might bridge the divide between school reformers who insist that magically good teaching can transcend poverty and realists who insist that substantial educational progress can only come with the strengthening of the families living in the culture of black poverty. Geoffrey Canada founded the Harlem's Children Zone in 1990 on the assumption that both the classroom and the neighborhood, both the student and the family, must receive coordinated attention if we are to see the change we seek. The schools in the Children's Zone resemble system schools in their curriculum, and in that they rely on public per-capita funding from the New York City public schools. The diverted funding, fortunately, doesn't doom the public schools as it does in so many other cities, because New York has managed thus far to keep the percentage of its students attending charters well under ten percent. What is different about the Harlem system is that it then raises an entirely new and equally large budget from foundations and private donors to provide the sort of health, counseling, parenting and other support services for children that can help provide a more stable and supportive home environment.

This new kind of charter approach could, in theory, be replicated in public schools through collaboration between school districts, social service offices, and private foundations and agencies. However, charter schools can act with more flexibility and speed than government entities, and have greater access to the additional private funding needed to make an impact. Although the federal government has made some grants to support similar efforts, for the time being, charters will provide the primary setting for this important type of program. Just don't expect magic and rapid results, because the Zone continues to follow the school reform assumption that college prep curriculum is the path to the future for the mass of young, poor, people of color. Its schools suffer from the same high teacher turnover and make the same modest test gains as KIPP schools. To return to Ravitch's conclusion, no charter system has shown that it can take on a full population of poor children and change their basic trajectory through high school and later life.

We should remain hopeful for and supportive of charter schools, if only because school reform laws and practices in high-poverty public schools have virtually guaranteed failure for students if they stay there. System schools, and many of the other charters, can't address the deeper fraud of the school reform movement, and in fact are based on it. This fraud is not the outright cheating and lying of Houston, Atlanta, and DC. It is not even the phony grades and diplomas that make the statistics for performance in high-poverty schools look like they might come from a weak, middle-class school. Rather, it is the pretense that this book has worked hard to dispel, the pretense that the challenges facing high-poverty segregated schools are the same as those facing middle-class schools. In fact, these challenges are different not just in degree but in kind. Using standardized tests on a middle-class, college-prep curriculum as the measures for teacher and school effectiveness in such a setting has brought only failure for over 30 years. It is high time to fix this mess. Read on.

* * *

PART 2. THE FIX

CHAPTER 10. TELL THE TRUTH: EVALUATIONS THAT WORK

The eight chapters of the previous section described the fraud of high-poverty schools. The six chapters in this section present the fix. The essence of the fraud is pretense, so the essence of the fix must be truth. Truth to students, truth to guardians, truth to the public, and truth to the press. Truth in goals, truth in grading, truth in testing, truth about graduation rates, and truth about the devastation of poverty.

Right now, the politicians and educators charged with preparing children in high-poverty communities to have the opportunity for a middle-class life are pretending that all of the children can succeed, and that most of them do. They claim that "research shows" that "zip code" is no barrier to achievement, because even if you pack poor black and Hispanic children into a segregated school, excellent teachers and a great college-prep curriculum can prepare them successfully for college. This book has argued, from the author's direct experience, that unless the high-poverty school is selective, and retains only those students with appropriate academic skills and behavior, the culture of poverty will be distilled and dominate the school. The 50 percent of students who are able and ready to reject the culture's dysfunction will be dragged back into it by the disruption of the more disaffected.

Researchers at Johns Hopkins University have found that students at risk of dropping out are "hyper-concentrated," with half of them attending just five percent of public high schools. The educational and social disaster occurring in these highly-segregated schools is obscured by the preservation of the well-known forms of high school: report cards listing grades, files for recording test scores and hours of required community service, sports teams and cheerleaders, modern buildings complete with a library and labs for science and robotics, clubs and assemblies, posters exhorting the excellence of ethnic scientists and the importance of ethnic pride, department meetings, and parent-teacher conferences. It all looks normal from the outside, but as with Tolstoy's description of a dying bee-hive, a close examination of the content shows a different reality.

Grades and test scores are manipulated to present a veneer of progress. Community service hours are fudged with increasing laxity as graduation approaches. Phony grades mask the fact that most of the athletes and cheerleaders are too far behind grade level to be anywhere near eligible. The library has a smattering of ancient books on its new shelves. The labs are unattended and non-functioning. The "robotics team" that earned that trophy consists of one student enticed by the promise of a free meal into coming to the district competition, which is filmed and edited into an impressive piece of propaganda. The classic after-school academic clubs like chess, history, yearbook, Spanish, and math exist only on paper, with perhaps one student sticking around for each, while the "step" and "fashion" clubs, both of which are celebrations of black culture featuring stamping or sashaying girls, are packed. The teachers in department meetings remain mute for fear of encouraging the "professional developer" from taking any more of their planning time than necessary, and one guardian in 50 shows up for the mandatory teacher conference for which teachers must sit and wait for eight hours.

The truth is that nearly all students in open-enrollment high-poverty public and charter schools are failing. Half drop out and the survivors are given degrees that mask their lack of effort and achievement. Rare attendance at college itself rarely results in graduation. Public funds and private donations in the billions are sustaining the teachers, administrators, contractors, suppliers, and staff who comprise the education business for high-poverty schools, but the payoff in students' knowledge, confidence, and middle class success is virtually nil. Everyone in the system benefits from lying about it, and everyone suffers from telling the truth. The first step in fixing high-poverty schools is the revolutionary act of reversing this incentive structure, and rewarding the truth.

We should celebrate failure, because it spurs us in a new direction to achieve success. A student failing a class should be seen as a good thing, because it tells us accurately how weak the student is. A school recording abysmal scores on a standardized test should be seen as a good thing, because it tells us accurately how inappropriate the curriculum is. These results are not something to be avoided by hook and technical crook. We should think of the truth as the data in "data-driven instruction." We don't know how to teach, what to teach, or even which curriculum to teach within until we know where students really are, academically, emotionally, socially, and personally. We need truth in goals, grades, and discipline.

Truth in goals: Right now the goal of high-poverty schools is to help students get a college-prep diploma. We have been told by everyone from presidents to security guards that graduating from high school gets you a bad job and that graduating from college gets you a good one. This claim confuses correlation with causation. What matters are the family connections, knowledge, and work ethic you have when you enter the work force, and how you use them to hold onto your job and grow into new ones.

The goal of graduation drives the current system. People get paid because their school graduates students. A massive conspiracy develops in the very first year of schooling and continues to the very last. It is a conspiracy to cajole school staff into finding a way to pass students, so they can build up credits toward that highly-valued diploma. A teacher who reports that most students are not ready for the next grade's challenges and curriculum is seen as a failure. The goal of graduation has obscured the goal of education. Our goal should not be to keep everybody passing so we can graduate helpless children. Our goal should be to identify, as soon as possible, those who are not passing, so we do not graduate helpless children, or let them hold back those who are ready to try.

Yes, we want students to pass and then graduate, but only those who have mastered the required material and learned the necessary social skills of effort, cooperation, and initiative. Unless we know what losing looks like we won't know who has won. Until we honestly identify the losers in the education race, there will be no winners. Teachers and administrators should be rewarded at every grade level not for lying about progress, as at present, but for truthfully identifying students who have not made sufficient progress. Succeeding chapters will consider what to do once we have identified those students, but the path to success surely must start with an honest assessment. Knowing what we do about the culture of poverty, we should expect a solid 50 percent of kids in high-poverty schools to come up short in the very first quarter of the first year.

Guardians should be brought into the discussion of school goals, so that they understand what it takes to prepare students to succeed in middle-class life. They probably need to come as far as teachers do in rejecting the presumption that passing and graduating, rather than learning the material, is the school's purpose. The first goal of a high-poverty school must be its students' survival. Each child who makes it to adulthood alive, healthy, not part of the juvenile or criminal justice system, and not already parent is a victory. The next goal, the next important victory, is developing a work ethic and the middle-class social skills of timeliness, cooperation, and perseverance.

The final goal, after these prerequisites are achieved, is for students to master whichever curriculum, college-prep or vocational, interests them. A dead last in our concern will be all the trappings of school, like sports, bands, clubs, dances, and admission to college. High-poverty schools should be judged on two measures, reflecting their main goals: students saved, and students prepared. We can call this the student-based approach, in which courses and requirements are constantly modified to address students' needs, in contrast to the current system-based approach, in which students are jammed into an inflexible scheme of college-prep courses and requirements.

Truth in grading: Central to success in saving poor students and preparing them for middle-class life is finding out quickly, through clear-eyed assessment, if they can handle the courses in which they are enrolled. As soon as it becomes evident that a student is not prepared for the curriculum in a course, he or she should be removed for remediation, and then placed in a class at the proper level. Grades have to be honestly recorded to identify such students. Just as teachers should never advance a failing student to the next level, administrators should never just place failing students in the same course again the next time it is offered. There is a reason why the student has failed, and repeating the experience will not address it. Rather, the student will need help in addressing academic gaps and social and cognitive challenges. Failure means that it is time to strengthen the students and identify an appropriate curriculum and level, not force them through the same approach to the same material.

Truth in discipline: Also necessary for students' success is an honest, rather than hopeful, assessment of their classroom behavior. Pretending that disaffected students are ready for the middle-class experience of a vocational or college-prep classroom is no favor to them, or to the students they then disrupt. Just as they honestly grade students' skills, teachers must honestly assess their actions. Students and their guardians need to know where students stand on the crucial social skills of middle-class life. Disruptive behavior should bring quick reassignment to remediation, but in this case to strengthen not academic skills but social ones. Intense counseling must be offered, involving guardians if possible.

* * *

How should we handle evaluation in our new system in high-poverty schools that seeks out rather than hides failure, so that it can place students in a setting that is based on their needs rather than a pre-determined structure? How can we measure progress when we stop looking for someone to blame, and agree that progress is never guaranteed because of children's uniqueness, even before factoring in the stressful culture of poverty? The complex systems that currently exist for assessing students, teachers, administrators, schools, and districts would be inappropriate for these tasks. These test-driven systems are all based on unrealistic assumptions about students' readiness for the college-prep curriculum, and are geared to pretending progress rather than reporting the truth. The student-based, save-and-prepare approach proposed in this book, which teaches survival skills and work ethic on either a college or vocational track, will clearly require new evaluation systems for high-poverty schools.

The old systems have become increasingly rigid, using percentages based on a false sense of objectivity. The first thing to do with evaluation is admit, openly, that education is a subjective business that relies on the judgment of experienced educators in every phase of organization, instruction, and discipline. An English teacher at a top private school was asked by a student, under pressure from his father, why a paper had earned a B rather than an A. "Because I've been teaching 30 years and I know a B paper from an A," was the teacher's response. There is a lot of wisdom in that response, which of course was backed up written comments and corrections on the paper. Even if the teacher had used a grading system in which fixed percentages were assigned to each of two, or ten, or a hundred individual categories of the writing of a paper, the teacher would have been the one to assign the scores in each.

Attempts to put evaluation of students, teachers, administrators, schools, and even a district on an objective basis are necessarily subjective, no matter how many scores they generate and average. It would be better to make the subjectivity truly explicit rather than falsely implicit. This recognition of reality will probably disappoint the testing class, which believes that education should be run like a business, with reference to numerical statements of profit and value, and that weak returns indict educators rather than the culture of poverty in which they work. It will certainly end much of the current employment in that class. Described here for the various parts of high-poverty schools are potential evaluation methods that could be used under the student-based approach.

Students

There are two main ways we evaluate students in high-poverty schools today: grades and standardized tests. They harm, far more than they help, students' progress. Teachers should be given the clear duty of deciding which students can handle the work required for the curriculum the teachers have been assigned, and which students have demonstrated the mastery of the material and the work ethic needed to move to the next level. Those who cannot handle the work would be referred out of the class, to remediation.

Those who have not demonstrated mastery would not be passed, setting up a decision by their guardians to retake the class or seek a different curriculum.

Grades are usually recorded on the five-point GPA scale, from a failing F to a masterful A, skipping E for some reason, and recorded as 0 to 4. These grades are of surprisingly little motivational value in the culture of poverty. Students may get briefly excited and outraged by seeing the components of their running grade displayed on a Smart Board, but the response is rarely to do anything about it, even when the chance is offered to regain points by correcting a quiz or exam. The students think of grades more on a two-point scale, pass or flunk, and even that distinction spurs little incentive. Despite being aware that homework is graded and that a grade-killing zero comes with skipping it, few students come to class with it. For those who do bring in homework, the likelihood is that it has been copied, fully, with random marks and personal notes, from another student.

An argument can be made for retaining the five-point scale for the college-prep track. It is used in admission decisions at selective colleges, and students will be familiar with it when they start getting grades in college. However, admissions officers have experience using a variety of evaluation systems, including narratives, and in any decent college a particular grade will mean so much more than in a high-poverty school that the comparison may be more confusing than helpful. Grades in a student-based high-poverty school — whether F to A, 0 to 4, 0 to 100, no or yes, not ready or ready — are useful primarily as information for teachers and administrators about whether a student is making sufficient progress to justify staying in the class during a year or moving to the next level in the next. Unless a school is committed to using grades for that purpose, rather than as a target to approach by manipulation in order to claim success, they are much ado about nothing. If the school is committed, then for high-poverty students, any grading system will suffice if it is used honestly. It can even be devised and altered at the school level.

For all their expense and rigor, standardized tests in their current incarnation provide surprisingly little new information to teachers. From the frequent quizzes they give, teachers already know who is weak and who is strong in the grade-level academic setting in general and in recently-taught topics in particular. If there is any lingering question about whether a student is strong enough to be enrolled in a course or a grade, there are a plethora of "show-your-work" grade level quizzes that any experienced teacher or administrator can interpret in a heartbeat. Standardized tests are useful to school reformers, not individual students. A return to the practice of 30 years ago, when a student might take an intelligence test once in their elementary school and then not see another until the College Boards, would make hundreds of currently-lost hours of instruction and testing time available to teachers.

A humorous aspect of those intelligence tests was that experienced teachers would often receive their packet of scored tests and simply put them in a drawer without looking, so as not to prejudice themselves against students who might have scored low. Many teachers today do much the same thing, ignoring administrators' lists of who tests as "proficient" and who does not, to avoid focusing on "bubble kids" to the exclusion of others. The only loss from ending the testing regime would be to the testing class, which needs piles of results from which to cherry-pick claims of progress.

Teachers

There have traditionally been two purposes of teacher evaluation. One is to help teachers improve their technique. The other is to decide whom to retain and whom to encourage, or if necessary force, to move on to a new school, or even to a new profession. The main method of improving technique for years was a simple one, and in fact it is the one still employed by most private schools: observation by an experience principal and a lengthy discussion of what was observed. The principal would offer some suggestions, and the teacher would try them out.

The decision on retention was separate from the observations. It too was based on the judgment of an experienced principal, who would let the teacher know well in advance of the end of the school year that there were serious concerns about effectiveness. That was usually enough to convince the teacher to move on voluntarily. Again, this continues to be the main method for termination in private schools. Contracts, even for the most experienced teachers, are individual and last one year. As long as private schools follow employment law in such areas as non-discrimination and working hours, they are free to hire and not renew at will, although fear of nuisance lawsuits and angry parents do, in practice, constrain administrators.

As associations and then in many cases unions of teachers became more common in the mid-20th century, things got a little more complicated in the public schools. I have seen the battle between school boards and their teachers' groups from both sides, as a school board member and as a teacher. I have felt the fundamental tension between the two groups that will always exist. There is no squaring this necessarily adversarial circle, and there is no need to. Management and labor require each other to make a modern industry, because their interests are opposed and would run out of control without a powerful counter balance.

There is no way around the conundrum. The teachers' groups want to protect jobs and benefits, while the school boards and administrators want to minimize financial exposure and dump trouble-makers at all levels of experience. Both sides see their actions as motivated by a desire to improve students' education, and both have the legal firepower to match the other and use it in almost every dispute. Both are here to stay, like segregation by wealth and ethnicity, and so must be factored into plans for improving public education.

Filing and negotiating grievances over working conditions and dismissals is where the teachers' groups earn their dues. Administrators have an institutional interest in adding duties until teachers' backs break, and in pushing out older, more expensive teachers and teachers who aren't "team players." The teachers' groups force them to use moderation. Unfortunately, the groups fight as hard for the bad as for the good, for the pedophile and the incompetent as for the defender of student needs. Unfortunately, school boards will fire the gay activist using the same powers and the same speed with which they fire the drunk. The teachers' groups use their power to slow down and undercut some of the craziest fads in school reform, but also to slow down and undercut some reasonable reforms. Even the most intransigent unions are not really significant barriers to success in high-poverty schools. The college-prep mission has been so misguided relative to the needs and the culture of the students that success, as open-enrollment, non-union charter schools with all-powerful administrations are finding out, would have been impossible in any regime.

Teachers originally organized to obtain the same sort of seniority guarantees as unions had fought for in other fields, so that teachers could not be punished for their views or affiliations and older workers whose salaries had increased over the years could not be fired in favor of junior ones to save money. Legal findings related to employment rights and due process were codified into group contracts that became more and more lengthy and detailed. Unions and associations began to promote a sort of super-seniority, called tenure, which they borrowed from universities in Europe and then America that wanted to retain distinguished scholars. Tenure is not technically a guaranteed position for life, since school boards may dismiss for irresponsible behavior if they can make the charge stick in court. But it is pretty darned close. Once granted, usually after a probationary period of a few years, tenure acts as collateral, allowing a teacher to sign a 30-year house mortgage for which the bank can rest assured that monthly payments are virtually guaranteed.

The primary goal of the teachers' groups then began to be to help probationary teachers gain tenure. They favored packaging the two purposes of evaluation together, so that favorable observations would be grounds for their lawyers to contest a decision not to renew a junior teacher's contract.

More recently the school reformers have gone the teachers' groups one better, and created long and complex checklists of supposedly essential teaching methods that teachers must use if they want to keep their job. The groups have generally acquiesced to these instruments, because the more complex the rules, the easier to find one that it can be argued, in grievance hearings and law suits, was not properly followed.

In nearly all open-admission charter schools and in public schools where reformers have negotiated evaluation instruments with unions or associations, teachers are observed early in the first half of the school year and given a numerical score that is the sum of the scores from the individual items on the checklist. The teachers' summed scores will fall somewhere on a scale such as ineffective, minimally effective, effective, and very effective. Teachers are then handed the list of the items on which they earned low scores. These items can range from the precise, like "ask follow-up questions," to the obscure, like "teach for understanding." Teachers must incorporate "best practices" for these items during future observations or face even lower scores for the full year, leading to dismissal.

These evaluation instruments increasingly factor into teachers' point totals their students' performance on the school's annual high-stakes standardized tests. In some cases more than half of a teacher's score is based on these tests. This practice represents a defeat for the common sense belief, in place since the very beginnings of education, that students are responsible for their effort and that their families are responsible for their behavior. It portrays students as interchangeable *tabulae rasae*, ready to have knowledge poured into their heads. It encourages students to be passive consumers, ready to complain about a defective product, the teacher, if for some reason the knowledge that has been poured into their heads drips out. The notion that teachers are responsible for students' performance infantilizes and disempowers students and their families, and undercuts teachers' authority.

The practice of linking teacher evaluation to test results also represents a singular victory for the reformers' philosophy, which is borrowed from the business-oriented model of education developed by governors in the 1980s: poverty is no excuse, therefore all students are able to excel, therefore if they do not excel it is because their educators are doing a bad job. Teachers can say all they want, in reference to a child's skill and behavior levels when entering their classroom, and to their attendance, behavior, and effort once they are there, "that's not on me." However, once test performance is tied to evaluation, it is indeed all on them, because a good teacher is defined as one who can overcome all deficits and motivate all children to attend, try, behave, and become excellent.

Many teachers, such as those in physical education and music or grades that are not tested, do not have standardized test results for their students. Other, such as special education teachers who visit their "inclusion" students only a few hours a week, are not their students' primary teacher in a tested subject. The reformers solve this problem by having all teachers in the school rewarded or punished with points based on how the school's population as a whole did on the tests.

As described in detail in Chapter 6, there are a variety of methods used to calculate how well students did. The judgment can be made by comparing proficiency rates in a class or grade to those of previous years. This unfairly allows fluctuations between the readiness and attentiveness of different groups of students to affect teachers' futures. The judgment can be made with a "value-added" model that compares individual students' performance with what was expected from their socio-economic background and their previous year's score. This unfairly allows fluctuations on readiness and attentiveness for individuals to affect teachers' futures. With either approach, teachers are at the mercy of random events.

The strangest version of basing evaluation points on test results arises when there are no standardized tests available for a grade or a class, and teachers are scored on the results of final exams they have drawn up themselves. The evaluation requires the teacher to state in advance, sometimes at the beginning of the year, a goal for the class, before they even know the students. The principal may lobby for an optimistic standard, such as "80 percent of students will receive a B or above on the final exam" in classes where 10 percent is more likely, and 50 percent are likely to will fail. Teachers can achieve such a goal by playing the definitional game like Houston administrators. They can write a simple exam, or grade it on the curve, or since attendance and learning go hand in hand, they can decide on an attendance rate that disqualifies most students from the calculation. By adjusting the principals' goal to read "80 percent of students who have attended 80 percent of classes receive a B or above." Only the best three or four students in a class of 25 attend that often, so success is guaranteed.

A recent variation on teacher evaluation in public schools links teachers' annual pay to their ratings on the previous year's evaluation. In such schemes a poor rating for a year results for probationary teachers in a pay freeze and a warning of termination if there is no improvement in the next, and a high rating opens the door to substantial bonuses. The schemes apply to tenured teachers as well, but they have many more layers of appeals and far higher standards of proof of incompetence to protect them. The reformers usually require a teacher to give up tenure rights to accept the larger bonuses, and in practice few teachers, probationary or tenured, take the deal. Charter schools require no such gymnastics to make employees "at will," because a fundamental motivation behind their creation was to create schools where administrators could hire and fire without worrying about teacher unions and associations, teacher rights, and tenure.

To their chagrin, and despite well-funded publicity and lobbying efforts in nearly every state, the school reformers have been unable to end tenure in public schools. Teachers see tenure as the bottom line, the security they obtain in return for the slings and arrows of their being, year after year, subjected to outrageous, sequential fads handed down from above. Interestingly, only ardent reformers, and not school districts in general, are fixated on ending tenure. The school districts, after all, are the ones who made the decision to grant teachers tenure after the two-year probationary period, so they must have thought they had pretty good teachers at that time. The additional experience since then has probably made teachers better, rather than lazier.

A possible chink in tenure's armor was found in 2014, when a California judge ruled in favor of school reformers who argued that tenure violated the rights of poor children to have good teachers. The case featured supporting testimony by the school reformer heading the Los Angeles schools, who fortunately has since then resigned his position, and the decision was hailed by President Obama's secretary of education, who unfortunately has not. The logic and the claims on which the decision rest do not appear likely to survive scrutiny during the appeals process.

The judge's decision claimed that an "expert witness" had testified that between one and three percent of teachers are "grossly ineffective," that a "value-added" study found that such teachers cost the students in each of their classes a total of $1.4 million in lifetime earnings, and that these teachers are disproportionately present in high-poverty schools. These claims led him to declare the tenure system that protects the jobs of these terrible teachers to be in violation of the right of poor students to equal protection in education under the California constitution.

Each of these claims dissolve under analysis. The expert witness did not make any judgment about whether teachers were grossly ineffective, the study is largely theoretical because its estimates of increased earnings are for fictional students whose improved tests scores are about five times higher than the improvements registered by students whose teachers rate in the top three percent, and the judge confused cause and effect in the case of low-scoring students and their teachers' ratings on, you guessed it, how their students score on tests.

The problem with the claim attributed to the expert witness, David Berliner of Arizona State University, is that he never made it. Berliner was willing to affirm, from common sense, the statement of a lawyer for the school reformers that a small percentage of teachers "consistently have strong negative effects" on test results. He made this judgment strictly as an artifact of statistical behavior in any large sample, and he notes that these teachers may well be effective in other ways. Berliner told Jordan Weissman of Slate magazine: "In hundreds of classrooms, I have never seen a 'grossly ineffective' teacher. I don't know anybody who knows what that means."

The problems with the study headed by Raj Chetty of Harvard that estimated $1.4 million in lost life-time earnings for a class taught by a grossly ineffective teacher are many and fundamental. First, the $1.4 million estimate for a class of 28 students does not account for inflation eroding the value of a dollar earned years from now in comparison to the value of a dollar today, which violates the fundamental rule of financial mathematics. It was included in the study along with the proper, inflation-adjusted figure of $270,000 in today's dollars out of concern that the public would not understand the meaning of "inflation-adjusted." That $270,000 works out to about $300 per year for students who score one standard deviation better on tests after the effects of parental income and previous achievement are accounted for. And the problem with that estimate is that the study did not find any teacher whose average student performed that well.

The largest gain in student performance found for the top third of the teachers in the study was about one-tenth the size of the unit of "value-added" impact used throughout the Chetty study, the unit that it claims, through many arguable assumptions required by difficult data, leads to the $300 per year increase in earnings. Even for the top three percent of teachers, the gain was about one-fifth of the value-added unit. Moshe Adler of Columbia and Chetty have published detailed exchanges on this issue on their respective websites. Finally, if high-poverty schools have more teachers who score low on adding value (and that was not established with data in the judge's decision), that is largely because these schools, as we have seen repeatedly in this book, are segregated not just by income and ethnicity, which the value-added procedures account for statistically, but by motivation, family dysfunction, and a constant flow of new, untenured teachers to replace the experienced ones who leap at the chance to flee to easier schools.

In summary, the judge explicitly took on faith the school reform claim that the most important factor in student achievement is the quality of teaching, and made no mention of the impact of social, economic, and parental influences, or of segregating the most challenged families into their own schools. Interestingly, the claim and indeed all of the findings and studies cited by the judge would be insufficient for his decision even if they were true, since he did not cite any figures for what percent of teachers were tenured in either the poor or wealthy settings.

Losing on tenure seems to have spurred reformers on with their alternative, already implemented in New Orleans and Washington, of simply replacing high-poverty public schools with non-union charter schools. Ironically, American universities have been winning the battle against tenure even as the public schools, for which universities had been the model, have been losing it. The share of professors on campus who are on what is called the tenure track has slipped from nearly all 40 years ago to well under half today, as universities have created "short-term" and "adjunct" and other new categories of less expensive professors with no right of renewal and often no benefits. Tenure slots are so rare and expensive, and so filled with white males and increasingly females from the previous generation, that many probationary professors who would have been granted tenure in the past for their publications and research are now being denied tenure by provosts and presidents after being recommended by their departments and faculties.

A return to the traditional system of observations and decisions by principals is the only way to implement an evaluation system in high-poverty schools that encourages teachers to report, rather than hide, failure. The check-list and results-based approach to teacher evaluation has to go, because it is based on failure being the teacher's, rather than the student's, fault, which makes it suicidal for teachers to report failure. Unions and associations will oppose such a subjective system, because it gives unlimited power to the principal, but they can be offered the same rights of appeal and arbitration they have now for non-renewals or dismissals under the checklist system.

The principal would have to justify the non-renewal of a probationary teacher with a lengthy narrative. Unions might negotiate a process in which the principal would have to convince an arbitrator to some stated degree of certainty ("virtually," or "highly likely") that the narrative shows that the teacher has not developed sufficient skill to run a classroom. Teachers' groups can perhaps be weaned from their fixation on winning tenure for all their new teachers after short probations with additional guarantees for those who do win it after a longer probationary period. For example, tenured teachers could be given the right to be in the final small pool being considered for an open job in another school in the district. Tenured teachers could be offered more pay, or perhaps the end of the deadly professional development sessions that were used to implement the old checklist, and their replacement with collaborative meetings within and between departments. Something has to be sweet enough to convince unions of what their teachers will tell them: the student-based approach is going to be much more successful than the old one, for teachers as well as students, and if it requires a narrative rather than a check-list for evaluation, so be it.

Administrators (and schools and districts)

The transition from subjective review to mindless, check-list madness has been even quicker, and more extreme, for principals and assistant principals in high-poverty schools than for teachers. In addition to their own checklist of categories, building administrators now typically have contract clauses that read like those of professional football players or college basketball coaches. Players get paid extra for gaining 1,000 yards or recording 50 tackles. Coaches get paid extra for making the Sweet 16, or raising their NCAA academic score. Similarly, administrators get substantial rewards if their school achieves certain results on the high-stakes tests, or if retention rates fall and graduation rates rise. These targets are usually what the district needs to retain federal funding and avoid restructurings.

Also like players and coaches, principals and assistant principals have limited job security. Principals in high-poverty schools usually last about two years before they are fired for failing to meet their targets. This sacrifice temporarily satisfies the gods of school reform and delays restructuring. Don't worry too much for the principals' mortgages, though. Administrators are paid a premium for the uncertainty of their status, and fired principals rarely go very long without a job. A sort of merry-go-round exists for them, just like the one for college and professional coaches who reappear after each disastrous run as the shining hope of another franchise. There are only so many people out there with the qualifications, the experience, and the desire needed to manage a high-poverty school, and they shuttle back and forth, from firing to hiring.

Building administrators in a student-based approach would need to have an evaluation method that rewards honesty and effort. Like principals guiding teachers, district-level officials would use a subjective approach of observation and suggestion to guide principals. Dismissal would be a topic of early discussion if incompetence was evident, but in general the district's goal would be to keep administrators in a building for as long as possible. Stability and connections to the community are particularly valuable in a high-poverty school, and can only come with years of routine and interaction.

How do you measure honesty and effort in principals, and in their schools and in the collection of schools in a district? With data on placements for instruction and support for remediation. Data should drive not just instruction, but the overall school program. They can be used to see if students are being accurately assessed, properly placed, and supported when they are unable to continue in a classroom due to their limitations on skill and behavior.

Under a student-based approach, classroom teachers would not have to try to reach parents for discussions and disciplinary solutions when skill levels or behavior problems disrupt their classes, or scramble to jury-rig placements in more appropriate classes and after-school sessions. Families would have chosen an appropriate curriculum, vocational or college prep, and those students who still were unable to cope in class would have passed to the care of the administrators and remedial teachers. Freed of disciplinary duties and impossible ranges of skill levels, teachers would be able to focus, like teachers in middle-class schools, on students who are within striking distance of success on the material in their course. It would be up to administrators to develop a system of remediation for students removed because of low skills, and a system of counseling and remediation for students removed because of disruptive behavior.

These curriculums and systems are discussed in detail in Chapters 12 and 13. For purposes of evaluation of administrators, schools, and districts, though, data would need to be collected on variables such as: percentage of students removed from each academic or vocational grade-level class for skill, and for behavior; overall percentage of removals for these two categories, individually and combined; percentage of students removed for skill who were later placed in an appropriate level course; percentage of those students who were successful in the new course; percentage of students removed for behavior who received family counseling; and percentage of those students who were successful in the course when they retook it. These numbers would be diagnostic, rather than, like the numbers in the old evaluation, punitive. Administrators would not be judged on them, because they reflect numerous variables about the students' realities. Rather, they would provide a snapshot of the success of the program, and give insight on how the administrators should modify it.

A major problem in assessing success in high-poverty schools is the frequent movement of students and the reluctance of families to share information with authorities. When a student disappears, how can you find out if it's a case of moving to a new town, or just to a new school, or of going into incarceration, dropping out because of family crisis or impending parenthood, or just plain dropping out? Communication between various schools and social service offices can be intermittent, although requests for transcripts do provide some information. Family members are difficult to reach even when a student is in the school because of changing phone numbers and addresses and a general avoidance of contact with authority. Once the student is gone from the school, tracking becomes even harder.

There is no easy solution to this problem, but under a student-based approach there would be a case manager in the school for each student removed from class for remediation. The case manager should have developed a decent profile on the family in home visits and meetings, and could try to maintain contact. At the district level, investigators could be tasked with tracking down students who have left the school, and then reporting their findings to the district and the original school. The purpose of all this checking and reporting would be to answer the most important evaluation question a high-poverty school can ask: what happened to our entering cohort? It is a question that needs to be answered not just during the high school years, but afterwards, for as long as possible.

Schools and districts need to develop measures that reflect success in life, such as arrests, sentences, college graduations and drop-outs, jobs held and businesses started, and salaries, so they can adjust their programs in light of long-term outcomes. Again, these measures should be seen not as punitive, or ways to demonstrate progress, but as diagnostic tools to help refine the educational program. A lost soul is not a cause for blaming the school, and a smashing middle-class success is not a cause for praising it. Too many variables play a role in a person's life for a school to take all the blame or credit. But we need to know if our overall goal of helping poor children become middle-class adults is being met. That's real evaluation. That is the truth or, to use Black English, "word."

* * *

CHAPTER 11. EDUCATION FOR (MIDDLE-CLASS) LIFE

In *Bleak House* Charles Dickens made much fun of social reformers in Victorian Britain. He contrasted the quiet charity of his wealthy heroes of the Jarndyce clan toward the poor they happen to come across with the pompous certainty of the reforming class that was personified by Mrs. Jellyby, the fundraiser for the Niger River village of Borrioboola-Gha whose work forced her to neglect her own family. The reformers promoted grand missions and well-reasoned techniques for saving all the souls who had become the wretched refuse of the industrial age, at home and in the colonies. Dickens wrote, in reference to a London ghetto called Tom-all-Alone's, "Much mighty speech-making there has been, both in and out of Parliament, concerning Tom, and much wrathful disputation how Tom shall be got right...And in the hopeful meantime, Tom goes to perdition head foremost in his old determined way."

Today's testing class, with its angry certainty that "we know what to do" for poor children and their devastated families, recalls Dickens's reformers. America's ghettos, with their continual resupply of failure and outrage despite grand and expensive school reforms, recall Tom-all-Alone's. All of us who have worked with the poor, whether we are wrathful in our disputations or not, should take heed that we respect the complexity of the social and economic systems that create and sustain poverty, and the necessarily minor role that our efforts will play compared to both the workings of these systems and the personal efforts of the poor themselves.

The proposals made in this and succeeding chapters do not pretend to be able to "end poverty" among Americans, as rock stars, UN officials, and other modern counterparts to Mrs. Jellyby claim to be able to do in the formerly colonized countries. Ending or even significantly reducing poverty must await dramatic changes in American economics and social consciousness. Black poverty, in particular, will probably remain disproportionate and resistant to erosion until there is some closure on the original sin of slavery through government reparations, the counter-balancing passage of a few centuries, or perhaps a few decades of heavy inter-marriage that obliterates America's ethnic distinctions. The best that the proposals in this book can offer is the hope that 20 years from now a somewhat larger number of young people will have a shot at a middle-class life than in the current system of fraudulent college prep for all.

The perfect, in this case, will certainly be the enemy of the good. We must take up the hoary mantle of triage, and offer to as many families as possible the opportunity for their children to succeed, without being unduly distracted by those who are unable to respond to it. The poor will always be with us, with the reasons for their poverty equaling their number. Our goal is to remove some of the barriers that impede their climbing of the steep and slippery slope from the black underclass to the American middle class. The completion of the climb itself will always be up to the climber.

In planning a curriculum, we must take students where they are, and where they are is in trauma. I told my students in high-poverty schools that it was a waste of time to work on math problems if they wouldn't first pledge to "take no life, make no life" each night — short-hand for staying out of violent situations and using a condom. To have even a chance of getting to the middle class as an adult, you first have to make it out of the teenage years alive, without a criminal record, without a baby, and healthy enough to work. This reality is one that high-poverty middle and high schools need to acknowledge by providing lessons and counseling for every child on these topics. The lessons can be combined into an "arrive alive" course that presents, discusses, and practices what students need to do to survive to a productive adulthood.

Once students have reflected on those issues and covered them in a structured curriculum, the next goal is to teach them the social skills needed to hold a middle class job: be ethical, cooperative, reliable, creative, perseverant, and confident in mainstream settings. Again, that is a huge challenge in a high-poverty neighborhood, and it must be met in a structured manner as in any course, with curriculum and assessment. This package of "arrive alive" and "social skills" might be called "education for life."

How does one go about structuring a curriculum for education for life? Very much like one structures an academic curriculum, with goals, courses that are appropriate for the experience and age of the students, components of the courses, activities to teach them, exams, and grades. "Arrive alive" is really a social studies course in which the society being studied is the students' own. "Social skills" is really a training program for work habits. Both can be justified as credit-bearing because they underpin school success. Studying plumbing or Shakespeare before you can show up on time and struggle through challenges without erupting or quitting is like a miler going straight to speed training without laying down the necessary base of long runs: a waste of time and talent for both athlete and coach. The education for life curriculum needs to start before the social and academic challenges of the teenage years, certainly by seventh grade, and then continue through high school.

There are many ways to cover the material. I would favor requiring the course every other year, say in seventh, ninth, and eleventh grades, with the material adjusted for the needs of that age. In schools where poor children are not in the overwhelming majority, the courses could be optional, although most parents and guardians of all economic levels would be well advised to enroll their students. "Arrive alive" would be offered in the fall semester, followed by social skills in the spring, so there would be 20 weeks of instruction in each. What is important, though, is not the particular structure chosen, but the acceptance by educators that the material is as important as classic academics, and must be taught in some fashion.

Unless you leave high school healthy, unencumbered by parenthood or a criminal record, and in possession of middle class social skills, you are unlikely to escape the surly bonds of poverty. Since that escape should be the goal of high-poverty schools, they must teach students how to do it. Many teachers are already teaching education for life, without thinking about it, when they discuss the barriers posed by pregnancy, and demand good note-taking, respectful silence when others are talking, that disputes be resolved in discussion rather than violence, and solid effort when frustrated by the material. This proposal recommends that the instruction not be hit or miss and offered just to some students, but a regular part of school, available for all students.

The "Arrive Alive" Course

In the "arrive alive" course, students could be deeply engaged and actually do much of the teaching. Children in high-poverty communities have a wealth of information about the conditions and the choices there, although they will never publicly offer examples from their or their families' lives. Even in private counseling sessions the code of silence about family matters usually keeps authorities, school and other, in the dark about the specific challenges facing poor families. As long as they are telling tales about the neighborhood without naming names, though, students are eager to present and analyze their information. Unfortunately, much of it is misinformation, comprised of gossip, error, and urban fantasy that need to be exposed and dissected.

I used to set aside ten minutes every period of math class to go over a topic of the day, like teen pregnancy, auto theft, a shooting in the neighborhood, or a dispute that escalated into a gang fight. These discussions could easily have spread over the whole period. The students could be sophisticated analysts one moment, offering all the arguments for and against various choices to be made in a crisis, and then ignorant gossipers the next, spewing bromides, often heard from guardians, about the need to be "hard" and the perfidy of "snitching." Just as in any course, "arrive alive" students would have to be guided through a curriculum that presents and comes to general conclusions about specific topics. If that sounds propagandistic, it's because it is. We make ethical judgments all the time in presenting academic courses, like social studies, history, or English. Nobody can take those courses without inferring that civil rights leaders were pushing for something good, Hitler was doing something bad, and Mark Twain was properly pointing out the absurdity of slavery. After listening to a student explain how he had to fight or be seen as a "punk" and "soft" in the neighborhood, the teacher will have to make a convincing case and demonstrate a credible method for avoiding the conflict.

Each year's "arrive alive" course would set out topics to be covered, updated for the age of the students and events in the neighborhood, city, and country in the past year. The theme of the course, though, would remain constant. The theme is that the culture of black poverty and the reality of white racism threaten students' chances to live and prosper, and that students need to be prepared to defeat the threat. Students need to be told, and indeed want to be told, what they know in their bones, that they are an endangered species under risk of personal extinction. They need to know, after Faulkner, how not just to endure, but to prevail. They need to confront the suicidal and self-defeating nature of many of the mechanisms that African-Americans developed for survival during slavery and segregation, and then have handed down for generations.

The material that I would cover in a 20-week course would include: good health, black male and female self-images, racial self-image and racism, how to avoid pregnancy and sexually-transmitted diseases, the meaning of respect and disrespect, how to avoid the judicial system, how to stay safe in a dangerous neighborhood, how to avoid fighting, and how to report violence in the street and the home. The order and combination of topics would depend on the needs of the school and the students. One way to structure the course, though, would be to cover each of these topics in two weeks.

This would provide time for students to discuss the topic, use activities to flesh it out, and be assessed.

Health: The diet of teenagers in the black underclass can only be described as suicidal. If you observe students congregating at the corner store before school, you will see them filling up on bags of red-hot chips and cans of sugared drinks, sapping their appetite for the free breakfast that awaits them. At lunch-time students again munch their greasy potato products as they wait to line up for their trays. Many will toss their soups and sandwiches, and even their beloved pizza, into the trash bin and just eat the desert. Milks are jettisoned in favor of sodas that students beg teachers to keep cold for them in faculty refrigerators. After school, waiting for sports practice, the athletes and cheerleaders buy hot dogs and sodas at a fundraising stand, and send friends out to the corner store for more junk food. In the homes, giant vats of Kool-aid, made by adding scoops of sugar to the mix, are drained during the evening. Dinner will likely be a frozen meal from the corner store or, if the family has a car, the one supermarket within a 20 minute drive. A special treat will be MSG-laden Chinese take-out or, yep, fried chicken from Popeye's.

Using measuring devices and nutritional references, students could log their diet one week and analyze it the next. Comparing their totals of various nutrients, empty calories, fats, and sugars to recommended levels would provide a window to start discussing the implications of diet for sound development and adult diseases. The epidemics of obesity, diabetes, and heart disease in the culture of black poverty start with childhood diets. In addition, there are strong links between the unhealthy diets of pregnant girls and the low birth-weights and health problems found in their newborns. This section of the course would focus on identifying and learning how to buy and prepare healthy meals. It could end with a cooking, and eating, exercise for one healthy meal students could remember as a model.

Most poor students have tried marijuana, cigarettes, and alcohol by the time they leave middle school. A few in every high school classroom have come to school high that day. A minority, mostly "runners" who carry drugs between neighborhood dealers and their customers, have tried crack, meth, or heroin. The sporadic level of use of these various narcotics in high school is not a major health problem, although arrest for possession or "running" is often the gateway into the criminal justice system. The course should demystify narcotics by presenting data on health effects as well as the link to a criminal record.

Gender issues: Students are confused about the social responsibilities of being a man or a woman. How do they act? What do they do? Gender differentiation in the poor black community is stronger than in the middle class. Slavery and segregation psychologically, and in many cases physically, castrated the black male. Backed by the threat of doing violence to him and his family, whites denied him the respect due a man. For 300 years it was a rare black man, South or North, who could speak his mind, seek his fortune, support and protect his family, or simply move through his day without insult, threat, and repression. Under slavery it was not only easier but safer to act shiftless than to show competence, because to achieve was to present a target. To protest, let alone resist, was fatal. Women were taught to defuse the ever-present undertone of confrontation, even to the extent of trading sex under duress to white men for the safety of their black men. From this trauma emerged the dysfunctional poor black family today, where men have disappeared, leaving overwhelmed women to pick up the pieces. The sound track for this tragedy is provided by the bitter, pathetic, cultural attack by male rappers on women as "bitches and ho's" who will give them "booty" for drugs or money, or just for the chance to stand close to their fame.

This component of the course, in which students come up with their own definitions for being a responsible man or woman, can be kicked off with a single word: "baby-momma." The whole complex of male irresponsibility and female enabling is contained in that modern substitute for "wife." The teacher should ask students why girls agree to the role of baby-momma, raising a child the father rarely sees, and why boys take pride in racking up as many baby-mommas as possible. What psychological security do these roles provide? Are the girls willing to do anything to gain the attention of boys because they have had little attention from their fathers? Are boys trying to claim manhood from parenthood, or perhaps replicate their fathers' insouciance toward family to try to convince themselves that it doesn't bother them? How can boys and girls avoid these roles? Everything in the culture around students tells them that this is the way of their world. This component would show them how pregnancy will trap both the boy and the girl in poverty, and would offer an alternative definition of gender roles that can be played out without being a teenage parent.

Race and racism: Being black is the constant preoccupation of African-American students in poor, segregated communities. It is what defines them, both within their culture and in interactions outside it. It is what keeps them from venturing out from their communities into the mainstream society, and makes them nervous and alienated when they are there. Developing a racial self-image is unavoidable in these circumstances, so students must be guided in assessing what theirs is and what difficulties it presents when entering the middle-class world.

A good way to start the discussion is to focus on the other side, the white side. Asking students for times when they have perceived fear and distrust from white people will bring out a storm of memories for analysis. This can lead to a discussion of preferences shown to whites, not just by whites but even by blacks, in hiring, promotion, and social settings. Equal opportunity commissions often conduct experiments with black and white actors who go to rent apartments or get bank or car loans with identical financial records, and they invariably find bias against blacks. And every child in the ghetto knows of the differences in access to taxi cabs, police observation, and arrest between whites and blacks. They know, and talk about, the disdain they perceive from the black middle class as well.

The purpose of these discussions would not be to reinforce black students' perception that they are victims who have the deck hopelessly stacked against them. Rather, it would be to exhume and demystify all the fears and insecurities about race and racism that they have, and discuss ways to be more successful in interactions with other ethnic groups and social classes. A teacher can turn the concerns around by having students adopt the role of white, Asian, or Hispanic people observing black students "acting out" in shared public places, like movie theaters and fast food shops. This allows the students to think about how they are perceived when they act like "just another black girl on the bus" — loud and intrusive, and cursing to show their fearful fearlessness.

Role-playing as employees of various races being treated rudely by supervisors can take some of the edge off of the inevitable conflicts students will have in the workplace. Perceived racism is often used by black students as an excuse for quitting, or not even taking, part-time and summer jobs. A question African-Americans are constantly asking themselves in a mixed ethnic setting at work or in a multi-ethnic college is, "Am I being treated this rudely because I am black?" The answer to this question is important, but usually impossible to decide. Accepting racial discrimination is out of the question for someone trying to preserve a healthy racial self-image, whereas we sometimes ignore common rudeness as the perpetrator's problem without any damage to our self-image. Given the numerous cases of rudeness, insensitivity, or misinterpretation we all observe or perpetrate ourselves in others' eyes daily, it would be foolish to consider all rudeness to a black person a form of racial profiling. Given the depth of racial identity and animosity in American history, it would be foolish to consider none of it as such. Students need to work through these issues and become more comfortable confronting them

Pregnancy and sexually-transmitted diseases: Teenage sexual activity is not by any means the exclusive province of black poverty. There are lots of men in all cultures who seem to be programmed to want as much sex as possible with as many women as possible. There are lots of men in all cultures who have bizarre excuses for not using condoms. What is different in the culture of black poverty is teenage girls' greater willingness to accept these conditions that appear to be so demeaning, and their more frequent decision to have and then raise the baby, rather than choose abortion or adoption.

Unless they are specifically asked, it is certainly not the business of anyone other than a family member to give a girl advice on whether to have an abortion. It is certainly not the business of a school curriculum or a staff member. However, it is the business of the school and staff to educate boys and girls, one hopes before they are sexually active but at all times nonetheless, about the psychological consequences of having sex, the physical consequences of having unprotected sex, and the facts about sexually-transmitted diseases, pregnancy, abortion, miscarriage, birth, and parenthood. Students are often a fount of misinformation on these topics, and they should be able to display their knowledge, or lack of it, and ponder the authoritative factual corrections that only a teacher can provide. Students are going to get their information somewhere. It is better if it is accurate and trustworthy, and can be discussed carefully with a teacher.

Disrespect and its dangers: "Respect," a pop hit by Otis Redding and then Aretha Franklin in the 1960s, could replace "Lift Every Voice and Sing" as the black national anthem. Not being "dissed," meaning disrespected, and getting proper respect, referred to as "propers" in the song and just "props" in current slang, are constant obsessions in interactions among poor black students. Why? Where does this need for validation come from? The answer is obvious, if troubling for young people to consider. It comes from the same place as the "joning" in which young blacks tear each other, and each other's mothers, down verbally: the trauma of violence and insult during slavery and segregation. You can often observe similar obsession and reactive behavior in young people of all ethnic groups and income strata who have been abused. In the culture of black poverty the abuse behind the obsession is a historical legacy that affects all families, the violent and the supportive, alike.

Given that black people were subjected to brutal disrespect that had to be accepted at pain of more violence to self and family, it makes all the sense in the world that once African-Americans were free of that threat, there was a tendency toward hyper-correction. Black riots in the 1960s and even those of more recent years are invariably triggered by a violent act by the police. A peculiar and pathologic consequence of segregation was that the riots of the 1960s damaged only the black sections of cities. Still, they were scary enough to white America to allow President Johnson to create the Great Society programs that still maintain the "safety net" that protects both the black poor and the white rich who fear their revolt.

Students are trapped by the wholly understandable need for external respect. They need to study its historical basis and its present consequences, and act out various roles in the drama with commentary from teachers. Unless this need can be demystified and discussed, the drive for respect can be counter-productive. This is particularly true for the strangest legacy of historical disrespect that survives today: joning. As noted previously, in past decades this practice of verbally tearing down not whites but fellow blacks was known as "doing the dozens." It seems to have started as a way for black slaves to balance their powerlessness by denigrating someone else even less powerful. Indeed, the term "dozens" itself may have come from the slave-owners' practice in Louisiana of grouping their least valuable slaves in lots of 12 for sale. During slavery and then segregation it was too dangerous to denigrate whites, so other blacks would have to do.

Beneath its creativity and undeniably humor, joning expresses the self-hatred of the individual and the ethnic group that Kenneth Clark and other psychologists have identified as the bitter fruit of slavery and segregation. In some ways, joning does the work of the Ku Klux Klan. Not only does it waste school-time by leading to fights and suspensions, but it certainly contributes to the black-on-black gang violence that has killed more blacks than Nathaniel Bedford Forest's progeny ever imagined possible. Joning is a way of establishing dominance, and such a challenge will usually lead to a response. Students need to be guided into considering the meaning and impact of joning. A good way to approach is this by having them write jones aimed at fictional friends, and then consider these historical roots of their wit.

Crime and punishment: As many as half of the ninth-grade boys you see in a black, high-poverty school have already entered or will enter the criminal justice system. A smaller, but significant share of black girls will do the same. How does it happen, and how can it be stopped? Students need to study these questions, so they can avoid this distinction, so respected among their peers as cool and so fatal to their chances for a middle-class life. The well-known claim that there are more black men behind bars than in college classrooms is no longer true, if it ever was. Comparing a pool of all adults to a pool of college-aged ones is a bit misleading in the first place, and according to Pew research there are actually about 1.2 million black men in college and about 840,000 incarcerated in prison or jail. However, this ratio of 1.4 is tragically about one-sixth that of white men.

This disparity between black and white comes largely on the criminal and not the educational side. The black college attendance rate of 36 percent of 18 to 24-year-olds in 2012 percent is close to the 42 percent registered for whites. Census Bureau data put the black poverty rate at 35 percent, and the white rate at 13 percent, so to have black and white college attendance rates this close speaks well for the access of the poor to college in America. Both ethnic groups have slightly higher rates for women than for men. However, there are significant differences in the college experience for whites and blacks. Black college attendance is heavily weighted to two-year and technical colleges. The disparity in attendance rates by ethnicity at selective four-year and open-admission two-year colleges is so pronounced that Georgetown University's Anthony Carnevale, author of a comprehensive study, calls them "racially separate and unequal institutions." In addition, once in college, blacks have a graduation rate of about 40 percent, much lower than the 60 percent white rate.

The black male incarceration rate of about ten percent in the age range 20 to 34 is six times that of the white one. This ten percent roughly triples if probation and parole are included to capture all people under the jurisdiction of the criminal justice system. For those without a high school degree, all of these percentages are much higher. For example, nearly half of young black men who have dropped out from a high-poverty school are incarcerated.

Criminal charges and incarceration are heavily focused on poor people. Department of Justice surveys estimate that the typical inmate is in the bottom quarter of national income before arrest, and does not have even a high school degree. As we have seen, blacks are almost three times more likely than whites to be poor. Even accounting for this higher black poverty rate, though, still this leaves blacks about three times more likely to be incarcerated than whites of the same income level. While some of this disparity comes from racial bias in police work and prosecution, much of it certainly comes from the prevalence of "hustling" in the black culture of poverty, which can lead to drug-related arrests, from dealing to assault.

A few poor black students are literally born into the life, which is what people call the criminal world. Their parents have been in and out of prison, and some even recruit them into the business, as runners, packagers, or prostitutes. These cases are decidedly in the minority, though. Most students who enter the criminal world, and then almost certainly the criminal justice system, do so either in secret or over the efforts of a guardian. The boys find companionship and protection in a set of friends. The "set" then evolves into a "crew" that might practice light delinquency until it is absorbed into a local gang that controls some limited part of the neighborhood drug business. This pattern reflects the lack of control by female guardians and absent fathers over their teenage boys.

Everything in this scenario conspires to force the boys to fight wherever and whenever insulted or challenged. The first step toward a criminal record is often a suspension after a fight in school. If administrators suspect a gang connection in the fight, they will lean toward a semester-long transfer to a special program in another facility to forestall retributions and escalation between the gangs they know are hidden in the student body. The next step will be an arrest for running drugs, meaning delivering and accepting payment for them. Students younger than 16 are preferred for this task, since the concept of legal culpability generally does not apply to juveniles, on the belief that they are not wise enough yet to be blamed for their crimes. However, committing a violent crime prior to turning 18 usually results in someone being charged as an adult.

Random stops and searches are prevalent in high-poverty communities, and young people caught in possession of illegal drugs are treated as if they were trafficking in them. As a result, many students are swept into the system without gang connections. A first arrest for a minor usually results in the minor irritation of wearing an electronic tracker as an ankle bracelet and a second arrest sends the boy to a juvenile home, but by the third they may be charged as an adult and remanded to the juvenile section of a jail.

This component of the course must aggressively trace the path from school to jail, and point out how to step off it. Role-playing and student research on employment and recidivism after a felony conviction can be powerful tools for reflection. Associations of former prisoners, which are active in many cities, can provide leaders for intimate discussions and counseling, which are far more effective than the belligerent harangues they usually offer in assemblies. However it is done, the reality that getting involved in crime harms both the criminal and the victimized community must be driven home. Disrupting the transmission of mass incarceration to yet another generation is central to the success of the mission of high-poverty schools.

Safety: Violent crime is concentrated in poor neighborhoods. Compare the media treatment of a gang gunfight on the city bus I took to the high-poverty school where I taught to that of a mugging in the wealthy, white neighborhood where I live. Both resulted in death, but the commonplace first story merited a five sentence blurb on page six of the Metro section of the Washington Post, while the rare second one dominated the front page for days. The statistics for any major city confirm that high-poverty students live in the midst of a constant crime wave that would mobilize a hysterical response if it were taking place in wealthier parts of town, and they need help in staying out of the line of fire.

Most young people who are shot are shooters themselves. They go looking for trouble, and it finds them. You can never tell which of your students is in this high-risk group. A veteran teacher told me that she had given up guessing which of her students might end up a shooter or shot, since she had lost both loud gang members and quiet, hard-working students to prison or death. Many of the shooters are in the life. Like the Mafia, they and their competitors use weapons in their crimes, and inevitably on each other. Many others are not in the life but feel the need to rent a gun and avenge a perceived wrong done to them or a member of their family. Usually sooner, but certainly later, those who pick up the gun will face it themselves.

Other categories of young victims include potential witnesses, robbery targets, and students whose guardians cannot keep them from being in the wrong place at what everybody knows is the wrong time. I have seen mothers, aunts, and grandmothers crying on television about their teenage son or daughter who was gunned down as a bystander in a drive-by shooting. The newscaster did not have the courage to ask them what in the world their child was doing at the playground at two in the morning on a school night, or standing outside a funeral home that had already been sprayed with bullets three times that year during gang funerals. Young people are drawn to likely scenes of risk and violence, and must be encouraged to stay away from them.

Students need to analyze all the categories of risky behavior, and be guided through discussions of ways to avoid them. If the goal of survival is made explicit, then the pursuit of that goal becomes a game that students can play. Students should be taught to think of themselves as a bodyguard with one client to keep safe until adulthood: themselves. The proper response to a situation is the one a bodyguard would recommend, which is to get out of there as soon and as far away as possible. The most intimate category of violence though, requires special treatment. That is violence in the home. The flip side of parents' lack of day-to-day control over young people is often an erratic attempt to force obedience and respect. The usually absent father, step-father, or boyfriend comes briefly and terrifyingly into the household, and takes umbrage at the resistance of the mother, or the teenage boy or girl. Hands, fists, feet, belts, sticks, and even rape are used to establish dominance. The psychological trauma of even witnessing, let alone being the target of, such abuse, can devastate the young person for decades, and will certainly hold back progress in school.

How can teachers help students avoid such situations? There is no easy answer, but the first step is to acknowledge their possibility and describe them as the crimes they are. Students can then be prepared to avoid these crimes the same way they are taught to move away from, rather than toward, likely scenes of violence.

Fights: Bullying and how to respond to it are common elements in many of the threats to survival for high-poverty students that have been discussed in this section. Gender and racial identity, the search for respect, crime, safety — all these issues are affected by choosing to fight as a response to verbal and physical provocation. It is such a common, central issue that students need to have it presented and analyzed on its own.

Many poor black children play out the cultural reaction to the denial of respect and outright degradation of slavery and segregation. They act aggressively, "getting up in the face" and space of other children, at first playfully and then increasingly seriously challenging them to fight or back down. It is the rare student who does not face this challenge at some point in their day. In addition, joning and friendly insulting are such common parts of interaction that these precursors to fights will constantly present choices to their targets. Students need the chance to think through these situations and their implications.

Do you have to jone back, and fight now, to avoid a reputation of being soft that will get you attacked outside of school? The answer can be broken down into practical and moral questions. Teachers can walk students through the practical consequences of fighting. Do you want a discipline or criminal record? Who is the punk, the man in jail who got there by always fighting, or the man on the job who got there by smoothing his way through challenges? Who "kept it real," the girl who was suspended for fighting and fell behind and dropped out, or the girl who laughed off the jones but made sure to hang out with friends who skipped them, and graduated. Like nations consulting their interests, students should be encouraged to think through whether at times the wiser course, the self-interested course, is to skip the fight and just dismiss a challenger as foolish, rather than set in motion an endless chain of dangerous tit for tat.

Teachers could also raise moral objections, rather than just practical suggestions. How would you feel if someone you were fighting fell and hit their head and died, or were paralyzed for life? How would you feel if that happened in a fight you were cheering on, rather than trying to stop? The point is not that there is a right and wrong answer to every situation a student may face, but that students who have never had the chance to consider the range of possible responses and consequences will always feel they have to take the course of action implied by their culture, their peers, and their guardians: fight.

Reporting violence: Another common element in many of the threats to students is confusion about whether and how to report violence to authorities. On the street, in the school, and in the home students see and experience violence. Schools have many good reasons to train them to report it. Affirming what they see gives them an important sense of control over their lives. Pretending they did not see something bad only weakens them, and reinforces a sense of helplessness and passivity. If you don't report something that scared and perhaps threatened you, you are saying that your feelings and your safety are not important. In addition, speaking up for what is right is powerful training for a middle class life. What distinguishes middle-class from high-poverty neighborhoods is the large percentage of people ready to complain, and demand change, be it from the police, the schools, or the city managers, at the drop of a hat. As recounted in Chapter 6, my colleague Caroline said in response to a student dismissing "snitching" that middle-class communities are completely composed of snitches. That's why criminals are cautious about operating there.

Reporting also allows students to get on with meeting their own goals. In school, the goal is to learn the material so you can move into a successful career. If your class is disrupted by students destroying materials, or fighting, or throwing things when the teacher's back is turned, it is your future that is being robbed. You have the best right of all to report the other students, your right to a future. In your neighborhood, you have your right to live without intimidation and crime. In your home, you have your right to live without violence.

Fear of retribution is what keeps most students from reporting crime and violence in the community, in the school, and in the home. Students need to learn how to report for each case and how to protect themselves afterwards. In school and in the home, they may well discover that the act of reporting protects them more than the acceptance of the violence would have. Being a witness or a complainant to criminal behavior is indeed dangerous, but letting criminal behavior continue is dangerous to the community, which includes you, your friends, your siblings, your parents, and your grandparents. Everybody knows James Brown's song that claims it's better to die on your feet than live on your knees. That was about black people needing to demand equal treatment from whites, rather than accepting second-class status. The same sentiments apply to people building safe communities, rather than accepting gang rule.

The "Social Skills" Course

The "social skills" course would review and practice the skills needed for success in middle-class life. It would be fine-tuned for the age of the students, and cover the particular skills they need for success in that year. For example, freshmen could be taught how to study, and how to maintain notebooks. Juniors on the college prep track could learn testing techniques for college boards. In the senior year, the vocational track could focus on applications for training and apprentice programs or jobs, and the college prep track could focus on college applications. The primary focus of the course, though, would be to learn how, more generally, to be ethical, cooperative, reliable, creative, perseverant, and confident in mainstream settings. These areas are constantly referenced already in high-poverty schools, but mostly on posters and slogans that students walk by without a second thought. They need to be taught in a structured fashion. Fortunately, there are examples and counter-examples in the culture of black poverty that can be used to spur discussion and provide material for exercises. Each component could be covered in about three weeks of classes.

Ethics: Psychologists of black poverty make much of black children's belief, reinforced by the words and actions of many of the adults in their lives, that nobody can be trusted, that everybody is cheating and getting over, and that people who play by the rules are suckers. For accurate historical reasons the children especially apply this belief to the white people and mainstream institutions they encounter. White middle-class families are far more likely to talk about and demonstrate what has been called the triumph of hope over experience, the belief that people and the institutions they populate are basically decent and can be trusted.

The mismatch of the two world views makes it harder for young African-Americans to fit in successfully when they enter a largely white work world. In mainstream institutions, people are expected to act ethically. We know they don't always do so. Otherwise we wouldn't need the many auditors, inspectors, enforcement officials, and other actors society pays to keep natural greed in check. The transgressions, though, makes ethical behavior even more highly-valued, and selfish behavior all the more suspect.

Ethical behavior is also, from Socratic times, widely recognized as being at the core of personal development. This gives schools another important reason to teach it. Students need to be challenged and guided in thinking through what is right and how to act in accordance with it. Teachers will need to approach the topic with sensitivity about the contradictions between the behaviors they are trying to teach and the words and examples that students' guardians are providing. The fact that guardians are often counseling students to "get theirs" and are openly bending and breaking rules in their lives is all the more reason to present an alternative vision of society and personal responsibility.

Empathy, the act of trying to understand another's perspective and emotions, is a requirement for ethical thinking. All teenagers, for developmental reasons, are challenged when it comes to empathy, but in the culture of black poverty the fight for survival and personal dignity has made it an unnecessary luxury even for many adults. Again, that is all the more reason to define it, value it, discuss it, and model it in role-playing. An option must be presented before it can be chosen.

Cooperation: Closely related to ethical thinking is the notion that we must be able to cooperate with others on tasks. Not everybody can, or should, do this. Mozart and Einstein, and modern counterparts James Brown and Steve Jobs, were not team players, yet they gave the world something we cannot, or in Jobs's case think we cannot, live without. Still, cooperation is a prerequisite for a successful middle-class career. Students have to be sold on the need for it, and taught the skills for it. Helpful exercises include those in which different people produce components for a project, or take on a physical or intellectual group task.

Cooperation is an area in which black culture provides examples that can be examined, valued, and transferred to the mainstream workplace or academic setting. The strong bias toward getting your own and looking out for yourself is balanced by various definitions of "self." After the obvious core definition, black culture, like all cultures, certainly defines family as part of self. The family can be as narrow as mother and child, and not extend even to the man who abandoned them, but it can also be as broad as the noteworthy black tradition of the extended family, where cousins and aunts are as close as mother and child. The family can even comprise the black nation as a whole, in which the self and the others share a bond of responsibility and camaraderie that is the strongest among America's many tribes.

In his 1960s anthem, "This is My Country," Curtis Mayfield of the Impressions sang, "every brother is a leader, and every sister is a breeder." Setting aside the sexism of the time, we can focus on the fact that everybody knows who the brother and sister are. In destroying the black family under slavery and segregation, whites created a super-family in which all blacks are kin. It is a pan-Africanism that Africans have never experienced. Cooperation can make sense to young people within the context of the black nation. That concept has to be seen as a way station, though, to learning how to commit to and cooperate with many ethnic groups at work.

There are a number of films black students in particular can analyze to delve into the concept of cooperation. "Lean on Me" is one, although it is an unfortunate glorification of the madness of the testing class. Joe Clark, as played by Morgan Freeman, turns a New Jersey high school upside down to raise tests scores and avoid restructuring. He tosses out the miscreants, sweetening his chances, and then bullies teachers into feverish test prep activities. From its title to its supposedly triumphant finish it focuses on black pride and cooperation. "42," the Jackie Robinson story, is a better motivator, since it shows cooperation on the job by people from different ethnic groups. "The Help" and "Glory" show black women and men, respectively, sticking together in the toughest of times.

Reliability: It's a joke we all know: CPT. Colored People's Time, meaning a lack of concern for the actual time of an appointment, or for a due date on a project. In Africa the imperialists called it African Time, usually in tandem with references to a general incompetence, like Wawa: West Africa wins again. In Latin America it is referred to in contradiction, where invitations that really mean what they say append the initials H.I. or H.S. for *hora Inglese* or *hora Suisse*, English or Swiss time. These joking terms have a serious history, because they obviously describe practices that blacks and Indians used to thwart their exploitation by powerful, violent rulers.

Nelson Mandela had an obsession with being prompt, because he knew the black practice of tardiness, like studied incompetence, was appropriate only for disrupting white rule and not for advancing black rule. Black students need to be exposed to his reasoning and his example, and to develop his habits. This will not be easy. Poverty itself disrupts homework and school attendance with regularity. Cars break down, cash is short, and cheap furnishings and household equipment fail. Still, until an ethic of pride in timeliness becomes as strong as CPT in black culture, young people will have a hard time lasting in college or on the job precisely because "it's a joke we all know" and so it is what white people will expect.

How do you teach promptness at schools at which there is a cultural tradition of skipping the first few weeks and the last few weeks, true attendance is around fifty percent, and most students dribble into school during first period and a good share only arrive for second? Part of the answer, removing chronically tardy students from the assigned class and placing them in non-credit remediation, will be discussed in Chapter 13. In the social skills course, though, the goal is to help students understand the benefits to the group of everyone being on time and the costs to the group of someone being late. One way this can be demonstrated is by putting students in groups and creating situations where what they want is disrupted by the teacher randomly pulling members out. It could be something as simple as having the whole group ready to go to lunch. Or students can be assigned a word game that requires each student, in order, to make up a word in category, such noun, animal, sport, town, or country. The catch is that the new word has to start with the last letter of the previous student's word. As the teacher pulls students out for classroom tasks or errands, their group will be delayed in finishing the required number of rounds and will lose. The disruption of the task by absence makes the point about the disruption of tardiness to a class.

Creativity: A crucial adult skill is the ability to solve a problem not by following instructions, but by figuring out a path oneself. Teenagers are generally oriented toward the present far more than the future, and the culture of black poverty accentuates this trait. As a result, many students lack the patience needed to generate options and think them through. This short-coming has certainly not been addressed by the heavily-structured lesson plans favored by the testing class, which occupy students with short, directed assignments rather than provide them with opportunities to wrestle with complex, longer tasks. They must be taught how to take the initiative, and to be creative in finding a way forward toward a distant goal, and in solving problems in general.

Fortunately, black culture has a tradition that can be called on to teach creativity. There appears to be a deeper need for a distinctive external identity in this culture than in the mainstream. One might search for the reason in the notion that the socially powerless subconsciously mask their condition with special trappings, leading to the somewhat apocryphal Cadillac obsession of an earlier black generation and the definite sneaker obsession of this one. Whatever the reason, though, students are used to plotting and then pursuing the basketball move, hair weave, crew sign and chant, tattoo, turn and tilt of the ball cap or other "styling" accoutrement that can distinguish them from the crowd. Even their names, often creative rather than mainstream, show the depth of this tradition.

In teaching problem-solving and creativity, teachers can call on this tradition and then urge students to be equally unique in their approach to solving a problem. Students can be asked to come up with a way to get a cargo across a busy city in the least possible time, or at the least possible expense, or to organize a field trip, from snacks to transportation to activities. They can then test out their plans in practice, and compare results in class discussions. There are many ways to teach and reinforce creativity through writing, including journals entries of personal experiences and plans, rhymed song lyrics, or letters on community, national, and global issues to officials and newspapers. The arts can used to promote creativity, through painting, dance routines, and making up and acting out dramatic scenes. Whatever the method, the goal of this component of the social skills course is to put students in mind to solve problems rather than wait for someone else to tell them how.

Perseverance: Of all the skills that lead to people being successful in college or career training, and to being hired and retained in jobs, there is probably none as important as perseverance. Yes, natural talent for some activity is a benefit, and lack of it is a limitation, but it is time on target that even allows whatever talent exists to emerge. It is perseverance alone that then gets the concept learned, the paper or book written, or the technique mastered. Teachers in high-poverty schools often hear "I quit... I'm done... I don't care" when a student hits a difficult concept and is discouraged from plowing ahead, or is just plain tired of working. A deep fear of failure explains some of this reluctance to try. After all, if you don't try nobody can say you couldn't do it; you just didn't feel like doing it. A fear of success also plays a role. After all, if you succeed, you'll be expected to do the same next time.

Teachers are shocked when they see the same students taking the floor for basketball warm-ups and taking part in a complex, lengthy set of drills, or running out with the cheerleading squad to perform a complex, lengthy dance routine to perfection. Clearly, these students can persevere for hours through repeated frustrations, and can learn simply by observation and repetition, almost without instruction. Why are these strengths not evident in class?

The motivation is, of course, far higher in the sport or activity, because there is group validation for success there, whereas students, as they say, "really don't care" about their academic grades. However, exercises that reward meeting clear goals of longer and longer perseverance in memorization or simple calculations can bring some of the same sense of accomplishment. Eventually, students have to be told and shown that perseverance on boring, even mind-numbing tasks, is a skill you have to master, and then be able to switch on and off at will. Initial success can be defined as holding on for just one minute of effort. That skill can eventually grow to the hours needed for college boards and vocational qualifying exams.

Confidence in mainstream settings: The isolation from the American mainstream of a student in a high-poverty community is almost complete. A guardian may cross over at times into the middle-class parts of town to work or conduct personal business, but the student has little call to leave the comfortable womb where everybody shares a single culture. When forced out of the womb, perhaps to see a movie, there being no theaters in the ghetto, or to go on a class trip to a museum, most students will be nervous and watchful, and feel like all eyes are watching and disdaining them. Some will lapse into silence. Some will cover up their fear and discomfort with louder, stronger, and fouler use of black dialect. All will feel a physical sense of relief when the subway or city bus brings them back into familiar territory.

The core of the problem is that these students don't spend much time in the mainstream, and certainly not enough time to start to see white people as individuals so they can put aside their alienation in speaking with them. They really don't know any white people other than their teachers, and they only know them in the context of the teachers coming down into their world. Students definitely develop strong connections with white teachers, and come to see their individuality and sense their respect, but for a variety of reasons it is difficult to bring this level of comfort along when entering the largely-white mainstream.

To be successful in multi-ethnic college or training settings and in their careers, students obviously need to develop confidence in interacting with people of different income and ethnic groups. This is a challenging task for teachers. Visits to the mainstream setting don't necessarily improve the situation. Going into the mainstream as a group, the students will cling together all the more for familiarity. The visits have to be structured to ease students into individual interactions, and this is not easy. Exchange programs with middle-class or private schools are hard to arrange. Academic levels are much higher in these schools than in the high-poverty ones, and for teachers to exchange shares of classes for a day would reinforce all the more the students' lack of confidence. In any case, parents put their children in middle-class or private schools precisely so their education won't be disrupted by the academic and behavioral lags of the high-poverty students. Woe to the teacher in those schools who puts the academic program on hold to engage in social engineering in the ghetto, or make the argument that it is also important for middle and upper-class kids to learn how to interact with kids in other social classes.

The most productive exchanges involve just a handful of interested middle-class students who are hosted for a few days in a high-poverty classroom, and then invite the students they connected best with to come visit them for a few days in their school. With the partner's support, the visitors from the wrong side of the tracks generally enjoy themselves and become acclimated and confident. This sort of exchange, however, doesn't reach many students. Somehow, teachers must build mainstream confidence outside mainstream settings.

One good way to build mainstream confidence is to train students to write and videotape presentations about themselves. The assignment is to prepare a video that introduces you to a general television audience, so students have to write and speak in standard English. Other options include taping a mock news cast, or a short documentary on some of your or your friends' skills, like singing, dancing, cheering, or playing sports. All of these can be posted to students' social media pages. As long as students keep in mind that they are presenting their work to a general audience, they will gain practice and confidence in working in a mainstream mindset. As is the case for all the social skills in this course, the particular activities can be created by teachers and students. What is important is for students to know what these skills are, why they need them, and how they can practice them. Because where they are going to practice them in the short term is in their regular classes, to which we now turn.

* * *

CHAPTER 12. THE CHOICE: WASHINGTON OR DU BOIS, VOCATIONAL OR COLLEGE PREP?

The overall goal of schooling for poor students is to be prepared to join the middle class. "Arrive alive" and social skills are central to achieving that goal, but students also need to add the appropriate intellectual skills. There are two tracks that can be taken to gain those skills, vocational and college preparatory. High-poverty school districts are largely failing to provide programs on either track that move students into the middle class. Politicians have increasingly defined individual success for poor children as going to college, so when they constructed the testing edifice to improve the schools, they did so based on a college prep curriculum. As a result, vocational programs in high-poverty communities have withered away for lack of funding and enrollment, and the college prep programs have been disrupted by incorporating large numbers of students without the interest or ability to go that route.

School systems owe poor families a real choice of different ways for their children to join the middle class. They must create sound programs in both tracks that can meet overall demand while providing the remediation described in the next chapter. Students may be denied admission to a specialized program in, say, plumbing, or pre-college science, because of limited space, but they should then be guaranteed a slot in another vocational or college prep program. The tracks should start around seventh grade, because this is where boredom and frustration become evident in incorrectly placed poor children. However, this should not be the only point of choice for guardians. There should be another systematic review for all students before 9th grade, and guardians should be able to move their children to another program or another track at any time.

To help guardians make their choice, school officials must honestly describe students' academic achievements. Guardians should be told that students who are years behind grade level in reading, writing, math, or behavior will need intensive remediation before they can succeed in either track. This will tend to encourage choosing the vocational track, because the academic courses there would be practical rather than college-oriented, and the remediation needed to succeed would be easier to achieve. However, highly-motivated students should never be denied the opportunity to try the college prep track. If they fail, their guardians can always choose at that time to move them to the vocational track rather than start the college prep courses again, as the remediation approach requires.

The choice between vocational and college prep reprises the dispute in the late 19th and early 20th centuries between two great advocates of black education and liberation, Booker T. Washington and W.E.B. Du Bois. Washington focused on vocational education, Du Bois on liberal arts. Washington was the dominant figure behind the growth of the Tuskegee Institute, which provided economic liberation for Southern blacks through agricultural and industrial training. Du Bois was the dominant figure behind the growth of the NAACP, which promoted political liberation. Much had been made of their dispute, but it largely concerned political tactics in confronting segregation and violence, rather than educational theory and practice.

Washington openly rejected Du Bois's agitation for civil and voting rights as premature and dangerous for Southern blacks, although he privately funded legal challenges to segregation. His rationale for focusing on economic rather than political progress was that it would strengthen the black hand in some future contest: "...I plead for industrial education and development for the Negro not because I want to cramp him, but because I want to free him." For his part, when Du Bois wrote that, "Mr. Washington's programme practically accepts the alleged Inferiority of the Negro race," he was referring to Washington's political program of accepting segregation in return for the opportunity for Negroes to work and profit, and not his promotion of vocational educational. Indeed, Du Bois was a proponent of vocational education for the masses, just so long as it did not preclude a liberal arts education for the "talented tenth," who he hoped would teach at colleges like Tuskegee and the 5,000 Negro schools that Washington built with the aid of Sears, Roebuck chairman Julius Rosenwald and staffed with Tuskegee graduates:

> I would not deny, or for a moment seem to deny, the paramount necessity of teaching the Negro to work, and to work steadily and skillfully...but I do say, and insist upon it, that it is industrialism drunk with its vision of success, to imagine that its own work can be

accomplished without providing for the training of broadly cultured men and women to teach its own teachers, and to teach the teachers of the public schools.

Du Bois's comment was meant to encourage Washington to ensure that the future school teachers being trained at Tuskegee studied not just the practical arts of agriculture, industry, business, and home-making, but also the ancient and liberal classics and the fundamental questions they raise. His dream was an uplifting of the race through an education that imparted, and allowed its recipients to impart to others, proper values along with sound information:

> Men we shall have only as we make manhood the object of the work of the schools — intelligence, broad sympathy, knowledge of the world that was and is, and of the relation of men to it — this is the curriculum of that Higher Education which must underlie true life. On this foundation we may build bread winning, skill of hand and quickness of brain....I insist that the object of all true education is not to make men carpenters, it is to make carpenters men.

Du Bois saw clearly, as clearly as we should today, that the children of a segregated and rejected minority will be growing up under duress, and will need clear guidance on the purpose of life and on the social skills to become successful in it, whatever their career:

> [H]uman education is not simply a matter of schools; it is much more a matter of family and group life — the training of one's home, of one's daily companions, of one's social class. Now the black boy of the South moves in a black world — a world with its own leaders, its own thoughts, its own ideals. In this world he gets by far the larger part of his life training, and through the eyes of this dark world he peers into the veiled world beyond. Who guides and determines the education which he receives in his world?
>
> His teachers here are the group-leaders of the Negro people— the physicians and clergymen, the trained fathers and mothers, the influential and forceful men about him of all kinds....Do you think that if the leaders of thought among Negroes are not trained and educated thinkers, that they will have no leaders? On the contrary a hundred half-trained demagogues will still hold the places they so largely occupy now, and hundreds of vociferous busy-bodies will multiply.

Even in the throes of brutal segregation, Du Bois would have had a hard time imagining the devastation and dysfunction in the poor black community today, where the middle class has fled, leaving behind virtually no examples for children of "physicians and clergymen," let alone "trained fathers," because there are virtually no holders of college degrees living within miles of the school and so few men living with their families. As he foretold, there are always leaders in a community, but now the "hundred half-trained demagogues...and hundreds of vociferous busy-bodies" are hustlers at best and gangsters at worst. This, of course, makes teachers an even more important source of both moral and practical knowledge than they were in Du Bois's day:

> It need hardly be argued that the Negro people need social leadership more than most groups; that they have no traditions to fall back upon, no long established customs, no strong family ties, no well defined social classes. All these things must be slowly and painfully evolved....If then we start out to train an ignorant and unskilled people with a heritage of bad habits, our system of training must set before itself two great aims—the one dealing with knowledge and character, the other part seeking to give the child the technical knowledge necessary for him to earn a living under the present circumstances.

Dubois wryly noted that Washington's Tuskegee vocational experiment made his point about the need for "broadly-cultured," meaning classically-trained, teachers, because it relied heavily on the leadership of a trained black elite: "Here he has as helpers the son of a Negro senator, trained in Greek and the humanities, and graduated at Harvard; the son of a Negro congressman and lawyer, trained in Latin and mathematics, and graduated at Oberlin; he has as his wife, a woman who read Virgil and Homer in the same class room with me; he has as college chaplain, a classical graduate of Atlanta University." Then, as now, both vocational and college prep programs are needed in the highly-stressed poor black community. The choice must be made real, rather than, as currently, chimerical.

* * *

What should vocational and college prep programs look like in high-poverty school districts? The details should be determined locally, rather than at the remove of state and federal legislators and administrators. The strengths, needs, and interests of poor communities vary widely. The schools of the Shenandoah Valley, the south side of Chicago, and East Los Angeles have one thing in common, which is a majority of poor children, but nearly everything else uncommon. Student interest in various paths to the middle class and a community's ability to provide and staff the facilities for those paths vary tremendously. Successful programs will differ locally on such fundamental academic issues as the grade at which they start, the core vocational and college prep curriculum and electives, how they assign students, and what it means to graduate. The principles, though, should remain the same: vocational programs provide a clear path to immediate employment in a job that is well above the poverty line, and college prep programs track closely the skills and knowledge needed to succeed in college.

Nearly complete local flexibility will be required to reinvigorate both vocational and college prep programs in high-poverty districts. The entire framework of No Child Left Behind and its state-level predecessors, the entire notion of distorting the curriculum to game up college prep test scores, and the mandating of a Common Core curriculum must be replaced with locally-created programs whose goal is to place students in situations where they can be engaged and reach the middle class. A local approach runs counter to the creeping federal and state financial control of the "No Child" and "Race to the Top" era. The more money the federal and state governments put into the public schools, the more control they gain, because school districts are loathe to give up the funds. Poor districts, in particular, rely on federal and state funding because they have a lower per-capita tax base in local real estate, which is the primary source of most school budgets.

The need for a reduction in federal control, in particular, also runs counter to some important successes in American education: desegregation from the 1950s, Head Start and Title I anti-poverty aid from the 1960s, and Title IX and Special Education from the 1970s. All these initiatives were subversive of state and local authorities who were lagging behind the national elite's consensus about equal opportunity regardless of race, poverty, gender, and special needs. The difference today is that the national elite's consensus about testing, accountability, and universal college prep is wrong, and has failed. It's fine to use financial incentives to promote national standards and practices. Just not these ones.

We now examine possible vocational and college prep programs in terms of their curriculum and electives, placement of students, and graduation requirements. However, all finals decisions should be made at the local educational level. Federal, state, and city politicians need to admit that they have been unable to move the needle for poor children, and let local educators regain their ability to meet their needs.

Curriculum and electives

There is great variety in successful school vocational programs in America. Districts offer instruction in different aspects of office construction and home-building, such as electrical work, plumbing, masonry, carpentry, heating and air conditioning, painting, concrete and foundations, and window work. Some programs collaborate to build houses as a group project, and sell them. Traditional programs like auto mechanics, auto body, aviation mechanics, nurse's aide, and cosmetology have been augmented with new ones in computer programming, information technology and software, web design, film-making, health technician, electronic game design, hospitality, food science and cooking, and social media. Nearly all vocational programs rely on a mix of educators and practitioners for instruction. In some programs the students take their academic courses in a home high school and their vocational courses in a different facility. In others they take both in the home high school, or both in the vocational facility. The academic courses in some programs are standard college prep and in others are more practical, and oriented to the world of work and community.

College prep programs are currently not as diverse as vocational ones. They have been severely homogenized by the time and curriculum demands of testing regimes. Art, music, physical education, and clubs have been minimized as the hours devoted to tested academic subjects have been increased. Most high-poverty schools prescribe a double dose of English, math, social studies, and science every day. These classes run for at least 80 minutes, leaving virtually no time for electives. However, there are a number of successful specialty middle and high schools serving poor students that have built enough political power to withstand, or at least compromise with, test-driven homogenization. Public schools offer programs in performing arts such as music, dance, and drama, visual arts such as painting, sculpture, and photography, written arts such as poetry, plays, and short stories, and academic disciplines such as science, pre-law, Latin, and ancient literature. Again, educators are augmented by practitioners in many of these disciplines.

Whatever flexibility has been achieved in vocational and college prep programs today should be greatly magnified. The path to employment in the non-academic vocational disciplines like masonry and web design should be eased by dropping certifications and requirements for teachers. Academic courses like math and English could work more and more alongside the non-academic courses, showing how to use their techniques in the field and awarding credit for doing so. College prep programs too should experiment with non-traditional courses and teachers in the arts and in community disciplines like government and advocacy, both to promote classic college skills and the hidden college skills of creativity and making connections between academic and real-life situations. As the federally-driven push for test-based accountability and a common curriculum recedes, unions and associations will be so relieved that they may be more open to compromising on experimental programs in which uncertified teachers handle special subjects, so long as they can represent these new teachers.

The elementary school preparation for both tracks can be the same, but would have to be significantly softened and broadened from today's mini-college prep approach. Test mania has captured the elementary school curriculum in high-poverty schools, pushing teaching of testing skills and content down into kindergarten, and even into pre-kindergarten. By second grade the curriculum typically mimics middle school college prep material, and throughout elementary school music and the fine and dramatic arts have become afterthoughts. For high-poverty children, elementary school should be a time to explore the books, engage in the discussions, write and present the stories, and create and discuss the art and music projects they don't have at home.

Students who might be ready for early college prep will not be hampered by waiting until seventh grade, and students who are essentially disengaged will be able to engage with school by relating it to their world. The Common Core focus on promoting a deep understanding of the construction of mathematics and language is inappropriate for the vast majority of elementary school students, in or out of poverty. It is far more important for them to use math in games and memorize math facts for rapid computation, and to use language in writing and presentations about their lives. There will be time enough for those choosing the college prep track to undertake conceptual explorations in secondary school.

Placement

Two fundamental issues must be addressed when giving families a choice between vocational and college prep schools at the middle school and then at the high school level. First, who gets to go to the various schools? Second, how do you graduate? The first issue is not so important for rural districts and small cities with one or two comprehensive high schools that everybody attends, although they will face it in assigning students to programs within a school. But in large cities or suburban counties with from dozens to over a hundred secondary schools it is crucial. These districts are so different from each other in their social and political history that it would be foolish to prescribe and enforce a single framework for placement. Schools can be successful with a wide variety of placement plans. Districts need to experiment to find what works for them, educationally and politically.

Most districts already have a few elite admission schools, usually for college prep but often for the arts. The success of those schools leads to the conclusion that as much as possible, all secondary schools should be admission schools. The concept of a "neighborhood" secondary school is inimical to the goals of high-poverty middle and high schools. The mission of a school district is to serve students, not the community as a whole. The drive to keep schools open for the benefit or pride of the neighborhood artificially sustains them with non-attending, non-performing students as well as a high share of transfer students. Principals try to keep enough bodies on the books to justify their jobs, and those of their teachers and staff. But it is students who should be saved, not schools. Low enrollment in an admissions scheme, like students failing courses in an academic scheme, should be welcomed, not gamed or denied. These realities are valuable data that help districts do their job. Principals and other staff from schools that close because of low enrollment can always seek employment at the schools whose enrollment has gone up.

There are many ways to provide family choice as well as school selectivity in secondary schools. Most large districts already have complex systems for assignment involving many of the components of the process proposed below, although they usually add in geographic assignment as a factor. A suggested process is offered here as an example, based on principles that address the needs of high-poverty students and schools. It would work roughly as follows:

Early in the sixth and eighth grades guardians would meet with school counselors to review their students' interests as well as their skill levels, as determined by whatever math and reading tests the district wished to use. They would learn about the various vocational and college prep middle or high schools in the district, some of which would be housed in the same building. The guardians could choose to include the student in the meeting, but it would not be required. They could then take their children to visit as many of the schools as they wanted before making their choices by a December deadline, and providing the district with an application listing their top ten or so preferences, in order. Students would also submit handwritten statements about their lives, their skills and interests, and their hopes for the future.

Schools would review the applications, grades, and tests of students who placed them first on their list, and decide within a few weeks which students to admit to reach their ideal size for their current space. Schools could hold interviews or auditions before making their decisions about which students best fit their mission. Students who were not admitted would be referred to the next school on their list. The process would repeat, for shorter periods of a week at a time, until all students found a placement by the end of March. This date would give schools an early start in finding teachers to meet their anticipated enrollment and interests. While it is likely that about half of low-income students will end up in a vocational school, it is possible that initially a higher share will choose, and be admitted to, a college prep school. The low-enrollment vocational schools should, at least for the first year, continue to operate, because failure or disillusionment with college prep work may encourage a significant number of families to ask for transfers during and after that first year.

Each district's experience over time will guide changes in the shares attending college prep and vocational programs. It is not even necessary that these programs be in different schools. For example, one building could encompass separate programs for college prep and for entry-level hotel work, or for college prep pre-engineering and vocational mechanics. However, it may be easier to organize classes in separate schools for college prep and vocational.

The howls of protest that would greet such a plan would come from advocates for poor families who prefer a pure lottery system rather than selection by the schools, and from wealthier families who want "neighborhood" preferences. Neither complaint withstands scrutiny from the perspective of maximizing the chances for success for poor children. Fortunately, these two complaints would balance each other out in operation, since elite college prep schools would be skewed toward students from wealthier families because of their higher achievement levels at the time of selection. As a result, these schools would give wealthier families the selective environment they desire.

A lottery system smacks of a guaranteed place regardless of student performance before or after enrollment, whereas education demands responsibility on the part of the student. Lotteries deny to principals the authority they need to run their schools, and place many students in situations where they are destined to fail. The insistence of white and wealthier families that their children attend "neighborhood" schools is no more logical than a lottery, but it will be politically tougher to resist. In fact many wealthier families choose their neighborhoods precisely so they can have their kids go to public school in them, with families "like theirs." Their motivation is not necessarily racist, and is probably more about class.

The wealthier parents are seeking the order and success, not the skin color, they associate with white and wealthy schools. Indeed, black middle-class families flee chaotic neighborhoods to seek the same order and success. Poor black families may like the convenience of neighborhood schools, but they have historically been willing and even eager for their children to travel well across town to obtain a better education. Ironically, for all their talk about the importance of a neighborhood school, many wealthy families exhibit the same behavior, making long drives or paying for a bus to take their children to distant private schools, from elementary school on up.

It would be certainly more democratic and probably more academically effective to place students without regard to geography right from the start, in elementary schools. Given the extreme residential segregation by race and class in American cities and suburbs, though, the political resistance to such a policy would recall either the flight of white families to private academies in the desegregated South in the 1960s or the violent protests in the Boston integration program of the 1970s. Whatever scheme district officials might cook up for integrated elementary schools, white families and wealthier families of all ethnicities will find a way, by hook, crook, moving, or private school, not to place their children in schools dominated by low-income children.

Recourse by the wealthy to private schools has already resulted in most big cities having too few white students in the public schools to provide meaningful integration. Eliminating geographic preferences for elementary schools would finish the job, weakening the districts' ability to justify their tax burden. While there are exceptions, and there could and should be more, most districts planning secondary school placements will have to accept that the students arriving from elementary school will have had a segregated education thus far. For secondary schools, though, an admissions-only policy would provide elite college prep settings in which the white and the wealthier would be over-represented, stemming their flow from the district.

The depth of the national phenomenon of white flight from city schools can be seen in Washington, DC. Over 40 percent of the population is white, and while the share of white students in the public schools has doubled in recent years, it is still only ten percent. This doubling is due to a spate of investment in heavily-white elementary schools in wealthier neighborhoods and the siphoning off of black students by the growing charter school system, which is only five percent white. The white share in the DC public schools drops off sharply in secondary schools, which have larger attendance zones and would be majority black and Hispanic even if white parents remained in the system instead of choosing private schools. Even within the few secondary schools that whites attend, the correlation of ethnicity, income, and parental educational status tends to re-segregate students, with whites being overrepresented in the more challenging classes and programs.

In every large city or suburban district the pattern is similar. White students are underrepresented in public elementary schools, and dramatically so in the secondary schools. The same is undoubtedly true for middle and higher-income black and Hispanic students, although the data are harder to obtain. Simply put, families who can afford to will find a way to avoid sending their children to school with the underclass.

The placement process described above would dramatically reduce disruption in classrooms and halls, because families will have chosen the school, and nobody will simply have been assigned. As described in the next chapter, schools would remove from class and place in non-credit remediation for a quarter any student who fails a quarter in a credit-bearing course or whose behavior disrupts a class. This approach would quickly pare down the college prep track by encouraging guardians to avoid a college prep placement in the first place if their students lacked the skills and more importantly the interest needed to persevere to success. It would also encourage those students to transfer to a vocational school, rather than languish in remediation or be constantly starting their courses over.

How would special education students be assigned under this process? Gingerly, with all due attention to their needs and the laws and lawsuits governing their conditions. Schools may not discriminate against students based on their learning, emotional, or physical difficulties. This applies to admissions as well. Guardians usually welcome special schools and self-contained classrooms for their severely-challenged children. They may choose such placements for their moderately challenged children, but they cannot be forced to do so. This reality places burdens on any school, but the social benefits to other students of helping their challenged peers can be tremendous. In any event, it's the law.

High-poverty secondary schools may have up to 30 or 40 percent of students categorized as special education. Most students gain this designation simply by being well below grade level in achievement, but some have identifiable disabilities that impede their progress. Under federal law, designation of a child as "special education" requires the writing up of an IEP, an Individualized Education Plan. In an IEP the school promises, but rarely delivers, a certain number of hours of special instruction, which can be provided in a regular classroom, in a "pull-out" session with a special education teacher, or in a separate class of special education students. These plans are generally honored in the breach, and their dozens of benchmarks, such as "student will learn all math facts to 12 times 12 with 85 percent accuracy," are rarely pursued and even more rarely achieved. Cumbersome and in need of reform as it is, the special education system represents a great advance, in that it operationalizes important rights that were previously unprotected. All schools, even the most elite college prep schools, should admit special education students who they believe can succeed with additional resources, and then provide those resources. At some point, though, failure must be acknowledged rather than hidden. Not everybody, special education or not, can succeed in competitive schools.

Graduation

What should a high school diploma represent? We can start with the awareness that for most high-poverty schools it represents nothing at present, because so many students who receive passing grades have not earned them or are simply graduated by a principal's waiver. Schools districts, and the colleges and employers who rely on them to certify readiness, have nowhere to go but up. A phony diploma is worse than there being none at all. The demand for metrics of success like graduation rate has obscured the underlying reality of failure. Failure is good, and should be accepted, because it means that success can be defined. It is a diagnostic that helps us understand our challenges. We are not shooting for 100 percent graduation, or any particular percentage because, despite the best of encouragement, 100 percent of students do not attend or try enough, and the percentage who do will fluctuate. The purpose of secondary school is not to graduate, but to learn. Graduation should be seen as a measure of learning rather than a goal in itself.

Rather than confront the culture of fraud that records unjustified passing grades, some states have sought to validate diplomas through exit exams like the New York State "Regents" or the Virginia Standards of Learning. Half of the states now require passing exit exams to graduate, and because these states tend to be larger in population and have larger cities, they contain 70 percent of students and probably an even higher percentage of low-income students. Because the institutional goal of getting nearly everybody who is attending to graduate remains the same, the exams defeat their own purpose. States respond to low passing rates by lowering the passing standards, and they provide various waivers and alternative routes, ranging from portfolios and work experience to on-line "general educational development" exams, so that students who fail exit exams can demonstrate "mastery" in some other way. Some states offer differentiated degrees, such as vocational, basic, and honors, and all, properly, have special degrees for special education that reward attendance and effort rather than achievement.

Many districts require a set number of hours of "community service" to graduate. This forced volunteerism is widely evaded and falsely certified in high-poverty schools. Even with credits being handed out to encourage attendance at after-school activities, few students focus on the hundred or more hours they must serve until well into their senior years. Then the guidance counselors are under pressure to award the credits in unjustified amounts. At the other end of the income spectrum, wealthy students can meet their requirements through package vacations to the Caribbean or Africa, where a few hours are set aside from tanning and scuba diving to help paint a local school. Schools should encourage, but not insist on, both community service and political action that the student thinks will address the root causes of the community's problems. It is more appropriate for schools to offer courses that explore why people are poor than to force students to help them in their poverty.

Strangest of all in the volunteering world is the day of service many schools and colleges offer, and some require, on the birthday of Martin Luther King, Jr. He never worked at a charity soup kitchen; he was a socialist who organized the poor to demand that the state be the employer of last resort, and that it provide relief directly. He never built houses for wounded veterans; he was an anti-imperialist who organized students and other citizens to march against the war in Vietnam that got them wounded in the first place.

What is most important for high-poverty students is that their degree be meaningful. The diploma must become an announcement to the world that they have demonstrated the ability to persevere. Without attendance and effort, most students will be unable to pass courses and graduate. A vocational diploma should also be proof that students have mastered their technical skills and attained a basic level of skill in reading, writing, and mathematics that will allow them to be responsible citizens and useful employees. A college prep degree should be proof that the graduate can successfully handle the demands of being a freshman at an open-admission community college. Honors degrees and college boards can provide additional information for more selective colleges.

Because curriculum should be locally determined, and vary between and within vocational and college prep programs, just as it does between private schools, so must decisions about whether a student passes a course, and how many and what type of courses are needed for degree, be made at a local level. Just as principals must be empowered to decide, without recourse to complex checklists, which teachers should find a new career, teachers must be empowered to decide, without recourse to national, state, or even district exams, which students have passed their course. There is nothing magic about a cut-off number, be it 60 percent for passing or 65 percent. In South Africa, the percentage score required is 50. On some state proficiency exams it is 33. The number is only meaningful when you know the difficulty of the exam, and teachers are the only ones who know their students well enough to write an exam that covers their material at an appropriate level of difficulty.

As long as teachers are rewarded, rather than punished, for recording as failures students who have shown they are not yet ready for the next year's curriculum, they will be the best at making that judgment. A nationally, state, or district-normed "end of course" exam is a good check for teachers to use on their judgment, but because some students who do grasp the material still test poorly, it should never be the sole criterion for passing. The same principle holds true for exit exams, and diplomas in general. Principals who are not under pressure to achieve certain graduation rates can go back to being educators. They can work with faculty to make both the overall judgment about what constitutes a degree and the individual judgments about which students are ready, and which need a little more seasoning before they can be presented to the world.

* * *

CHAPTER 13. TRIAGE: REMEDIATION FOR MISBEHAVIOR AND ACADEMIC SHORTFALL

The two greatest barriers to success in non-selective, high-poverty secondary schools are inappropriate behavior and a lack of academic preparation for the assigned course. On the behavioral side, disruption, from talking to fighting, absence, and lack of effort by about half of the students keeps the other half from getting to their business. Worse, they set a low standard for behavior and effort to which, to quote George Washington on false patriotism, the more promising half retires. On the academic side, most students are five or more years behind grade level in reading skills and math. Through no fault of their own they slow the rest of the class to a frustrating crawl. Even after students move closer to a good fit for their interests as proposed in the previous chapter, with a choice between viable vocational and college prep schools with locally-determined curriculums, most high-poverty schools will still need a revolution in thinking about the problems of misbehavior and academic shortfall.

The previous chapter made a plea to permit failure, and to make the goal of school not to graduate students, but rather to give them the opportunity to graduate. Similarly, the goal of a single course should not be to pass students, but rather to give them the opportunity to pass. If they don't pass it should be seen not as a failure or tragedy, but rather as good information and an opportunity to meet their needs. Students who disrupt others, who attend little or make little effort, or who fall behind badly during a 10-week quarter or fail at the end of it should be referred out of the class for non-credit remediation for whatever ails them. This will allow the students who are following middle class norms of behavior to succeed, and allow those who are not to following these norms to grow by finally getting intense attention for their challenges.

There would be no returning to the same class after disruption, chronic absence, weak effort, or failure, as is now the case. Students referred from a class for behavioral or academic remediation would leave that cohort forever, so as not to slow it down on their return. If referred for misbehavior, meaning disruption or lack of attendance or effort, they would first receive behavioral and family support from an expanded corps of social workers. When released by their social worker they would be tested for grade level in math, reading, and writing, and then receive appropriate remediation for the rest of the quarter from math and English teachers assigned for that purpose. Students referred for academics would go straight to the tests and academic remediation. The quarter spent in remediation would not provide credit toward graduation. Students would restart the course from which they were referred, or another course, with a new group in the following quarter if their remediation social worker and teachers judged them ready for it.

Students referred for disruption in public spaces, such as the entry space, the halls, the cafeteria, or a sports event, would be referred to remediation during the lunch period for the entire quarter. They would take their meals in a separate room, with a social worker, who would work with them for the lunch break. The details may vary by school, but the principle behind the remediation would be clear: nobody is allowed to disrupt another's education.

Particularly in the first year, as perhaps half the students in a high-poverty school were referred for remediation, the school would have to adjust its staffing. Classes would shrink throughout the first quarter as disruptive students and those refusing to do assigned work are referred to social workers and those functioning at years behind grade level are referred to teachers. At the end of that quarter the classes would shrink even more as students were referred for academic remediation because of a failing grade. The shrunken continuing classes would then have to be combined, with the excess teachers assigned to help the referred students get to an academic level that would allow them to be successful in the course from which they were removed, or in a more appropriate course. Many of those teachers would then be assigned to the new credit courses as students emerged from remediation for the new quarter.

This system of triage, in which students who are ready are moved right along with their cohort and those who are not are taken off the credit track and placed in remediation, sounds cold and callous at first. On reflection, though, it should be clear that this system is far kinder to far more students than the current one. At present hardly anybody has the chance to succeed.

Under a system of strict referral and remediation, everybody would. It would allow half to learn and the other half to grow. It would certainly encourage a share of students, discouraged by constant referral and unable or unwilling to take advantage of remediation, to drop out. However, under the current system of pushing students into classes for which they are not behaviorally or academically ready, about half the students in high-poverty schools eventually drop out anyway. Even worse, they drag down the behavior and achievement of the other half before they go.

The principle of referral for remediation should virtually eliminate suspensions and expulsions. By enrolling students, schools have declared responsibility for their education. They cannot shirk this responsibility because it turns out to be difficult. Suspension only drives a student farther behind, and expulsion is an abdication of responsibility that transfers the burden on somebody else. Charter schools, which have far higher rates of expulsion than public schools, should be required to care for their students in precisely the same way as a condition for taking public funding. The only exception to a ban on expulsion would be for a crime of violence against another student or staff member, since the victim should not be required to be reminded of the crime daily.

By referring students to remediation rather than suspending or expelling them, schools would be showing students that they are committed to them, and will educate them no matter how they behave or perform. Failing to behave, attend, or make an effort in remediation will only bring more intense remediation and attendant counseling and family support, not punishment. Students fail for a reason, and remediation makes finding and correcting the reason the priority for the school and the student. Instead of mindlessly placing students in their grade-level courses where they will be frustrated and fail, remediation tries to take the students where they are and prepare them to be successful when they begin those courses with a new cohort.

Remediation could take place in the school or in a specialized center elsewhere. Different schools and districts would make that choice differently. Wherever you were referred for remediation, the same principle would apply: you would not return to your original class after the quarter or more of behavioral counseling or academic support, but instead wait for a new course to begin. Whether on-site or at a different location, students in remediation would remain part of the original school until their guardians decided to apply elsewhere or the students reached the age when they are permitted to drop out or seek a general educational development degree.

Remediation for disruption and lack of effort

Strictly applied, a "no disruption" rule for remediation would just about clean out every classroom in a high-poverty school. Nearly every child, at some point in the year, and indeed in the week, will reach their particular threshold for frustration and act out or resist working. The sweetest, most hardest-working student can surprise a teacher by suddenly becoming volcanically angry and stubborn. The cause of the melt-down can be clear, like having seen a friend killed or a mother beaten the night before, or obscure, like reaching a personal limit for the pressures of poverty and adolescence. The first few times it happens, the teacher may even think it is a joke, that the "good" student is engaging in tongue-in-cheek play-acting to make the humorous point that he or she too knows how to act tough.

"Emeraldia" was one of my star math students. She was a big girl, popular and quick with a quip, always happy and smiling, always cheered loudly by the other students when performing with the "step" team, as if they especially appreciated the extra effort she had to make to keep her bulk on the beat. A retired principal who was visiting our class to describe a college tutoring program interrupted her presentation to tell Emeraldia to stop checking her cell-phone in her bag. Emeraldia erupted, screaming, "Get the (expletive) out my face. Ain't no black (expletive) tell me what to do!" This forced me to walk her out of the room and keep her out, as my rules required, until a guardian brought her back for a conference. Stunned by this behavior, I sent her to her favorite person in the school, the social worker who was her coach on the step team. The social worker told me that some "family issues" with her mother the night before had left Emeraldia feeling raw, that she was staying with an aunt, and that telling her mother about the disruption would probably result in a beating. The three of us talked over the incident, and nothing like it occurred again. The retired principal was just the wrong black woman at the wrong time telling Emeraldia what to do.

Sending a generally successful student like Emeraldia to remediation for this outburst, which would set her back by at least a quarter in math, might seem counter-productive. On the other hand, just because the disruption is understandable does not reduce its impact on the other students' ability to do their work, and on their general understanding of what is acceptable in the classroom. It would also give a social worker the chance to counsel Emeraldia and perhaps even help firm up her living arrangements or strengthen her relationship with her mother. Teachers and administrators would have to make judgments about real cases like these when deciding whether to refer a student to remediation. There is always a reason for disruption, for talking, for laying your head down on the desk and refusing to work, for a rotten day. Maybe a teacher could institute a two-strike or three-strike rule. There are no easy answers, but schools need to err on the side of referral if they are to have any hope of helping the greatest number of students succeed.

Referral is not punishment. It is placement in a more favorable environment for the student's needs, thereby making the class itself a more favorable environment for the other students' needs. Consider the problem of homework, which is needed to cement concepts learned in class. Completed homework should be the ticket for admission to the classroom every day. Otherwise, students will not do it. Students who consistently don't do homework should of course be taught how to organize the task and helped to plan a time and place to do the work. They should be given a teacher's phone number to get help if they are stuck. But if they persist in not doing the homework, perhaps by no fault of their own in a chaotic house and life, they simply don't belong in the class, and should be referred to remediation. The social worker there may be able to address some of the issues in the students' lives that keep them from succeeding. Another benefit to the referral is that the class as a whole, and many of the students who initially do not do homework, will rise to the challenge if the rule is clear.

In the remediation setting the social workers would help students write and talk about, and think through, their challenges. They would reach out to guardians and other family members to try to resolve conflicts and establish systems for supporting the students. There will need to be many more social workers hired to make a referral system credible. And they will need more tools at their disposal, like cash for short-term emergencies and a low enough case-load to allow them to visit and work with the guardians and relatives. There is really no way around this financial burden for the schools. To reach and help troubled teenagers, you have to allow social workers time to get to know them, and to get outside of school and work with them where they experience their problems.

Academic remediation

The academic remediation program in a non-selective high-poverty college prep secondary school will have to be substantial. Particularly after grades are posted for the first quarter and even throughout the first year, as policies of challenging tests, honest grades, and referral out of the classroom for failing build credibility with students and guardians, up to half of a college prep school might initially be placed in academic remediation. In vocational schools, the less rigorous academic work and vocational courses would not require as strong a background, and so there would be less academic referral.

After their social workers judged them ready to handle their behavioral challenges, students who had been referred for behavioral reasons would, like those referred for academics, be given grade-placement tests in math, reading, and writing. It would be clear from the results that many would need significant academic remediation before they could be successful in the classroom when they started a course again in the next quarter. Many teachers in the school would have to be assigned to remediation duties in the early part of the year, many of them for the entire day.

The remediation teachers would not be working on grade-level content in math, English, social studies, or science, because the remediation period would not provide academic credit. The goal of the remediation period would be to strengthen basic skills in math, reading, and writing so that the students could be successful when they start their credit courses again. A teacher's remediation classroom would resemble a tutoring session, not a group instructional session. The student would have very different deficits, which they could address with work on assignments that are appropriate for their current levels. The initial assignments would be at levels even easier than students' current achievement levels, so they could be successful and learn how to manage the assignments.

Numerous computer and on-line programs exist for math and reading that students can work on at their own pace to move from lower to higher levels of skill. Teachers would assign and supervise the work, moving between children rather than teaching concepts to the group. Both students and teachers would be working to get back into regular academic classes in courses that would start with the next quarter. With the start of each quarter, fewer and fewer students would be referred for academic failure because the additional time spent learning basics would have given them a stronger background for the grade-level work. Some, though, would continue to fail, and be referred again and again for academic remediation. At a college prep school their lack of progress would eventually convince their guardians to try the vocational track.

The logistics of remediation

What would remediation look like at the school level? At selective high-poverty schools, for academics or for the arts, it would barely exist. Students who are successful enough to be admitted to such schools tend to have positive behaviors that match, and are partly responsible for, their achievements. Compared to other poor students, they also tend to have guardians who are able to enforce good behavior at home and solid effort at school. Remediation would be required, though, in non-selective schools, meaning the majority of schools in a high-poverty district that take students regardless of academic level.

Let's imagine a cohort of 200 seventh graders who have just started a non-selective, high-poverty middle school that offers the classic college prep curriculum of math, English, social studies, and science. For the first few years of a remediation approach, this scenario would also apply to a non-selective college prep high school. After that, with students who have less motivation and strength in college prep already heading for vocational programs after middle school, a college prep high school would largely consist of students who can meet expectations for behavior and effort, so remediation would be focused on middle schools of both varieties and on vocational high schools.

Of our 200 seventh graders, probably 90 percent live in a single-parent household, with a mother, aunt, or grandmother who has chosen college prep over vocational for the child's middle school placement. The average math and reading levels are around second grade, and the students typically come to school less than 60 percent of the time. Assuming that classes meet daily in four periods of about 80 minutes each, class size is 25, and each teacher has three periods of class and one of preparation, there are three teachers for each of the full-year subjects: math, English, social studies, and science. These 12 core teachers are augmented by those for whatever music, gym, art, language, ROTC, or other courses are offered by the quarter, and probably three full-time special education teachers who visit classrooms to support students.

Let us predict that 80 of these 200 seventh graders are referred for behavioral reasons during the first quarter, some for more than one period. They come to remediation during all the periods for which they have been referred. Those who have been referred for disruption in a public space, like the entrance, halls, or cafeteria come to remediation during lunch rather than join the rest of the students in the cafeteria. The school has to hire at least four full-time social workers to review the referred students' behavioral needs and work with them and their families during the quarter.

During the period for which students have been referred they are assigned to a room with a social worker, who meets with them one at a time. When not meeting with the social worker, they work on writing assignments for the social worker about their lives and challenges. The period feels long, boring, and quiet. Guardians are asked to come in at least once a week to meet with their children and the social worker. This motivates both adult and child to get the problem solved so it would not simply occur again, and result in referral again from the new class in the next quarter. We can assume that guardians for 20 of the 80 referred students transfer them to another school, generally a vocational one, during this first quarter.

After a few weeks of remediation, with their behavioral issues addressed to the social worker's satisfaction, the 60 remaining referred students take low-stress, grade-placement tests for math and reading. They are then transferred over to academic remediation for the remainder of the quarter to work on material that is appropriate to their achievement levels, so they can gain strength for their new classes. Let us assume that ten students who disrupt in their remediation assignment by misbehavior or absence move to a more intense level of remediation, with referral to a family therapist for misbehavior or to local child protective services for truancy. As these interventions are successful, perhaps five of these ten students rejoin academic remediation. The other five transfer to another school.

During this first quarter perhaps 20 of the 120 students remaining in the regular classes are referred directly to academic remediation because they are failing badly on early quizzes and clearly not able to participate with the rest of the class. Again, some are referred for more than one class. They join the 55 behavioral cases that are staying in college prep rather than transferring to vocational schools. Let us assume further than 10 of these 20 academic referrals soon transfer to a vocational program as well.

By this point in the quarter 35 of the 200 students have left the college prep seventh grade for another school, 65 are in academic remediation for one or more subjects, and 100 remain moving forward in all their credit bearing classes. Only half as many core teachers are now required for the remaining 100 on-pace students, so there are six teachers available for assignment to remediation for the 65 students. As a result, the remediation classes are smaller than the credit-bearing classes, with about 20 students in each. Math and science teachers are assigned for the math remediation, and social studies and English teachers for the reading and writing remediation. The students who were in the classes that were cancelled when those teachers went to teach remediation have been added to the remaining classes, taking up slots opened by referral to remediation.

All of this requires creative scheduling by administrators and flexibility by teachers and students. When the results of the first quarter come in, things get even more complicated. Perhaps 20 of the 100 students who remained in their classes throughout the first quarter failed, and so are referred for academic remediation. This reduces the on-pace cohort to 80, requiring a little more consolidation and the movement of one final teacher to remediation. However, nearly all of the 65 remaining students who spent part of the first quarter in remediation are now ready to start their course again, and most of the remediation teachers now return with those students to the classroom and the new core classes. For subjects like gym, music, or language, students may have to wait until they are offered again the next semester or year.

From this point on, things calm down, because the students who were referred during the first quarter now have better academic skills and, more important, the knowledge that disruption and lack of attendance or effort will lead to referral and another one-semester delay in their progress toward graduation. Fewer and fewer will be referred during the rest of the year, so fewer and fewer social workers and teachers will be needed in remediation. Perhaps ten students remain in remediation at the start of the third quarter, or second semester. Perhaps more five transfer to vocational or other programs at that point.

So, what is the likely situation of the 200 students half-way through the year?

- 80 are working hard and behaving well, and are on pace with the original cohort.
- 70 are working hard and behaving well, and are one quarter behind in one or more of their classes. It is likely that at some point in the years before graduation they can pass a summer school course that is designed to teach and test the final quarter of the course for which they referred.
- 40 have left the college prep program for a vocational or other school, where they are more likely to be working hard and behaving well. They are less likely to be referred for remediation at that school, both because the academics are easier and more relevant to their interests and because they have had the referral experience, and want to avoid having it again.
- Perhaps 10 are still in remediation, and are one or two quarters behind in one or more courses.

This tally necessarily ignores the unpredictable and significant movement of poor families in and out of a school district during the year. In addition, there will always be a small number of families who either disintegrate or actively resist the tracking efforts of school authorities and then child protective services when their child is chronically absent, and has effectively dropped out. However, of those students remaining under the district's jurisdiction, more than 95 percent are now in a setting where they can be successful, compared to virtually none under the original scheme. By allowing failure, accepting delay, prohibiting disruption, and remediating academic and behavioral deficits without credit, we can give nearly every child a chance to succeed. The rest is up to them and their family.

* * *

CHAPTER 14. STRENGTHENING THE FAMILY: JOBS AND EARLY SUPPORT

Families in distress produce children in distress. To have stronger students, we must have stronger families, and that requires a new approach to addressing the challenges of poverty. All educators know of rare cases of poor children overcoming crippling family conditions of neglect, abuse, and homelessness to graduate and join the middle class. The numbers, though, are not large enough to count on as a matter of policy. The root of the problem of high-poverty schools is poverty itself, which enervates, drains, and complicates families' ability to raise capable children. Fortunately, there are ways to strengthen the families of the poor students of both today and tomorrow, if we are willing to invest a fraction of the money we are currently spending, to little effect, on their education.

The physical, cognitive, and social damage suffered by children raised in poverty is indisputable, and must be addressed if we want to make noticeable progress in moving poor students into the middle class. That damage starts before birth, and is largely accomplished before children turn two. However, even at the high school level a struggling student from a high-risk background can be dramatically more successful with support from a more involved and more stable family. The school-based proposals in this book of a choice between vocational and college prep, true grading, and referral based on behavioral and academic level can give many children a chance for a middle-class life. Many more will have that chance if they start school with stronger bodies, minds, motivation, and self-discipline than they do today, and are raised by parents with regular, decent-paying jobs.

Attacking poverty, like educating children, is a humbling task. There is no silver bullet, many unique structural and historical barriers must be addressed, and any approach that works at one time and place may be inappropriate for another. Consider the efforts by Western countries, the World Bank, and private organizations to "save Africa" by "ending poverty" since the days of colonialism. Despite a trillion of dollars of donated cash, goods, and services, most Africans have not escaped grinding poverty, nor joined the rest of the world's path to longer life expectancy.

The World Bank cannot address some of the underlying causes of this failure because it is actually run by the world's wealthiest countries, and they keep Africa from sharing in the wealth of refining and manufacturing by paying off dictators for exporting raw materials. Poor governance, corruption, civil war, loyalty to one's ethnic nation rather than one's country, lack of investment, and myriad other domestic explanations are offered, but the core reason that Africa is underdeveloped is because the historical seizure of Africa's political and economic power by brutal colonialism has not been reversed. Former colonial powers, the United States, and more recently China have simply replaced colonial administrators with local ruling partners, and continued to arm them so they can rule in return for access to raw materials and markets.

Whatever the political context in which people, ethnic groups, and countries find themselves, experts debate whether international anti-poverty efforts should focus on spurring economic growth that gives governments and residents purchasing power so they can eventually afford clean water and modern medicine, or focus on simply delivering the water and medicine right away, often through foreign aid programs. The answer is both, of course. China has seen a tremendous reduction in poverty and a similar increase in life expectancy through rapid, capitalistic economic growth. Socialist Cuba reduced the worst effects of poverty with direct services that were heavily subsidized by the Soviet Union. These lessons from international efforts are relevant for the United States. While the early support and jobs programs proposed below and strong overall growth can both help break the grip of poverty, irreversible progress will come only when the poor dramatically increase their political power.

A remarkable boost in political power has occurred twice for African-Americans, first during Reconstruction, when their rights were guaranteed from the end of the Civil War until 1876 by military occupation of the South, and then during the 1960s, when fear of black protest and violent revolt brought a host of voting reforms, economic benefits, and opportunities for jobs to the urban ghettos and the then-tiny black middle class. Until another boost is forced upon the political system, the two best ways to strengthen poor black children — and poor children of other ethnic groups as well —

will be by finding jobs for their parents, and by supporting their parents in improving health and intellectual stimulation in the crucial pre-natal period and infancy.

Jobs

America's poverty rate remains high, upwards of 20 percent, despite significant spending to lower it. In addition to a proliferation of efforts by private foundations and individuals, there is no doubt that taxpayers are doing their share. A credible compilation by the libertarian Cato Institute identifies a trillion dollars of annual spending by all levels of government, 75 percent of it at the federal level, on programs specifically targeted to help the poor. That amounts to $20,000 each year for every person in poverty, raising for Cato and others the obvious alternative that perhaps those funds should simply be given to the poor as cash, rather than spent on programs.

This concept surfaces repeatedly across our political spectrum. It hearkens back to one of Daniel Patrick Moynihan's proposals, which was endorsed by both President Nixon and his challenger George McGovern in the 1972 election but never implemented, of a guaranteed annual income to help people rise out of poverty. Liberal economist James Tobin, conservative economist Milton Friedman, and anti-poverty crusader Michael Harrington all endorsed the concept then, but it foundered on the American public's moral problem with solving poverty directly by just making the poor wealthier. That approach seems to offend our sense that the "deserving" poor should be helped, but not the dissolute poor. This sense found expression in the 1996 Republican Congress and its "welfare reform" bill that imposed minimum wage work requirements, cutting off support to adults who were unable to find or hold these jobs. The bill also instructed poor women to get married before having babies, and reinforced the order with various cash penalties and incentives.

Unlike King Canute of legend, who facetiously commanded the tide not to come in to make a point to his courtiers about the limited power of government over natural phenomena, the Republican leadership actually seemed to believe that their demand that the poor work and get married would succeed. All it succeeded in doing was dramatically reducing the cash provided to the most challenged poor families. President Clinton "triangulated" politically and signed the bill, which led to the resignation of his top anti-poverty aides over the counter-productive nature of these moralistic restrictions.

Political problems aside, how credible is the concept of converting today's poverty funding to cash transfers? Half of all poverty spending is for Medicaid, one of Lyndon Johnson's creations that has been, literally, a lifesaver for generations of Americans. Health insurance would be just about as expensive for individuals to buy themselves, so if we want poor people to have access to medical care, there really is only $10,000 per person left to consider as a cash grant. Many of the remaining poverty programs are already cash-like, including the next five largest ones: Food Stamps (now called the Supplemental Nutrition Assistance Program) at $75 billion, the Earned Income Tax Credit and the Child Tax Credit, which each return about $60 billion to minimum wage workers, Supplemental Security Income for the elderly and disabled at $50 billion, and Welfare (now called Temporary Assistance to Needy Families) at $30 billion. There are some programs that do not put cash directly into poor people's pockets, such as college tuition, aid to high-poverty schools, housing subsidies, job training, and care for the homeless. Distributing these small funds as cash is unlikely to make much of a difference in upward mobility.

So if a guaranteed income is not on the table, what should be done? What is missing in all these spending programs is the source of all family stability: the job. Moynihan's analysis returned repeatedly to the benefit to family structure and strength of a well-paying job. In the social context of the 1960s, he focused on the need for the man in house to be employed, and that focus is if anything more relevant today after the dramatic increase in absent fatherhood. We can always hope for the sort of strong and broad-based economic growth that reaches down to the lowest economic strata with living-wage employment that disrupts the transmission of poverty to new generations. In a global economy, though, it is virtually impossible for a single national government to arrange that. In the meantime, we should pursue the areas of direct spending that has the most impact on poverty, which is assuring living-wage jobs for parents,

Like the Cato Institute, House Budget Committee chair Paul Ryan in his March 2014 budget proposal continued to make the mistake the Republican leadership made in 1996, confusing correlation with causation. They argue that if poor people stayed in school, did not have babies until they were married, and took any job and kept it, they would rise out of poverty. Yes, middle-class people have far higher graduation, marriage, and employment rates than poor people, but that is as much an effect as a cause of their income. The sort of meaningless high school degree handed out in a high-poverty school today gets you at best a minimum wage job, which pays well below the poverty line. A living-wage job, along the lines of $15 an hour, or about $30,000 a year in 2014 dollars, is the surest way to strengthen a family.

Most developed countries consider it a recession, requiring direct government employment or government subsidies for private employment, when official unemployment reaches about seven percent. During America's depression, unemployment soared to 25 percent, and President Roosevelt responded with a bevy of employment and assistance programs. For the past 50 years black America as a whole has always had an unemployment rate in the mid-teens, so it is always between a recession and a depression. The black rate is always twice that of whites, across all levels of education, and the Hispanic rate is only a quarter of the way from the white to the black rate. The higher black rate is probably partly due to blacks being discriminated against, consciously or unconsciously, by employers and managers. Some of the difference, though, is also probably due to the tendency of young black people to reject low-paying jobs because they perceive them as demeaning. Black high-poverty areas in cities often top 25 percent unemployment officially, which is a depression in itself, but so many people are not searching for jobs that this often translates to well over 50 percent. Where are the crash jobs programs for these recessions and depressions?

Local governments and non-profit organizations have years of experience in training the jobless and placing them in public or private sector positions. They have a backlog of such positions, just waiting for funding. Public sector jobs can range from data entry and school support to infrastructure repair and maintenance using basic skills. Private sector jobs, which are created with public subsidies, can be as varied as the needs of local businesses require. Both sorts of jobs can evolve into regular employment, but even if they don't, they provide the social benefit of strengthening the family's ability to develop and support its at-risk children. The same is true even if the jobs are "make-work" positions like maintaining and supervising a nearby park or playground. A number of families might be able to move to a middle-class black or integrated area, which is the hidden, unspoken goal of poverty programs.

How much would it cost to offer one of these jobs to every family of a poor school-aged child? For about $100 billion each year in additional federal spending every poor family that wanted it could have a $30,000 public or private sector job. In a two trillion dollar federal budget, in which public, political, and real winds can suddenly blow $100 billion into special programs, this would be a manageable commitment to meeting the needs of the children whose educational status we constantly bemoan. Examples of politically-popular programs on this order of magnitude that are of dubious public usefulness include the rebuilding of shore residences after hurricanes that owners knew were likely when they first built them, the collection of subsidies, studies, and foreign aid programs based on the unwarranted belief that we are suffering a "climate catastrophe" from industrial gases, and the refurbishing of our old but functional nuclear weapons and delivery systems.

Surely we could provide the same funding for something as important as helping poor families give their children a shot at the middle class.

The Census Bureau estimates that there are 16 million children living in poverty. Slightly more than 2 children live in each poor household, on average. That makes about eight million pairs of parents or guardians. If every pair were to be offered one slot in a living-wage jobs program, perhaps three million might provide a participant who could then hold onto the job by showing up consistently and performing well. Custodial parents or guardians would have preference, but if they left the program for a better job or were removed from the program for non-performance, then the other parent or guardian in the same family could have that slot. At $30,000 per year, uncounted for taxes and social services so as not to reduce existing assistance such as Medicaid, food stamps, or welfare, this would put $90 billion in the pockets of poor families, with another $10 billion or so required for administration and evaluation. Participating families with school-aged children would have to bring them to school on time each day. In addition, participating parents would have to stay up to date on any court-ordered child support commitments.

Let us imagine the impact on a poor family if the present mother or absent father goes to work daily and then every month can cash a $2,500 tax-free check monthly that does not reduce existing medical, food, or cash assistance. The financial benefits are obvious, since a frugal household can almost immediately start planning a move to a safer neighborhood. The psychological benefits may be even more important. Men and women who have been at the bottom of the social ladder will become familiar with daily work responsibilities and the respect and stability it brings both on and off the job. Their children will see them as active agents in their lives rather than defeated actors, and will base their behavior and their sense of the future on a successful rather than a struggling mindset. How can we afford not to try this approach?

Pre-natal and infant support

Some of the damage done to the health and intellect of poor infants in America is unavoidable. Even accounting for them having, on average, lower income and less pre-natal care, teenage girls give birth significantly earlier in pregnancy than adult women. As a result, their babies have, on average, more of the physical and cognitive problems that are associated with prematurity. Recent Brookings Institution research by Melissa Kearny and Phillip Levine demonstrates that broad cultural trends, rather than government programs, have cut the teen motherhood rate in half in America over the last 20 years. However, the research also shows that there continues to be a strong association of teen motherhood with both minority status and poverty. While teenage girls whose parents have lower economic and educational attainment are no more likely to be sexually active than their wealthier peers, they are much more likely to be mothers. Kearny and Levine attribute this difference to more poor girls being "ambivalent" about avoiding motherhood, and so eschewing contraception and abortion.

As always in American sociology, race and class are confounded in these data. One in ten white girls versus two in ten black or Hispanic girls will be mothers as teenagers. This difference almost certainly reveals an ethnic dimension to teen motherhood, because it is too large to be explained solely by white girls coming disproportionately from wealthier families. Girls in the high-poverty schools in which I have taught have rates that reflect both the economic and ethnic disparities, with up to half of them becoming mothers before turning 20. Changes in the association of poverty and minority ethnicity with teen motherhood are occurring, but like the overall trend they too are guided by culture more than policy. For now, it is common for the children entering high-poverty schools to have been born prematurely to a teenage mother.

Some of the dangers of prematurity can be mitigated during pregnancy with better pre-natal care, such as visits to the doctor and visits from visiting nurses. However, some damage will remain simply due to the age of the mothers. In addition poor mothers of all ages suffer from higher levels of stress that may have a negative effect on pre-natal development. Poverty and the lack of resources and support it implies are strongly correlated with infant mortality. Black infants, partly because of their disproportionate poverty, have twice the rate of white infants. But consider this strange finding by the Centers for Disease Control: college-educated, well-paid, married black women also generate twice the infant mortality rate of their white peers. The Joint Center for Political and Economic Studies calls this result, which controls for income and education, the stress effect of being black in America. Under this eminently reasonable interpretation the constant pressure for these middle-class women of being black in the mainstream white culture of their professions and the constant worry about how their children will be treated by society combine to stress their bodies during pregnancy, resulting in increased prematurity and resulting low birth weight.

Most of the gap between the cognitive abilities of poor and wealthier children does not come from pre-natal factors. The real problem is intellectual, and the culprit is a parental language gap. Poor families use far fewer words and engage in far less verbal play with their infants than wealthier families. There is strong evidence that poor black parents have an additional deficit in words and verbal play compared to poor white parents. The cognitive benefits for infants of hearing, mimicking, and responding to language are certain, as are the cognitive costs of not being so engaged. Recognizing this problem, a number of public and private programs have begun to send trained visitors to poor parents and parents-to-be to collaborate, teach by example how to interact to increase stimulation, make suggestions about healthy living, and simply help navigate the burden of being a parent of limited means.

These programs have a variety of names, such as Parent to Parent, Nurse Family Partnership, Early Head Start, Parents Helping Parents, and the Maternal, Infant, and Early Childhood Home Visiting Program. Some use professional staff and some use volunteers; some are focused on children with disabilities rather than poor families. They all, though, can all be collapsed under one rubric: Voluntary Home Visiting Family Support Programs. They are supported by half a billion federal dollars a year, provided by the law that authorized "Obama-care."

The purpose of home visiting programs is to help parents become more effective at child development, from pregnancy through the first birthday. Given the rigors of poverty and race, even an excellent program with wide coverage will be no panacea. No amount of home visiting, of course, will remove the stress of being black or poor in America, but it should certainly help in the longer term for individual children. The impact on school achievement would be far greater than that of Head Start or pre-kindergarten. The most rigorous longitudinal studies show that high-quality stimulation programs with infants and their parents have longer-lasting and stronger effects than school-age programs on social variables like high school graduation, delayed parenthood, and special education status.

For perhaps $20 billion each year the federal government could support a corps of home visitors large enough so that one could be offered to every first-time expectant father and mother in poverty. The visitor would come for a few hours, perhaps twice a week, from the middle of pregnancy to the middle of the first year of life. The visitor would become a partner, a sounding-board, and an advisor to parents both on their own health and well-being, and that of the baby. Most importantly, the visitor would model how to talk to and play with the baby, skills that are not automatically displayed by many poor parents. The intent is that the stimulating parenting behavior, once taught by example by the home visitor, would be taken on by the parents themselves after the visitor leaves the home, and after the visits stop.

Most parents, especially young parents, would agree to take part in the program. They would come to look forward to the visits and be eager to mimic with their children the activities they are shown by the visitor. However, some of the neediest parents may choose not to take part, out of fear of getting any agency close to their business. This is similar to the resistance by poor high school students to telling anybody anything about one's family, because that might lead to investigation and trouble. This is a good point to note in closing this proposal. We are working with individuals, each different and each with their own set of strengths and stresses. A little humility about our limitations and theirs, a little attention to what real people are telling us about their lives, would go a long way in the high-stakes debate over educating the children of poverty.

* * *

CHAPTER 15. THIRTY YEARS IS CERTAINLY ENOUGH

So, where did it all come from, the college prep curriculum for high-poverty kids and the testing mania to enforce it? First, let's assume that it all came with the best of intentions. Yes, we might be suspicious of the politicians who have found education to be a fertile area for their popularity, and the philanthropists, foundations and policy entrepreneurs who have found it a fertile area for their profiles. But who could argue against helping children, "creating world-class schools," seeing access to a good education "regardless of zip code" (which in segregated American cities is a code phrase for ethnicity and income) as the new "civil rights struggle," and giving everybody a chance to go to college? There is no reason to think that the members of the testing class don't believe they are doing right by the kids with their school reforms. What is intriguing, though, indeed stunning, is how quickly and thoroughly they have imposed their beliefs on the public schools through state and federal mandates.

The story is about 30 years old. Until the 1980s, curriculum was controlled at the school district level by elected boards of education with just a few state and federal constraints, and standardized intelligence tests were administered perhaps once in elementary school for their intended diagnostic purpose of helping teachers understand their individual students better. (Some teachers, though, recall simply putting the test results in a drawer without looking at them, so as not to prejudice themselves against students who might score poorly.)

It was during that decade that federal funding for poor and learning disabled students began to grow more important to states and school districts, and state-level elected officials began to take an interest in the hitherto local responsibility for education. These officials, who in the natural progression of politics often became elected at the national level, began to speak of education like a business in which the product of viably-educated adults was dependent on the input of top-flight teachers and principals. They promised to improve the product by improving the input. The improvement was to come from testing the output, and then holding the input "accountable" for the results. Foundations became interested in the topic, and began to pump money into it, attracting a whole class of "school reformers."

There is no single politician, foundation, or reformer one could point to as being indispensable to the beginning of the testing movement. As Charles De Gaulle liked to say when he was praised, the graveyards are full of indispensable men. The same can be said for the explosive growth of school reform. By the mid-1990s the ideas of the testing class had percolated down to influence both the curriculum and the evaluation of administrators, schools and teachers in every school district in America. By the mid-2000s, the capture of the system by the reformers was complete, achieved by threatening cut-offs in federal funds under No Child Left Behind and by changing laws to use public funds for charter schools and to take control of high-poverty school districts away from boards of education and give it to mayors and city councils (and governors and legislatures, if the locals couldn't turn around the dismal results). There were many cooks in this kitchen, all encouraging each other.

But if there was a single starting gun, a first cannon shot, in the school reform revolution, it came in 1983. This book has sounded a cry of alarm about the fundamentally wrong direction of high-poverty schools. Three decades ago another cry of alarm was sounded about the fundamentally wrong direction of public schools in general. I can only hope that my cry is as effective for good as that one was for ill. The 1983 Reagan administration report titled "A Nation at Risk: The Imperative for Educational Reform" contained a number of good ideas, most of which were ignored, and a number of bad ones, most of which were not only adopted but expanded upon.

The report's negative impact emanated, above all, from its tone of crisis. President Reagan went on a national tour to publicize and popularize the notion that America's public schools were failing so badly that "America's place in the world" might well be "forfeited." This claim was based on the report's use of comparative but poorly examined statistics. The commission noted a steady decline in SAT scores and international test rankings while ignoring the increase in the share of poor and minority students taking the SAT and the larger share of poor test-takers in America than in other countries. Poverty, as often shown in this book, is both primary cause and correlate of low test scores. The discontent that Reagan fomented, or perhaps simply galvanized, fed the growth of the school reform Beowulf that guards the barriers to progress in high-poverty schools today.

Of course, all was not well by any means in high-poverty schools until "accountability," standards, and the related misuse of testing to evaluate teachers and school rather than students burst upon the educational scene in the decade after publication of "A Nation at Risk." These schools were already reeling from the alienation of their segregated clients when the report was published. However, it is clear that the report provided important educational justification and political cover for the school reform movement that has further battered and distorted high-poverty schools ever since.

* * *

"A Nation at Risk" was the brainchild of two Utah educators. Both were devout Mormons with virtually no experience in high-poverty education. Former Utah education commissioner Terrel Bell had been chosen by President Reagan to be Secretary of Education. Bell then selected University of Utah president David Gardner to chair a National Commission on Excellence in Education that would counter right-wing charges that Bell was too moderate, and too easy on the public schools, to serve Reagan faithfully. Bell filled the commission with administrators and advocates of science and business. The 18 members included five college presidents or administrators of college systems, three members of state or local school boards of education and their associations, two principals, one superintendent, one governor, and a state commissioner of education.

Only two people made the team as teachers: a professor of the history of science and a high school teacher of French who had won the National Teacher of the Year award in 1982. Both were teaching at elite institutions, Harvard and the New Rochelle, N.Y., schools. Both, coincidentally, were survivors of Nazi extermination efforts. A third teacher, Berkeley professor Glen Seaborg, was also on the commission, but he is counted here as an administrator for his previous term as chancellor of the University of California and his work on science education for military applications. Seaborg had been a bomb-maker at Los Alamos, the chairman of the Atomic Energy Commission, and a leader of the post-Sputnik science education initiative.

The final three members of the commission were the chairman of Bell laboratories, the leader of an organization that advocated teaching economics in schools, and the wife (and promoter) of the crusty conservative theorist Russell Kirk. It is noteworthy that not a single commissioner represented the perspective of organized teachers. The American Federation of Teachers and the National Education Association were not invited to this party. Perhaps Bell and Gardner knew in advance that they planned to advocate linking teacher evaluations to measures of performance, which the tenure-protecting unions and associations could never support.

As was appropriate for a report by an administration aggressively pursuing the Cold War abroad and tax cuts, deregulation, export support, and restrictions on unions at home, "A Nation at Risk" was unabashedly nationalistic and pro-business. There was no John Dewey left in its portrayal of children as resources rather than as souls. Students were to be trained to guarantee America's economic dominance and international might, rather than provided with learning skills and knowledge to improve the quality, economic or spiritual, of their own lives. Consider these calls to the ramparts in the report's introduction:

- Our Nation is at risk. Our once unchallenged preeminence in commerce, industry, science and technological innovation is being overtaken by competitors throughout the world...The educational foundations of our society are presently being eroded by a rising tide of mediocrity that threatens our very future as a Nation and a people.

The capitalization of Nation in this excerpt takes on an almost religious aspect, making the "challenge" of our "preeminence" an attack on an amorphous deity that must be rescued from evil "competitors." The "very future" of the Nation would be threatened unless the pool of trained workers, researchers, inventors, and business executives was increased. The report clearly holds that a primary purpose of American education is to preserve our "very future" by dominating the international economy.

- If an unfriendly foreign power had attempted to impose on America the mediocre educational performance that exists today, we might well have viewed it as an act of war...We have even squandered the gains in student achievement made in the wake of the Sputnik challenge... We have, in effect, been committing an act of unthinking, unilateral educational disarmament.

This combative excerpt, with its latent xenophobia and overt military references, is of a piece with President Reagan's intense disputes with the Soviet Union over nuclear weapons and American hegemony in Central America. The mention of an early Soviet-American competition, the space race of the late 1950s, makes the implicit explicit. The report here is making clear that a primary purpose of American education is to win the Cold War with the menacing Soviet Union.

- America's position in the world may once have been reasonably secure with only a few exceptionally well-trained men and women. It is no longer...The risk is not only that the Japanese make automobiles more efficiently...that the South Koreans recently built the world's most efficient steel mill...that American machine tools, once the pride of the world, are being displaced by German products. It is also that these development signify a redistribution of trained capability throughout the globe....If only to keep and improve on the slim competitive edge we still retain in world markets, we must dedicate ourselves to the reform of our educational system.

This listing of countries of concern provides the details of the perceived challenges to American corporations in the early 1980s. Backed in some cases by the unions, the corporations were busy stoking public concerns about rising imports and foreign trade barriers in order to gain government subsidies and tariff barriers themselves. The report here is putting some meat on the bones of its earlier claim that only better education can save the Nation from defeat, albeit economic, by a foreign power.

In the report's recommendations we find the source of the core of the school reform paradigm: performance-based teacher evaluation and compensation, "rigorous and measurable standards" for students, and a standardized college prep high school curriculum for all. The report hoped to multiply the number of students qualified for and interested in careers in science and technology, whether as better-trained workers or innovative inventors. Business leaders had been complaining loudly that they could not find enough of either one to compete with their new foreign challengers.

Other recommendations, which unlike the core of school reform fell by the wayside, are almost identical to some of those proposed in this book. Already weary of grade inflation, the commissioners argued that: "Grades should be indicators of academic achievement so they can be relied on as evidence of a student's readiness for further study." Standardized tests were implemented to obtain a truer measure of student achievement than inflated grades. However, with politicians demanding excellence and prohibiting failure in "No Child Left Behind" and similar laws, administrators began to cheat on, game, and misreport tests results just as they had grades and graduation rates.

The report highlighted a true crisis in attendance, and advocated the use of clear incentives and sanctions for students and their families. It also called for schools to place, promote, and graduate students based on achievement levels, and not age. Both of these recommendations, if implemented rigorously, would have kept a large number of students from moving along with their initial cohort. That result would have been contrary to the institutional interests of high-poverty schools in keeping enrollments up, masking weak performance, and claiming high graduation rates. It is understandable that these unpopular reforms were never the focus of a politically-driven movement.

Similarly, the report called for discipline policies that were "clear and consistent" and proposed the creation of "alternative programs" to meet the needs of "continually disruptive students." Again, removing students from schools was never on the agenda of the testing class. As argued in this book, making these proposals work will require close attention to incentives rather than penalties for administrators and teachers and to engagement with parents, guardians, and the public in explaining the benefits they provide to all students.

* * *

Politicians rather than local school boards were the first to respond to the new public mistrust of schools. While politicians and school boards are both elected, the boards and their superintendents came late to the "school reform" consensus because they drew their feedback from parents and students rather than the general public. There was little sense of "A Nation at Risk" among these constituencies, as opposed to the national media and general public. The movement by politicians to control local education exploded in the 1980s. President Bill Clinton and his successor George Bush were just two of the many governors who promised voters that they would save the poorly-served children, and began to assert powers in curriculum and administration previously reserved to the elected school boards.

As governor of Arkansas in the 1980s Clinton officially turned the reform project over to the state's First Lady, Hillary Rodham. Presaging her appointment to run a federal task force on health care reform when he was president, Clinton appointed his wife as head of a state Educational Standards Committee. She barnstormed the state, collecting statistics showing its generally poor outcomes in graduation rates and college attendance. Instead of focusing on the challenges of poverty and race, she argued that the cause was bad teachers. Rodham proposed a package of content tests that teachers would have to take to get and hold onto their jobs, and with her husband's help hammered it through the legislature. According to her "business" approach the resulting improvement in education would be measurable, and the state soon began requiring tests for students that could be used to measure the effect of teachers.

In 2013, thirty years after the Clintons' initiative, a school reform organization analyzed national testing data and ranked Arkansas 45th of the 51 states (including the District of Columbia) on a measure of "achievement and gains" for poor students. According to University of Arkansas education professor Gary Ritter's analysis of Rodham's recommendations: "Just about all of those high-profile moves were cosmetic, superficial endeavors that didn't begin to tackle the underlying problems and were quickly weakened or undone."

As governor of Texas in the 1990s Bush claimed to be spurring the "Texas education miracle" led by Houston's school superintendent, Rodney Paige. He later brought Paige to Washington to be his secretary of education and architect of the No Child law. The miracle wrought in Houston by Paige, a former college football coach who was elected to the school board and then engineered his own selection as superintendent, turned out, like the entire genre of school reform miracles, to be due to the inspired gaming of test results and graduation statistics. The school district redefined drop-outs as students "seeking alternative education" and adjusted test eligibility and proficiency cut-offs to guarantee temporary growth in cherry-picked results.

As president, Clinton worked with school reform advocates to pressure state school authorities to adopt test-based curriculums. Congress has control over the District of Columbia, so its captive schools became the first to feel the heat. I know because my son was in first grade in one of the largely white, middle and upper class DC neighborhood elementary schools in 2000. I began to hear from his teacher, and indeed from the pre-kindergarten and kindergarten teachers who had taught him in the two previous years, that standardized tests were taking over their curriculum. The principal told me that she had been relegated to a back row seat at the annual school district convocation in an attempt to shame her for not having made her progress targets, which was tough to do in a wealthy neighborhood where most of the kids were already "proficient" when they walked in the door. The principals who had reported success, probably through gaming and cheating, sat on the stage and were fêted and showered with bonuses.

Looking into the matter, I found out that Clinton administration education officials, backed by Congress, were forcing the district to give written standardized tests to first graders, despite the fact that most of them were just learning to read, and many could not read at all! Nothing like this had occurred at my daughter's all-black, low-income DC neighborhood elementary school in the 1980s. I wrote and spoke about the policy in local media, and during the call-in portion of a radio show I managed to get the DC superintendent to agree that it was illogical and frustrating. He soon moved the testing start up to second grade.

A sad coda to this incident was that the wonderful young first grade teacher who called the matter to my attention repeatedly failed to pass the math section of a Hillary Rodham-style content test for teachers, and lost her contract. Backed by her principal, she argued that her longstanding inability to grasp advanced math content should not rule her out from teaching addition and subtraction to first graders. Tough luck. The district stood by its teacher test to show federal officials its commitment to improve teaching, so she had to move her family to a state that did not require teacher testing.

Bill Clinton was just the warm-up act. George Bush outdid him in spades, appointing Paige as his education secretary and making a deal with liberal lions Ted Kennedy and George Miller in which their support for the "No

Child Left Behind Act" and its penalties for weak test results was exchanged for Bush's support for increased federal funding for public schools. It is arguable whether Bush kept his end of the bargain, but in any event their fond hopes for improved performance by high-poverty kids did not materialize in the ten years that was set aside to bring all students into "proficiency."

The No Child law violated the laws of statistics by ordering schools to make all students above average. If we moved just ten percent of students each year into the "proficient" group on tests, it reasoned, at the end of ten years, we'd have 100 percent proficiency! Schools that failed to make the required "annual yearly progress" would be "restructured" and eventually taken over by school reform corporations. Of course, at the end of the ten years, the law had to be waived because so many schools and districts had found that, surprise, poverty rather than bad teachers lay at the core of the income and ethic "achievement gaps." Rather than recognize the pathetic result of the massive school reform experiment, President Obama and his favored local school superintendent made secretary of education, Arne Duncan of Chicago, "doubled down" on it. In a "Race to the Top" they offered the waiver and additional federal funds only to states that included students' test scores in teachers' evaluations and implemented the Common Core curriculum.

School reform has been an unstoppable political reality since the 1990s. Nearly all governors had won legislative approval to impose "accountability" measures on local districts well before the No Child law extended the concept to federal control in 2001. The National Governors' Association has raised tens of millions of dollars, much from Microsoft founder Bill Gates, to promote these measures, and was the leader of the drive for a Common Core curriculum. Mayors have gotten into the act as well, pushing laws to take control of their public schools from elected boards of education. About 20 mayors of generally larger cities, including New York, Chicago, Philadelphia, Boston, and Washington, DC, now direct their schools.

These governors and mayors, in league with their legislatures and city councils, stimulated a demand for reform into which tax-exempt donors and entrepreneurs flowed, creating the testing class that took over the public schools and created the charter schools. For high-poverty communities, this movement has achieved little after 30 years other than trapping their schools in a descending spiral of impossible demands for improvement. Its ideology of "no excuses" reveals a quasi-religious belief that with its very wording dismisses the debate about the role of poverty as a barrier to achievement in a college prep curriculum. This conveniently absolves politicians and citizens from addressing segregation and lack of opportunity. Because income is so strongly linked to success on standardized tests, school reform inevitably leads to apparent failure on the part of teachers and schools, despite strenuous and systematic distortion of the curriculum and "gaming" and outright cheating, as in Atlanta and DC, on test results. These apparent failures then lead to the gutting of public schools by charters, vouchers, and the flight of more able teachers and students to private schools, all of which in turn starts a new series of impossible demands and apparent failures.

* * *

The pendulum has swung way over to a mania for "school reform" and its package of standardization, phony progress, and charter schools. This book makes proposals, based on the reality of the trenches in which I have labored, for an appropriate curriculum, true grades, vocational choice, and referral for disruption and academic deficits. These proposals cannot be successful, in fact not even legally undertaken, until the pendulum swings back toward the center. High-poverty schools can then be freed from the federal, state, and even local school reform laws and regulations that followed in the wake of the 1983 report, and returned to the control of locally-elected boards of education.

High-poverty communities are unlikely to be able to carry out such a revolution on their own. Their schools were dragged into school reform by forces outside their control, and will probably be liberated the same way. They never asked to be at the core of the movement to "reform" America's public schools, but they were placed there anyway. Even though "A Nation at Risk" lambasted the public schools in general, the evidence that school reformers since then have cited to support their agenda has come from the high-poverty arena. A general awareness that "Johnny can't read" certainly did not arise in Winnetka, Illinois, or Mt. Vernon, New York, or any of the wealthy school districts that far outnumber the urban and rural districts in America.

Segregated living patterns, exacerbated by private schooling for the white and the wealthy, have packed the weakest families into schools, and in some cases into districts, that are almost entirely composed of families under stress. These schools and districts provided the horror stories of opportunity denied, of soaring drop-out rates and chaos in the schools, of tenured teachers reading the newspaper and showing movies. When reformers repeat their mantra that "zip code" should not determine a child's educational chances, they are not talking about Beverly Hills 90210.

Fortunately, a movement against school reform has been growing in wealthier communities that have the political clout needed to derail it everywhere. As documented and encouraged by FairTest, dozens of parent and teacher revolts over testing at middle and upper class schools have begun to discredit the tenets of school reform. These critiques generally come from the leftish, liberal side of American politics. At the same time, the right-leaning outcry against the Gates-funded Common Core curriculum has also called the school reform model into question. These protests from both wings of the political spectrum have not yet shaken the firm opposition of the testing class, nor of the mainstream media and politicians who continually and bull-headedly sings the praises of allegedly "high-performing" school reform projects. But cracks are appearing in the edifice.

In 2013 New York City elected a mayor, Bill de Blasio, who campaigned as an advocate of reducing the influence of the extreme school reform dogma imposed by his predecessor, Michael Bloomberg. De Blasio appointed as school chancellor a long-time opponent of the misuse of standardized tests and curriculums, former teacher, principal, and administrator Carmen Fariña. The appointment could not have contrasted more strongly with Bloomberg's serial, and in some cases outright bizarre, appointments of chancellors with little experience in high-poverty education, or in education or any kind. Their only qualification seemed to be a willingness to implement Bloomberg's ideological bias toward a business model of "no excuses" punishment of principals and teachers for the weaknesses of their students. Fariña quickly made good on de Blasio's campaign promise to replace Bloomberg's test-heavy system of grading schools and labeling them failures in need of mass firings. Her new system did away with A–F grades for schools, replacing them with judgments about whether they were "meeting targets" in such areas as curriculum development and making efforts to meet students' needs.

In 2014 the legislature in Washington State refused to include student test scores in teachers' evaluations, despite the threat by the federal Department of Education to deny a waiver to the impossible demands for 100 percent "proficiency" that had come due after ten years of the No Child Left Behind act. The federal government did indeed deny the waiver, costing Washington $40 million in federal funds, but the legislature held firm in refusing to mandate that all public school districts use, or misuse as this book argues, the test results as part of teachers' evaluations for continuation and pay raises. Oklahoma also lost its waiver, and some federal funds, for refusing to agree to the new "Common Core" standards. In New York State 10,000 parents "opted out" of school reform tests for their children, and teachers in Chicago and Seattle boycotted the administration of such tests.

At a minimum, these beginnings of turn-arounds in the nation's largest school district and far-flung states indicate that a battle of ideas about public schools has finally been joined. This intellectual battle will gradually shift in favor of the notion that schools must be based on the realities and the needs of students and parents rather than the bromides and hopes of politicians and administrators. Then the realization that children in high-poverty communities live in a reality that is quite distinct from that of middle class children will make it logical for the public to support the freeing of high-poverty schools from the cookie-cutter standardization of a college-prep curriculum. This standardization has doomed to failure all the children of poverty, both the half whose family background and personal alienation and damage make them unwilling or unable to follow it, and the half who have emerged from a challenging background able to do so if they are freed from the disruption of the alienated.

When high-poverty schools, along with public schools in general, are finally freed from the 30-year "school reform" experiment and returned to the control of local school boards, the federal government will still play an important role in education. If educators adopt the proposals in this book in an attempt to increase dramatically the share of poor students making it into the middle class, they will need federal funding for special education and for strengthening the child-rearing capabilities of poor families. Particularly with severely handicapped children, local school boards often lack the funding and the specialized services needed for special education. Similarly, it will be beyond the capacity of most school districts to provide public sector or subsidize private sector living wage jobs for the families of poor students and to fund local prenatal and infancy support for parents.

How can we hope to achieve these true reforms? At present, the task certainly seems overwhelming. Simply ending federal, state, and city control is daunting, let alone dumping the testing class and starting over with a focus on the needs of students and their families. But policy can change, and will change, because the reality of failure is too strong to resist. When we reject the concept of schools as a silver bullet for poverty, and punishment of teachers for the test weaknesses of poor children as a silver bullet for those weaknesses, we will be on our way to a more logical framework.

In *War and Peace*, Tolstoy's protagonist, the thoughtful Count Pierre, expresses amazement and then horror at the way people are transformed into machines when called upon to perform an unthinkably inhumane task, like executing prisoners. He realizes that you cannot change this tendency of humans, once in a system, to act in accordance with it, even in violation of their certain knowledge that it is wrong. That is why the revolution in high-poverty education proposed in this book probably will not come from within the system, from an expansion of the brave acts of teachers and administrators who refuse to teach to or give more standardized tests, or of local lawsuits and victorious school board races. These important acts certainly help call the prevailing paradigm into question, but the system's actors will respond as Tolstoy predicts, demoting or firing critics, dragging out lawsuits, and threatening progressive school boards with funding cut-offs. The revolution will have to grow just as "school reform" did, from a public consensus that the current system is terribly off-track.

To borrow from Tolstoy's sly portrayal of the aristocracy tacking in its opinions in response to prevailing public winds, once the education paradigm begins to shift under the influence of public opinion, the firmest cheerleaders for school reform will be the ones making the most rapid transition to being the firmest cheerleaders for student-centered education. When the pendulum swings back, everybody will want to ride it. That is why everybody, not just teachers and parents, can play a role in saving our high-poverty schools and their students from another generation of failure. All of us simply have to laugh at, to ridicule, to question, and to cast doubt on the false claims of the testing class. The claims are so obviously silly, so obviously contrary to what we know about people, especially poor children and their families, that in the end they will not be able to withstand this barrage. Today it is a sub-Nation that is at Risk, the sub-Nation of the poor and especially the black and Hispanic poor. They are counting on all of us to laugh, to refuse to accept, and to offer a better way, grounded in reality rather than ideology, that can become the new consensus.

INDEX

Made in the USA
Middletown, DE
01 May 2015